MANY

IET

I N

SECTOR

MANY

British zone

HAMBURG

BERLIN

POLAND

HANNOVER

W E S T

EAST GERMANY

BONN

G

E

French

FRANKFURT

zone

American zone

M

A

N

Y

MUNICH

N

0   50 km
0   30 ml

Air corridor   Major road

EAST BERLIN
WEST BERLIN

N

0   1   5 km
0   1   3 ml

✕✕✕✕✕✕✕✕✕   Berlin wall

✈
Tegel   Airport

Autobahn

┼┼┼┼┼   Railway

THE BERLIN WALL

NORMAN GELB

THE BERLIN WALL

MICHAEL JOSEPH
LONDON

To Boris and Helga

First published in Great Britain by Michael Joseph Ltd
27 Wright's Lane, London W8
1986

British Library Cataloguing in Publication Data

Gelb, Norman
The Berlin Wall.
1. Berlin (Germany)—Politics and
government—1945–
I. Title
943.1'55087   DD881

ISBN 0 7181 2739 0

Filmset by Wilmaset, Birkenhead, Wirral.
Printed in Great Britain by
Billings & Sons Ltd, Worcester

Contents

1

The Wall

GRIM AND FORBIDDING, the Wall snakes through the city of Berlin like the backdrop to a nightmare. In certain respects, that's exactly what it is. Tears have been shed here, curses uttered, threats snarled, blood spilled, lives snuffed out. The Wall has been standing a long time now – more than two decades. It has become part of the political architecture of modern times, a concrete barrier planted across the middle of the biggest city between Paris and Moscow, a dramatic statement as well as a grotesque edifice. It is an awkward thing, outlandish and unloved, a numbing fact of life, a fortification thrown up in panic to keep people in rather than out.

What follows is the story of the Berlin Wall and the circumstances surrounding its erection. But it is more than just an account of the splitting of a city. It is a story also of power politics and thermo-nuclear threat. It was played out in Washington, Moscow, London and Paris as well as Germany. Berlin was, after all, the place described by Soviet Premier Nikita Khrushchev as 'the testicles of the West. When I want the West to scream, I squeeze on Berlin.' It was the place about which President John F. Kennedy growled, 'If Khrushchev wants to rub my nose in the dirt, it's all over.' Berlin was where the Cold War had begun with a Soviet blockade, where Soviet and American tanks faced each other virtually snout-to-snout for the first – and hopefully only – time, and where the grisly game of nuclear brinkmanship was introduced.

For a brief moment, the Berlin Wall was the focus of the whole world's attention. Spawned in an atmosphere of bluster and defiance, it generated a mood of deepest anxiety and profoundest

despair. Everywhere, hawks and doves debated its significance
and consequences. In Moscow, the Russians, who had authorized its erection in violation of international agreement, kept
nervous watch as this most remarkable, most presumptuous
urban redevelopment scheme – chopping a city in two – was
implemented. They needn't have worried. In Washington,
despite rumours of secret American connivance, the White
House, State Department, Pentagon and Central Intelligence
Agency, having expected something else, struggled but failed to
fix on a suitable response. Deplored and reviled, but unchal-
lenged, the Wall stood and grew and grew.

Swarms of journalists and news photographers descended on
Berlin to see and record the erection of what was quickly designated either the 'Wall of Shame' or the 'Wall of Peace' – depen-
ding on where you stood ideologically. Pundits and politicians,
generals and spymasters converged on it like impious pilgrims
come to marvel at a blasphemous miracle. People marvel at it
still and wonder – did its erection halt a downhill tumble toward
a catastrophic war which might have engulfed the globe, or
would the world be a better place today had it been immediately, unceremoniously, defiantly demolished?

The great Wall of Berlin is more than just an emotionally-
charged geopolitical spectacle. Made of reinforced concrete,
ten to thirteen feet high, it is a very remarkable structure.
Meandering through the heart of the metropolis, turning corners, winding and bending, it hacks the old capital of Germany
into two distinct entities, and then curls to enfold all of the
western half of Berlin in its concrete embrace. If straightened,
the Wall would measure 103 miles long, which is greater than
the distance from New York to Philadelphia or London to
Calais. But that doesn't give a truly accurate picture of the
situation.

There is more to the Wall than this one edifice. Behind it, one
hundred yards deeper into Communist territory, is another concrete barrier, almost as formidable. The levelled area between
the two is a desolate, dangerous no-man's-land, patrolled by
kalashnikov-toting guards, dotted with free-fire machine-gun
emplacements, and sown in places with landmines. It is punctu-
ated by 285 elevated watchtowers, more suited to prison camps
than city centres, and by a series of dog runs where ferocious,
long-leashed alsatians effectively run free. It is not a safe place
to be.

Before reaching the Wall from the East, a person would have to get over the interior concrete barrier, evade the guards, dogs, minefields and/or automatically-triggered guns, and sidestep strategically positioned devices designed to set off both sound alarms and light signals when activated. When that person finally reached the Wall on the border undetected, he would have to get a firm grip on it to lever himself over, despite the thick, smooth-surfaced, ungrippable cement tubing affixed to its top to prevent him from doing just that. Some would-be escapers, having remarkably got that far, have been foiled by this last refinement.

Floodlights and searchlights are positioned along the Wall to illuminate it at night – an eerie sight. Specially reinforced obstructions have been erected at the handful of official border crossing points to discourage people emboldened by pipe-dreams of crashing through in vehicles, which a daring few did during the Wall's early days.

All this vigilance is not directed against criminals. The object of these extraordinary precautions are the people of East Germany. When the Iron Curtain was lowered by the Communists along the border between East Germany and West Germany after the Second World War, Berlin – though deep within Communist East Germany – was spared this division. It remained under joint control of the victorious Russians, Americans, British and French, each with their own sector of the city, each with their own military garrison stationed in that sector, but with right of unrestricted movement throughout the German capital guaranteed by East–West agreement.

That meant that East Germans, seeking more from life than they believed was being offered to them in their Communist homeland but unable to cross the Iron Curtain directly into West Germany, could still find a way out. They could make their way to East Berlin – the Soviet Sector of the city – and then cross without fuss or ceremony into West Berlin, where the dividing line between the American, British and French sectors had become largely irrelevant, where freedom of speech, belief and mobility was protected by law, and which was recovering from the war's devastation at a dazzling pace. American correspondents in Berlin at the time called their cross-over the 'five cent subway ride to freedom'. Having come across, the refugees could stay in West Berlin or, if they wished, they could be flown out to West Germany – to waiting jobs and new lives well beyond reach of the Communists from whom they had fled.

They came in the thousands over the years, tens of thousands, hundreds of thousands, millions. So great was the flight that the continued existence of the Communist East German state was threatened. The Wall was erected around West Berlin to stop the exodus and thereby save the Soviet Union and its East European empire from the consequences of an East German collapse.

Many things have happened since that summer's night in 1961 when, in a blitz operation, thousands of armed guards took up positions along the border and the first barbed wire was strung across the middle of the city to mark the spot where the Wall would stand. But East Berlin is still walled off from West Berlin. The people behind the Wall are still being shielded from the temptations and distractions so glitteringly displayed just a few minutes away. They are still locked in.

Not all people in East Berlin and East Germany have accepted this situation. Despite all the obstacles, many have managed to get across the Wall, over it or under it, since it was built. But more than three thousand East Germans are known to have failed in their effort to escape and to have been arrested by the Vopos (*Volkspolizisten* – People's Police) for trying to get across town to West Berlin. At least sixty persons are known to have been shot dead in the attempt. How many more have lost their lives or have been wounded trying to escape is just a guess. The East German authorities do not publicize such things. People wounded and caught are led or carried away by the border guards. Rarely is news of their subsequent fate made public. However, it is known – through observation from afar and reports brought across by successful escapers and western visitors – that dozens of persons have been wounded in abortive, often foolhardy bids to break through to West Berlin.

The Wall has regularly been strengthened, with points deemed penetrable reinforced and other sections merely tidied up. There is continuous maintenance along its entire length. So efficient has this maintenance been that escape attempts have now practically ceased, though a reckless or desperate person still occasionally tries to find or make a way through, and occasionally still succeeds. Not long ago, an East Berlin border guard was jailed in West Berlin for shooting dead another guard before fleeing over the Wall. He said he had not wanted to kill the man, only disable him so that he could make his get-away without fear of being shot himself. Two East Germans soared over the Wall on a pulley attached to a steel cable strung from the roof of a building in East Berlin and fixed by a friend to a car hidden behind a West Berlin house. The East German authorities are continually alert for new schemes, new devices, new subterfuges for trying to get over the Wall. Not for nothing have they outlawed hang-gliding.

While writing this book, I experienced a curious feeling of going down a distant, winding road I had traversed before, at least part of the way. In fact, I had. I went to Berlin as correspondent for the Mutual Broadcasting System a little more than a year before the Wall was built. I remained in the city for two years, till the Wall crisis had just about petered out, before being shifted to London. For practically that entire period, it was one hell of a story to cover. The city was, at the time, politically turbulent, emotionally charged, and unceasingly eventful. I have sought in the following pages to capture the drama of that traumatic moment, as well as to tell the story of the Wall, and of the circumstances that led up to and grew from the construction of that gruesome monument to human discord.

2

The Stage is Set

FIFTEEN AND A HALF years before the Wall went up, as the Second World War drew towards an explosive close in the winter of 1945, Soviet troops battling their way to Berlin reached the Oder River, a mere thirty-five miles east of the city. There they were brought to a halt. As the Germans desperately struggled to forge a defensive line between the Red Army and their capital, the Soviet commanders whose men would have to pierce that line were ordered by Moscow to stay put and consolidate their positions. They were to wait for their supply lines to catch up with them, for their units to re-group and for orders to crash finally through to the Berlin nerve centre of Adolf Hitler's Third Reich.

The Soviet commanders were mystified. It was true that their supplies were running short, their tanks were having to cope with the mud of an early thaw, and many of their units had been decimated. But their goal – the capital of the hated enemy – was so close and their men, having built up a head of steam, were anxious to push forward to seize it. However, Soviet leader Joseph Stalin had other things in mind. Stalin realized that capturing Berlin would end the war. He therefore held his Berlin-bound troops in check while his other armies pressed forward to overrun as much of German-occupied East and Central Europe as possible before peace was declared. They would thereby guarantee Soviet control of the region after the war.

Stalin was confident his troops could take Berlin whenever he gave the order. In terms of distance, his forces were less than an hour's car drive away, while the western Allies were a safe 300 miles from the city. In addition, the Americans were still recovering from the Battle of the Bulge, the daring but ultimately abortive German Christmas-time counter-offensive in the Ardennes. While they sorted themselves out, there was still Budapest for his troops to take, and Prague and Vienna.

Prime Minister Winston Churchill had also begun to examine the prospects for the post-war world. The British leader was convinced that whoever captured Berlin would have a trump card to play when hostilities were brought to an end. He and his generals proposed that the western Allies roar across the north German plain to take the city with the kind of thrust operation which the Wehrmacht had earlier used to devastating effect.

Everyone knew that the capture of Berlin was the primary objective of the Allied forces – or so it seemed. General Walter Bedell Smith, Chief of Staff to Supreme Allied Commander Dwight Eisenhower, declared, 'From the day our invasion broke over the beaches of Normandy, the goal of every Allied soldier had been Berlin. The Supreme Commander, the staff and all the troops shared a driving ambition to seal the defeat of Nazi Germany by seizing the capital of the Reich itself.' A planning memorandum at Supreme Headquarters Allied Expeditionary Forces (SHAEF) had been unequivocal: 'Our main objective must be the early capture of Berlin.' Eisenhower himself had called Berlin 'the big prize'.

Two crack American paratroop divisions were in advanced training for a drop on Berlin at short notice to support a ground assault on the city. Newspaper headlines in America and Britain blared out reports of the diminishing distance between Allied forces and Hitler's Berlin headquarters. A popular American song crowed *We'll Be Singing Hallelujah, Marching Through Berlin!*

Nevertheless, Eisenhower was not much taken with the idea of racing his forces forwards to take the city. As a strategist, he inclined towards an advance on a broad front, rather than the narrow thrust preferred by the British. Though it would make movement towards the German capital a much more protracted operation, it was less risky. With the forces under his command still a good distance from the city and the Russians practically within artillery range of Hitler's Berlin bunker, talk of the western Allies taking Berlin did not overly impress him. If the Russians were capable of capturing the German capital more easily – and it seemed they could – there was no reason to engage in a race with them.

To Americans at the time, the Russians seemed to pose no

threat whatsoever. On the contrary, they were seen as gallant allies who shared their desire to wind up this ugly war as soon as possible, and who would join with them in guaranteeing that peace, harmony and justice would prevail in the post-war world. Getting to Berlin before them, just to be there first, would not be warfare but a shabby, pointless form of politics, and American soldiers fighting a war did not play politics, shabby, pointless or any other kind.

Eisenhower shared Bedell Smith's view that 'battles are fought to defeat armies', as if war was simply a military exercise, remote from other considerations. The Supreme Commander considered that his mission – his 'crusade' – was to destroy the enemy forces, thereby sealing the defeat of Germany and ending the conflict. And that was all! He was prepared to concede that Berlin had symbolic significance. But he turned his attention to what he believed was a more pressing matter.

A flurry of reports told of élite German forces converging on the mountainous region of southern Germany and western Austria. There, it was said, the Nazis intended to hold out indefinitely with new miracle weapons at their disposal and an abiding faith in their Führer. This Alpine bastion proved to be nothing more than a fantasy, existing only in the feverish daydreams of a handful of Nazi leaders whose grotesque world was crumbling about them. Instead of gathering élite troops to man this 'National Redoubt', the Germans were piecing together whatever forces they could find – including elderly Home Guard soldiers, Hitler Youth units of teenagers, army labour battalions, untrained administrative staff, stranded navy personnel and planeless airmen – to reinforce the defensive lines facing the Russians on the Oder.

American military intelligence was, however, completely duped, both about the Nazi Alpine bastion and the size of the enemy's remaining resources. The strength of remaining German military capabilities was highly exaggerated in the reports Eisenhower and his aides received. General Omar Bradley wrote later, 'Not until the campaign ended were we to learn that this Redoubt existed largely in the imaginations of a few fanatic Nazis. It grew into so exaggerated a scheme that I am astonished that we could have believed it as innocently as we did.'

But they did believe it and the Supreme Commander acted on that misinformed belief. He decided that rather than head for Berlin, which he now dismissed as 'only a geographic location', his troops, once they reached the Elbe west of the capital, would turn south along the river to link up with advancing Soviet troops well away from Berlin. Hitler's remaining forces would thus be split in two, making them easier to take on and finally crush completely.

That was the plan as winter began to give way to spring. But in March, a dramatic transformation on the field of battle raised tactical questions. The Russian forces east of Berlin were still where they had been at the end of January, on the Oder, and the Germans were busily bolstering their defences against them. At the same time, it was evident that the Germans were rapidly losing both the ability and the will to challenge the onrushing armies of the western Allies, now fully recovered from earlier setbacks. Resistance to American and British forces was disorganized and crumbling fast after the German failure to blow up the bridge at Remagen permitted American forces to get across the Rhine without the delay and huge casualties that had been anticipated. There were still battles to be fought, but American and British troops were encountering far less resistance than had been expected as they surged forward across the rubble of western Germany. German soldiers were surrendering to them in droves, sometimes whole units at a time, sometimes even by telephone to frontline headquarters positions. Countless others simply shed their uniforms, threw away their rifles and drifted homeward. The Rhine well behind them, the forces of the western Allies faced no major obstructions on the road to Berlin except the River Elbe.

Eisenhower had sixty divisions to throw against the German capital if he wanted to do so. There were more than enough supplies to meet any situation in the field. German airfields east of the Rhine had been quickly adapted to receive Allied transport planes which were ferrying 2,000 tons of supplies in each day. It could no longer be said that the Russians were necessarily best placed to capture Berlin.

The British did not hesitate to hammer that point home. In view of America's far greater contribution of troops and supplies, they were prepared to accept American military leadership in the offensive that began with the D-Day landings. But they had ideas of their own on how the war should be run. Having fought longest against Nazi Germany and, during some dark, worrying months, having stood alone in that struggle, they had hoped that their troops would have the privilege of administering the death blow to Hitler's Reich by taking Berlin. They were riled when that privilege was denied them by Eisenhower, who diverted the

Berlin-bound forces under the command of Field Marshal Sir Bernard Montgomery, the victor of El Alamein and Britain's most popular war hero, northward to capture the German ports and liberate Denmark. To learn, in addition, that Eisenhower was contemplating letting the Russians capture the German capital, when it seemed that the Americans could easily get there first, left Prime Minister Winston Churchill dumbfounded and furious. It was no longer a matter of national pride. It concerned the long-term fate of Europe and the world.

Devoutly anti-Communist, profoundly suspicious of Soviet intentions, Churchill insisted that international political considerations had to be taken into account on the battlefield as the war approached a climax. Like Stalin, the British leader knew that the shape of the post-war world would be strongly influenced by developments in the final stages of the conflict. The Allies might share a common objective in a war, but each country had interests and aspirations of its own. Agreements had been reached with Moscow, but there was no guarantee that they would be honoured, any more than the Nazis honoured the pre-war non-aggression pact they had signed with the Russians. There would be much bargaining, much haggling, much jockeying for position. All sorts of factors neglected in the heat of battle could turn out to be of critical importance.

It had been pointless to raise questions about the fate of Berlin when the forces of the western Allies had barely begun making their way in that direction. But with western troops now scudding across Germany as fast as their tanks and trucks could take them, Churchill strongly challenged Eisenhower's contention that Berlin was of secondary significance. How could it be when the very name Berlin had become synonymous with Nazi Germany? There was still time. Berlin was within reach. Churchill insisted it could and should be taken by the western Allies – by the Americans if not the British.

His arguments made no impression on Eisenhower. The Supreme Commander remained haunted by a vision of an invulnerable Nazi stronghold in the mountains to the south. Berlin was not an important military target and, therefore, was of little interest to him. When, at the end of March, instead of going through channels as he had done previously, the Supreme Commander directly informed Stalin of his intention to leave the German capital to the Russians, Churchill saw it as a blatant ploy to shut him up, and he was outraged. Field Marshal Sir Alan Brooke, the British army commander, noted bitterly in his diary that Eisenhower had 'no business to address Stalin directly'.

Eisenhower may have wanted to preclude bureaucratic interference in his strategic planning. But his main reason for contacting Stalin was far from devious. It was known that gunfire had accidentally been exchanged between Russian and German troops when, after the Nazi–Soviet pact had been signed, their forces made contact with one another as they went about splitting Poland between them in 1939. As the forces of the western Allies and the Soviet Union rapidly approached each other in the middle of Germany in March 1945, it became vital to liaise quickly with Moscow to establish link-up points and contact procedures so that confusion would not lead to tragic incidents when they finally came within shooting distance of each other.

In his controversial message to Stalin, Eisenhower informed the Soviet leader that, as they neared the climax of the war in Europe, the main thrust of his forces in Germany would be southward towards the region around Leipzig. There, he suggested, the Russian–American link-up might take place. There was no specific mention of Berlin, but the unmistakable implication was that the Americans would be leaving the city to the disposal of the Russians.

The Soviet leader promptly replied to Eisenhower that his plan 'entirely coincides with the plan of the Soviet High Command . . . Berlin,' he added gratuitously, 'has lost its former strategic importance.' He told Eisenhower he had assigned only 'secondary forces' to move against the German capital. However, Stalin was convinced Eisenhower was trying to deceive him. Having for months considered Berlin his own for the taking, he was both worried and angered by the military circumstances which had appeared to open a path to the German capital for the western Allies. He was convinced that, despite Eisenhower's assurance to the contrary, the Supreme Allied Commander was planning a major assault on the city, to claim it before the Red Army could. The Soviet leader did not intend to be so easily bamboozled.

He immediately summoned to the Kremlin Marshal Georgi Zhukov and Marshal Ivan Koniev, his two crack military chieftains, and asked them challengingly, 'Well, who will take Berlin, we or the Allies?' Neither had any doubt about the answer. Playing them off against one another, Stalin ordered Zhukov and Koniev to draw up plans for an all-out offensive against the city. They were given little more than two weeks to complete preparations for the assault. Stalin was determined to capture Berlin before the Americans could get there. Though he had told Eisenhower he was assigning only secondary forces to the Berlin front, he was taking no chances. More than one million troops and more than 20,000 heavy guns were to be earmarked for the job.

Churchill, meanwhile, shared none of Stalin's doubts about Eisenhower's candour. Convinced more than ever that the Supreme Commander's determination to bypass Berlin would prove to be an historic blunder, and unable to budge him, the British Prime Minister appealed over Eisenhower's head to Washington. Cabling his concerns directly to Franklin Roosevelt, he tried to impress the President with the consequences of what he believed would be, in effect, needlessly handing the German capital to the Soviets:

> The Russian armies will no doubt overrun all Austria and enter Vienna. If they also take Berlin, will not their impression that they have been the overwhelming contributor to our common victory be unduly imprinted in their minds, and may this not lead them into a mood which will raise grave and formidable difficulties in the future? I therefore consider that from a political standpoint, we should march as far east into Germany as possible, and that should Berlin be in our grasp we should certainly take it.

Churchill's warning and advice earned him nothing. Roosevelt believed that, though leader of a totalitarian regime, Stalin was essentially a reasonable man whose aim was identical to his own – the defeat of Nazi Germany and the establishment of conditions that would guarantee that Germany would never again be a threat to world peace. There was much sympathy in America for the Russian people, whose horrific suffering in the war was extensively reported in newspapers across the country, as were the heroic deeds and accomplishments of the Soviet armed forces and guerrilla fighters.

Suggestions from London that Moscow's designs might be less than honourable were not well received in Washington. Many Americans who knew little or nothing of Russia referred affectionately to Stalin as 'Uncle Joe' (which infuriated Stalin when Roosevelt told him about it at Yalta) and thought of him as a kindly national leader who wanted nothing but peace and freedom for his people. They would have been deeply offended had it been widely known that Churchill thought the Russians to be potential adversaries and that he was urging Roosevelt to think the same. Misgivings about allies, where they existed in Washington, were instead directed primarily against the British, who kept talking about their precious Empire. It seemed to some Americans that their British cousins were striving to maintain unjustifiable rights and privileges in far-flung territorial possessions which they ruled through conquests in the distant past and which, like their American colonies two centuries earlier, were being denied the right to choose a government of the people.

George Kennan recalled that, when the leaders of the victorious nations began parcelling out the zones of Germany they would occupy once the war was over, Roosevelt was far more interested in whether Britain or the United States would gain control of the coveted north-western industrial zone of the country than in the dimensions of the area which was to be the Soviet Zone. Unlike Churchill, he was not at all worried that Russia was gaining its first ever toehold in Central Europe.

Also, while for operational purposes unity remained firm among the western Allies, there had for some time been growing mutual disenchantment between British and American generals. The British thought of Eisenhower as a good organizer, but indecisive as a supreme commander. They believed that 'Ike' tended to be excessively influenced by the last person with whom he had conferred, which was hardly a quality to be desired in a military leader.

The Americans, meanwhile, were offended by British efforts to complicate the war by injecting non-military considerations. In addition, United States Army Chief of Staff George Marshall, who had nominated Eisenhower as Supreme Commander, was irritated by criticisms of Eisenhower's performance, conveyed to him privately, and not always tactfully, by some British military leaders. At the same time, American generals thought very little of the talents of Field Marshal Montgomery, the senior British officer in the field. They considered him an overly cautious tactician, who had missed several important battlefield opportunities in Europe with costly consequences. They also thought of him as a blowhard. According to General James Gavin, commander of the American 82nd Airborne Division, they were tired of the publicity Montgomery was claiming 'for battles fought and won by the Americans'. At one point, Eisenhower was so enraged by a self-serving public pronouncement by Montgomery (he told a press conference that he had tidied up for the Americans after the German Ardennes offensive) that he was on the verge of insisting that the British recall him to England. British advice about strategy might have been more effective in swaying Eisenhower – who, as the British rightly believed, was not that hard to sway – had personal friction not been an element in Allied relationships.

There was, in fact, beginning to be a feeling in Washington that Soviet intentions were indeed questionable. Despite carefully spelled out understandings that free elections would be permitted in countries liberated from Nazi rule, the Russians had already imposed a Communist government on Rumania and were in the process of doing the same in Poland. There were other disturbing developments as well. The Russians went back on an agreement to let the United States use airfields in Hungary just liberated by the Soviet army, and were dragging their feet on co-operation in setting up the United Nations, upon which Roosevelt pinned his hopes for peace and security in the post-war world.

But the American President remained reluctant to offend Stalin by challenging Soviet actions, other than to issue mild expressions of concern. He feared that to do so might undermine post-war unity. When it was suggested to him that Stalin could not be counted on to keep agreements, Roosevelt replied, 'I just have a hunch that he is not that kind of man.' When pressed, he replied confidently, 'I can handle Uncle Joe.'

He was, however, to be denied the chance to try. No one outside his immediate entourage knew that the President was desperately ill. By the time British objections to Eisenhower's intention to leave Berlin to the Russians reached him, Roosevelt was dying. Ambassador Robert Murphy, summoned to discuss the situation in Germany with the President, found him 'in no condition . . . to offer balanced judgments upon the great questions of war and peace'.

For some time, messages to Roosevelt related in any way to military operations, as was Churchill's about Berlin, had been going instead to Chief of Staff General Marshall. Concern in London about Eisenhower's strategy received from him little more than scorn. Marshall agreed with Eisenhower that political considerations should not intrude upon the primary task of winning the war in the quickest possible way with the least possible casualties.

If things had gone as expected, that would have ended the controversy. But the dispute over who should take Berlin had flared and then apparently been settled before the full significance of the German military collapse in the West had been grasped. In its closing days, the war had taken on astonishing dimensions. The forces of the western Allies had cut off the

Ruhr, trapping a third of a million German troops, whose commander, Field Marshal Walter Model, was soon to commit suicide. A gap 250 miles wide had been opened in German defences and Allied forces had stormed through it.

The Allied advance had taken on steamroller proportions. Eisenhower's aide, Captain Harry C. Butcher, recorded in his diary on 8 April, 'I told the Supreme Commander that I had heard comment from the correspondents, officers and GIs that they wanted to keep going until they got to Berlin. This desire was rampant.' Three days later, on the evening of 11 April, American troops, having raced a remarkable fifty-seven miles through disintegrating German defences in the previous twenty-four hours, reached the Elbe River, the last natural obstacle on the road to Berlin and only fifty-three miles from the German capital. Advance US army patrols swept into the riverside city of Magdeburg, terrifying after-work shoppers, who had no idea the enemy was near, and creating a traffic jam. Two days later, the Americans planted a bridgehead on the Berlin side of the Elbe.

This was an historic opportunity. The Russians were closer to the German capital than the Americans, but they still had no orders to advance and they faced formidable resistance from German defenders, who had been reinforced and had dug in at strongly fortified positions. In contrast, there seemed to be little to block an American spurt forward to seize Hitler's capital and finally bring the Second World War to a dramatic, irreversible conclusion. Years later, General William ('Big Simp') Simpson, commander of the United States Ninth Army, said, 'The only thing that moved faster than [us] those days was a comparatively few fleeing remnants of the battered and broken German army . . . [We] had ample supplies to drive on and capture Berlin. There was no question in my mind that we could do it, and do it with little loss.'

Nor was Simpson the only one who thought his men would soon be in Berlin. General Walther Wenck, commander of the German forces positioned between the Americans and the city, had little hope of blocking their way. Assigned the task just a few weeks earlier while still recovering from serious injuries suffered in an automobile accident, Wenck examined the situation, despaired at the sight of scratch units which had been stitched together to fashion an 'army' for him to command in this endgame, and told his deputy, 'If the Americans launch a major attack, they will crack our positions with ease. What is to stop them? There is nothing between here and Berlin.'

Eisenhower was faced with a renewed dilemma. Although he had decided to pass up the city, and had told Stalin of this intention, his men had spurted hell-for-leather to the Elbe and had actually crossed it. The situation had to be reviewed.

If Eisenhower's plans were not going to be altered, Simpson's troops at the Elbe had to be braked hard and braked quickly, because neither they nor their commander knew anything about Eisenhower's intention to leave Berlin to the Russians. There had been no need for them to know. No one could have anticipated the rapidity of their advance or the extent of the German rout in the West. But now, having reinforced their bridgehead on the Berlin side of the Elbe, the Americans were about to storm out of it to claim 'the big prize'. Patrols had whisked forward, had reported little to worry about, and were already less than fifty miles from Berlin. Simpson had already instructed his staff that they were going 'hell-bent for Berlin', and expected to be there before another full day had passed.

No delay was now possible for Eisenhower. He again had to make a decision about Berlin. As Simpson finalized his plans for taking the city by roaring down the autobahn Hitler had built for his Third Reich, the Ninth Army commander was summoned by General Bradley back to Army Group headquarters at Wiesbaden, where he expected to be asked to outline those plans. Instead he was told by Bradley to 'Stop right where you are. You can't go any further.'

'Where the hell did this come from?' Simpson demanded.

'From Ike,' Bradley said.

Simpson was to clean up his flanks, link up with the Russians to the south, and deal with remaining German forces there. His forces across the Elbe were not to break out of the bridgehead; they were parked in a dead-end. Simpson was baffled and angry. 'All I could think of,' Simpson recalled later, 'was, "How am I going to tell my staff, my corps commanders and my troops? Above all, how am I going to tell my troops?" '

Eisenhower had been under strong pressure to change his mind about Berlin. Examining the change in battlefield circumstances, he had asked Bradley what it would cost to take the city. Bradley replied it might cost 100,000 casualties, "a pretty stiff price to pay for a prestige objective'. It seemed not only exorbitant but pointless in view of the Allied agreement which placed post-war Berlin within the Soviet Zone of occupied Germany. When widely criticized later, Eisenhower was to ask, 'If I were to seize Berlin at a very great cost in lives, and a day or two later we were ordered to withdraw to comply with the post-war occupation plan, what would the troops think of it and what would the American people think of it?'

General Gavin later said, 'Every soldier I know of who has analyzed the fighting during the month of April 1945 is troubled by the fact that Eisenhower's armies stopped on the Elbe.' Eisenhower himself later told Willy Brandt that if he had to do it over again, he would have permitted the American troops to roll on to Berlin. But, essentially, it was a political decision and, with Roosevelt dying (he died the day after Simpson's men reached the Elbe), America's acting political leadership was incapable of making such a decision. It was left to the military, and they were qualified to make only military decisions.

It is impossible to say what casualties the American forces would have sustained had Simpson been given the green light. No doubt there would have been a price to pay. The Russians suffered 300,000 casualties in taking Berlin. But by that time, while resistance to the Soviet forces remained fierce, many Germans prayed to be captured by the Americans rather than the Russians, whom they had been led by pathological Nazi bigotry to think of as sub-human Asiatic fiends, bent on rape and plunder. Some German units on the eastern front fought on fiercely against the Russians in the hope that the Americans would advance fast enough to take their surrender. Without knowing Simpson had been ordered to halt his forward momentum, General Wenck shifted his makeshift army, originally assigned the task of stopping the Americans, to the east to fight the Russians instead. In the end-of-war chaos, some German officers had been deluded into believing that when the Americans arrived, their own units would join them to go on to fight the Russians together.

On 16 April, three days after Simpson's men had futilely crossed the Elbe, the Russians, who had been hunkered down on the Oder since January, finally launched their drive to break through to the city. On 2 May, they completed their capture of the German capital, effectively ending the Second World War in Europe.

3

Discord in the Ruins

LENIN ONCE SAID that whoever controls Berlin controls Germany and whoever controls Germany controls Europe. The Russians had now taken possession of that once great city. But they couldn't keep it – not all of it. Though it was located deep inside what was, by agreement of the victorious powers, to be the part of Germany occupied by the Soviet Union, the city itself was to be divided into four sectors. Like the four zones into which vanquished Germany was being split, each sector of Berlin was to be occupied and controlled by one of the four powers – the United States, Britain, France and the Soviet Union.

At the time, like most of Germany's main cities, Berlin was in ruins. Willy Brandt, later to be mayor of West Berlin, described what he saw when he returned from exile in Scandinavia:

> Craters, caves, mountains of rubble, debris-covered fields, ruins that hardly allowed one to imagine that they had once been houses, cables and water pipes projecting from the ground like the mangled bowels of antediluvian monsters, no fuel, no light, every little garden a graveyard and, above all, like an immovable cloud, the stink of putrefaction. In this no-man's-land lived human beings. Their life was a daily struggle for a handful of potatoes, a loaf of bread, a few lumps of coal, some cigarettes.

By carrying out their occupation duties alongside each other in this rubble of humbled Germany, it was expected that the wartime allies would demonstrate and preserve international harmony in a world they had liberated from the horrors of fascism and the ordeal of war. As it turned out, there was trouble practically from the beginning.

Within days of the end of the war, the Russians demanded that the United States immediately evacuate Soviet Zone areas which American troops had overrun in the closing days of the conflict. It had been understood that such a withdrawal would take place once the fighting was over. But the tone and urgency of the Soviet demand seemed unnecessarily severe, amounting almost to a suggestion that the Americans, no matter what they had earlier agreed, intended to make squatters' claims to parts of the Soviet Zone unless shooed out on the double.

As always when dealing with the Russians, Churchill was suspicious of their designs. He advised Harry Truman, who had succeeded the deceased Roosevelt as President of the United States, to delay withdrawing the American troops from the Soviet Zone until details of various agreements with Moscow about post-war Europe could be worked out and, where appropriate, implemented. 'It is vital now,' the British Prime Minister warned, 'to come to an understanding with Russia and see where we are with her.'

Truman was indeed dismayed by things the Russians were already up to. He objected to their imposition of Communist rule in parts of liberated East Europe. He was angered by their presumptuous claim that a provisional government they had established in Austria had authority over the entire country, though it had been agreed that Austria was also to be divided into four zones of occupation. Nevertheless, the American President who, at the end of the war, had cabled Joseph Stalin America's congratulations on his 'splendid contribution to the cause of civilization and liberty,' maintained that the western Allies were still obliged to fulfill commitments they had made. Despite Churchill's latest call for vigilance in dealing with Moscow, he saw no reason during his first weeks as President to make major changes in previously hammered-out plans. Nor did he wish to spurn the advice of his newly-acquired military advisers who couldn't see why American troops, having completed their mission in Europe, should mark time in parts of Germany from which they would anyway have to be evacuated before long.

There was still a war in the Pacific to be won. There was also strong domestic pressure to 'bring the boys home' if they weren't being shifted half a world away to take on the Japanese. In addition, Washington, hoping that concerted Allied occupation arrangements for Germany and for Berlin might be quickly implemented, had been signalled by Moscow that there could be no such thing until American troops withdrew from areas of Germany 'they illegally occupy.' With these pressures building up, Churchill's forebodings were easily outweighed and Truman informed the British leader, '. . . our State Department . . . does not believe that the matter of retirement of our respective troops to our zonal frontiers should be used for . . . bargaining purposes'.

Nevertheless, western officials having to deal with their erstwhile Soviet comrades-in-arms found their behaviour inexplicably hostile. Colonel Frank Howley, later to be American commandant in Berlin, said, 'We went to Berlin in 1945 thinking of the Russians only as big, jolly, balalaika-playing fellows who drank prodigious quantities of vodka and liked to wrestle in the drawing room.' But Howley and other American officers were baffled by undisguised Russian antagonism, particularly in view of the vast quantities of military supplies the United States had sent the Soviet Union during the war, without which the horrendous Soviet casualty rate would have been greater still.

However, allowances were made for the gallant ally whose people had suffered so horribly at the hands of the enemy. An estimated twenty million Russians – one in every ten – had been killed. Countless numbers of them had simply been murdered by Nazi execution squads. Another twenty-five million Russians had been made homeless. Russia had been ravaged as no country ever had been before. Almost two thousand of its cities and towns had been flattened.

It was understandable that Soviet leaders would now be wary about anything happening in Germany. If their suspicions seemed exaggerated when they were dealing with their friends, that was perhaps understandable too, after what they'd been through. Nor was it really strange that individual Soviet officers with whom western officers came in contact were undiplomatic in behaviour and speech. If they deviated from conventional standards of courtesy in their dealings with their allies, they were, after all, a different people. And, as the British observed, Americans were themselves no sticklers for etiquette or conventional courtesies.

Besides, there was very little concern among the Allies about what fate awaited Germany and Germans at the hands of the Russians. Details of what had transpired in the Nazi concentration camps were being widely publicized for the first time. Millions of people had been methodically slaughtered. American and British troops had liberated Bergen-Belson, Dachau,

Buchenwald and other concentration camps and had been literally sickened by the stacks of emaciated bodies, the rows of emaciated survivors, the crematoria, the blood trenches, and the gallows. In some cases, they had been so enraged by what they had found that they had unhesitatingly shot down camp guards on the spot. Surviving inmates, who had been robbed of virtually all vestiges of human dignity in the excruciating struggle to stay alive, told the most horrific stories of the treatment inflicted on them, not only by those guards but even by German doctors in the camps, some of whom had engaged in grotesque experiments on humans. Eyewitness testimony and documentary evidence could not be denied.

Germany had become a dirty word and Germans were thought of as scum. The important thing was not to spar with the Russians about this or that triviality, but to make certain that Germans would never again be able to perpetrate crimes against humanity. Allied 'denazification' courts and procedures were established. Nazi officials were arrested, imprisoned and, in some cases, executed. American occupation troops who fraternized with German girls were court martialed. Even anti-fascist Germans had a hard time persuading Allied personnel that they did not share responsibility for Nazi crimes. A climate was generated in which people in the West did not care what their long-suffering Russian allies had in mind for Germany, or how they went about it.

There was some surprise when American troops, acceding to Russian insistence that they withdraw from positions they had overrun in the Soviet Zone of Germany, found themselves shadowed and scrutinized by the Russians, as if they were thieves absconding with property belonging to the new rightful owners – the Russians. There was some irritation when the western Allies were told, after the Americans (and the British too, reluctantly) had bowed to the Russian demand that they withdraw their troops from the Soviet Zone, that it was not yet convenient for them to come to Berlin to assume control of their sectors of the devastated capital. It was almost as Churchill had forecast and it was finally realized that, by ignoring his caveat, the Americans had thrown away the only card the West had held for inducing the Russians to honour their agreements. Nevertheless, it didn't seem to matter much at the time. The war with Germany was mercifully over; the war with Japan was still to be wrapped up. However, frustrations in dealing with the Russians in Germany gradually accumulated, and they centred around Berlin.

On 8 May 1945, the Germans had formally surrendered to the four Allied powers at a ceremony in Berlin. A week later, the Soviets had unilaterally appointed a German civilian governing body for the city, responsible to themselves alone. Two weeks after that, an advance party commanded by Colonel Howley, en route to Berlin to size up the sector the Americans were to occupy and administer, was halted by the Russians fifty miles from the city. Howley was told that a Berlin agreement restricted his party to thirty-seven officers, 175 men and fifty vehicles. Despite Howley's protests that there was no such agreement, the Russians refused to let his party through until he complied with the Russian restrictions.

The reduced American party was then made to bivouac in a suburb of Potsdam, ten miles from Berlin, and were escorted through the ruins of the capital by a Soviet guard who tried to keep them from districts which the Russians were methodically stripping of factory machinery and other valuables. Howley was left with the impression that the Russian officers and men with whom he came in contact 'had been briefed that we were their enemy, merely enjoying an armistice, and they regarded us as such'. He was startled when an angry young Russian officer asked him, 'Why are you Americans going to fight us?' Gregory Klimov, an officer in the Soviet Military Administration of Germany recalled, 'Even at [the] first meeting with the Allies, one could not help noticing a great difference between them and us. They welcomed us as joint victors and sincere allies in war and peace . . . We, on the other hand, regarded the "Allies" as the opposing party, as enemies with whom we had to sit at the one table only for tactical reasons.'

Even when units of General Simpson's Ninth Army, which had been halted at the Elbe in April, were finally permitted by the Russians on 4 July to join them in occupying Berlin, the Soviet commandant raised a technicality which, he said, would unfortunately delay a United States take-over of what was to be the American Sector. Thoroughly annoyed by now, Howley, without Soviet permission, sent United States officers and troops to take control of the American Sector at dawn on 5 July, taking command of the borough halls in the sector and informing borough officials that they would from then on be responsible only to the American commandant. The Russians protested angrily when they realized what had transpired but, faced with a *fait accompli*, they acquiesced. The Americans boasted at the time that they had learned finally how to deal with Russian intransigence. In fact, they were just beginning to learn what Russian intransigence was.

Despite this unseemly bickering, western leaders clung to a vision of a Germany and a Berlin which, though divided into different zones and sectors, would be administered as units and overseen by joint commissions, on which the occupying powers would be equally represented and where harmony would be the ruling principle. It did not occur to them that their line of contact with Berlin through the Soviet Zone of Germany would present a problem and they neglected to insist that access be specifically defined by treaty. They assumed that the right to occupy their sectors of the city automatically included the right of access.

Again, they were mistaken. It was quickly apparent that, rather than a right, the Russians considered use by the western Allies of the access routes to Berlin a privilege, which they could control and grant or deny. When eyebrows were raised at such an obstructive attitude, the Russians made it clear that they considered Berlin theirs by right of conquest. They chose to ignore the corollary: that one-third of what was now the Soviet Zone of Germany, overrun by western troops in the closing days of the war and evacuated by them in accordance with agreements, should have been under western rather than Soviet control by the same right of conquest. It was then that the Americans finally came to the conclusion that, as suggested by Churchill, the Soviet attitude was: What's mine is mine; what's yours is negotiable.

Nevertheless, the Americans and the British (the French, still to be assigned a sector, were not yet deeply involved in the controversy) felt that, to avoid complications, they would for the moment accept much more limited access routes to Berlin than they wanted. Changes could be made later after the dust had settled. What they did not realize was that in also agreeing that all decisions of the joint control commissions set up by the victorious powers would have to be unanimous, they had given the Russians a veto to block any alteration to agreements previously made and procedures previously established. Churchill had warned them but, for the Americans, it was like suddenly finding themselves in a shoot-out, when all they had expected was a sing-along.

The Russians made no secret of the fact that they considered the German capital their own, regardless of its official four-power status or the proceedings of the 'Kommandatura', on which the commandants of the four occupying powers were supposed to have an equal voice in running the city. Communists and others prepared to act exclusively on Soviet orders had been deployed in positions to control the workings of the city's civilian administration. Berlin's reconstituted police force had also been put under Communist command. The Berlin radio station was supervised by the Soviet military. Non-Communist newspapers were rigidly censored. A food rationing system was devised which enabled the Russians to downgrade the ration card of any Berliner who displeased them. They established a trade union association and kept tight control of it. While the western powers devoted their energies to introducing an elaborate (though hardly immaculate) denazification programme in Berlin, the Russians concentrated on the instruments through which they intended to establish long-term control of the city.

As the months passed, the Allies, and particularly their representatives in Berlin, began to grow exasperated with Soviet presumptions and obstructions. The difficulties they encountered could no longer be shrugged off as a product of post-war confusions and dislocations. It was now obvious they were part of a deliberate Russian policy. But Britain, where Churchill was no longer Prime Minister, and France were caught up in sorting out formidable problems of their own generated by the war and its wake. They were preoccupied with making good wartime damage, creating jobs for demobilized servicemen, and finding enough food and fuel to go around. Their tables of priorities left little room for concern over rumblings of discord in Hitler's old capital city. They left it to the Americans, with their infinitely greater resources and infinitely fewer hardships, to take the lead in dealing with Soviet shenanigans. But the Americans at that stage were bent on getting along with the Soviets, for the greater good of all concerned.

General Lucius Clay, then American Deputy Military Governor in Germany, said, 'We were quite willing to start off on their terms.' Diplomat George Kennan has written of 'dreams of a happy collaboration' with Russia which he vainly tried to convince others in Washington were 'quite unreal'. Caught up in the spirit of the budding United Nations, American leaders tended to believe there was a natural harmony of interests among nations. They weren't going to let a handful of minor frustrations disrupt that harmony.

Accordingly, every effort was exerted to make the joint four-power occupation of Berlin function smoothly. If it meant a few compromises, it seemed a price worth paying – until it became unmistakably clear about a year after the end of the war that the Russians saw things and did things very differently. The Soviet military administration in Berlin was, in fact, engaged in a systematic campaign to stifle western-oriented political movements which had begun to re-emerge in the rubble of the city.

The Soviets had re-established a German Communist Party in Berlin within days of the end of the war. The Germans who were to be its leaders had been flown in from Moscow, where they had spent the war years. However, the Communists had been required by the presence of the western garrisons to share the political stage with non-Communist parties. These were led, for the most part, by men and women who had been interned by the Nazis or who had returned from exile abroad. They, their movements, and their potential popularity posed a serious threat to Soviet plans for Berlin and Germany, far greater, it seemed, than the threat posed by the western garrisons, which Moscow expected to pack up and go home in due course.

Barely had the non-Communist parties surfaced in the city when it became evident that the Communists did not intend to confine themselves to conventional political action to compete with their rivals. Activists were kidnapped and disappeared forever into the Soviet Sector. Others were beaten up. Some withdrew from politics after being warned in the Communist press to cease their 'reactionary' activities. Not only political figures were at risk. Three judges who had refused to hand down decisions urged upon them by the Communists also disappeared. Students were expelled from the university for commenting unfavourably on the Communist leadership.

In a tactical move, the Communists disbanded their own party. In its place they created a new organization, the SED, an acronym in German for Socialist Unity Party. Through a merger, the SED was meant to gobble down the newly-established Social Democratic Party which, because of its appeal to the working class in what had once been a strongly socialist city, was seen as a threat to Communist control of Berlin. The resulting 'merged' political organization was to be kept under strict control of a Communist caucus answerable to the Soviet military authorities. Some Social Democrats were drawn into the SED through dreams of working-class solidarity or because of intimidation. The Social Democratic Party had to struggle against Soviet-backed pressure to retain its independent existence. People were shouted down and roughed up at meetings called to discuss the proposed merger. The courage and vigour with which some Social Democratic leaders openly defied Communist bullying persuaded previously sceptical right-wing American army officers in Berlin, who looked on in admiration, that there might after all be a difference between Communists and socialists.

Their defiance also persuaded the Allies to call for city-wide elections at the end of 1946 to see exactly how Berliners felt about the pace and direction of events in their city. The results left them in no doubt. Ignoring Soviet warnings and bribes (the Russians provided the SED with food and coal to distribute in a city desperately short of both), the voters administered a humiliating snub to the Communists. The non-Communist parties took more than eighty percent of the votes. The SED made embarrassingly modest showings even in staunchly working-class districts of the city. A prominent East German Communist who later fled in despair and disgust explained, 'To the man in the street, we were known as the "Russian" party . . . Our leading officials lived in large country houses hermetically sealed from the rest of the population and guarded by soldiers of the Red Army.'

The Russians saw nothing wrong with that. Scorning the rebuff at the ballot box, they persisted in their efforts to dominate the city so many of their soldiers had given their lives to claim. Through manipulation of municipal personnel under their control, direct intercession by their military officers, intimidation, and stonewalling at the Kommandatura, they were partly successful. But the Allies decided they had been swept along far enough by the tide.

The Kommandatura soon lost the image it was supposed to have of a council of common purpose and camaraderie and became bogged down in wrangling. The western commandants found ways around Soviet obstructions. They cleaned out remaining vestiges of Soviet control of the police and municipal administration in their sectors. RIAS (Radio in the American Sector) was set up as a counter to the Russian-controlled radio station in the Soviet Sector. Non-Communist newspapers were supported, as was the Free University set up in the American Sector by students and instructors who could no longer endure Communist ideological rigidity and bullying at the historic Humboldt University in the Soviet Sector. Non-Communist activists were encouraged in their bid to end Communist control of the Berlin trade union organization.

Their plans and expectations increasingly thwarted by these tactics, the Soviets fought back. To frighten non-Communist political activists and media personnel, Communist-run newspapers ran rumours of an impending western withdrawal from the city after which, it was ominously hinted, scores would have to be settled. While reporting western denials, the *New York Times* frightened a lot of Berliners when it reported, 'It is a matter of common knowledge that many military government officials openly discuss the probability of a three-power withdrawal.' Soviet officers took to touring parts of western sectors where Allied personnel were billeted, as if preparing to take over their accommodations. The Russian commandant in the city, in public pronouncements, repeatedly referred to Berlin as part of the Soviet Zone of Germany, which it was not.

Soviet harassment of Allied traffic between West Germany and West Berlin became habitual. Western airliners flying to the city through the agreed air corridors were buzzed by Soviet fighter planes. Restrictions were imposed on civilian train travel through the Soviet Zone to and from West Berlin. When the Russians tried to check personnel aboard Berlin-bound American military trains, General Clay, now American Military Governor in Germany, posted armed guards on those trains to keep them off. The British did the same. It drew warnings from Moscow that Allied trouble-making over a place the Russians had paid so steep a price to conquer was testing Soviet patience.

Roosevelt had once told Stalin he thought United States troops were likely to remain in Europe little more than two years after the war ended. But by 1948, three years after the German surrender, the Americans – the main obstacle to the consolidation and expansion of Soviet influence in Europe still showed no signs of going home. Indeed, the countries of Western Europe, France in particular, were pressing the Americans to join with them in a mutual defence alliance which would guarantee that United States forces would remain planted on the continent indefinitely.

The Russians were also bitter at what was happening in West Germany. The American, British and French Zones were moving towards a merger into one nation. What was more, with substantial American economic aid, a remarkably rapid recovery from the devastation of the war was taking shape. It spawned a spectre that haunted the Russians: the emergence of a strong, hostile, vengeful West Germany. Wartime memories, hatreds and fears remained vivid. That problem had to be dealt with. And Berlin might be the place to deal with it.

Deep within the Soviet Zone of Germany, encased by Soviet military might, Berlin was an ideal place to begin prodding the Americans into their overdue withdrawal from Europe. If Stalin could bring that about, first from Berlin, then from West Germany, the West Germans would have to think again about who their friends should be and to whom they should tip their hats.

As Soviet pressures mounted, the idea of a strategic Allied withdrawal from Berlin was given close consideration in Washington. Realists at the Pentagon, whose job it was to weigh up military possibilities, pointed out that a city so far behind Soviet lines was indefensible and, if it came to the crunch, impossible to supply. Realists at the State Department pointed out that the Allies were in a no-win situation in Berlin. They were in no position to take any credible diplomatic initiatives there and could merely respond to Soviet moves.

In Moscow, where such American views were closely monitored, it was debated how much harassment the Americans would endure before throwing up their hands in despair, pulling up stakes and abandoning the city. The prevailing view was that it was only a matter of time and sustained pressure. However, some in Moscow were not so sure. Painfully aware of the monopoly in nuclear weapons the United States still enjoyed, and plagued by the chronic Soviet mistrust of foreigners, they believed their country was exposed to even more horrendous destruction than the Germans had inflicted. Still grieving for Russia's staggering wartime losses, they were convinced that there were Americans sufficiently hell-bent on destroying Communism to welcome a Soviet challenge in Berlin. Such a provocation could be used to justify an American assault on the war-weakened Soviet Union. That was what Hitler, in his last days, had forecast would happen.

There were indeed people in the United States who thought the time was right to destroy Communism, but they were neither in positions of influence nor to be found in any great numbers. However, there had emerged a group of Americans who had been dealing with the Russians over Berlin, or had served with the United States occupation forces there, or had been connected with the city in some other way, and they had grown passionately devoted to guarding its freedom. This 'Berlin Mafia', as it would later be called in Washington, did what it could to convince the White House as well as the upper echelons of the State Department and the Pentagon that Berlin should not be handed over to the Communists, no matter how vulnerable it seemed. It was argued that the American garrison there, though not nearly a match for the Soviet forces deployed around it, was a perfectly credible deterrent, a trip-wire the Russians would not dare to stumble across, no matter how fiery their rhetoric.

The most influential of the Berlin Mafiosi was General Clay, who had come a very long way from the days when he had amicably agreed to questionable Soviet demands simply to avoid a row. He had once told State Department Soviet affairs expert Charles Bohlen that the key to getting along with the Russians was, 'You had to give trust to get trust.' But as the one who negotiated with the Russians about the arrival of American occupation troops in Berlin in 1945, it was Clay who had failed to secure written assurances from them on the inviolability of the access routes to Berlin. He had publicly accepted blame for that mistake and was now vengefully mistrustful. In a message to Washington early in 1948 about Soviet pressure on the Allied presence in Berlin, he warned, 'If we mean to hold Europe against Communism, we must not budge.'

Whether the Allies would budge was soon to be tested. Stalin was determined to force a showdown with the West over the last remaining patch of territory within Communist East Europe in which the Soviet writ did not run and, in the process, show the Americans they no longer had any business being so far from home. In June 1948, the Russians laid seige to Berlin. Rail, road and waterway access to the city from the West was severed. 'Technical difficulties' was given as the reason for the blockade. But the timing was dictated by a currency reform which the United States, Britain and France had authorized for their occupation zones in West Germany, where runaway inflation was threatening trouble.

Once blockaded, the western garrisons in Berlin and the people who lived in the western sectors of the city would be without food and fuel, all of which was shipped in from West Germany. Denied the necessities of life, West Berliners would clamour for those garrisons to pull out and for the Communist East German regime to meet their needs, as it promised it would. The West would have to beat a humiliating retreat.

Like the Americans, the British and French condemned this attempt at geopolitical extortion. But the people of Britain and France were still suffering the consequences of the war and most of them still hated Germans because of it. They themselves had not long before endured a glacial winter, during which food had been scarce and fuel had been in such short supply that people had died from the cold. They displayed little enthusiasm for risking renewed war and additional hardship by challenging the Russians on behalf of Berliners, no matter how pro-western those Berliners might be.

In Washington, too, voices were again raised questioning the advisability of standing fast in a place which was bound always to cause trouble, which was a lost cause militarily, and which was likely to be more of a diplomatic liability than it was worth. Fearing the Berlin situation might easily escalate into war at a time and place of Soviet choosing, several influential figures, including members of President Truman's cabinet, counselled caution.

But blocking a Communist take-over of Berlin had become as much of a crusade for General Clay as crushing the German armies had been for Eisenhower, and he wanted action. He proposed sending an armoured column through East Germany to West Berlin to break the blockade and show the Russians that Americans could not be bullied. That idea was quickly quashed by the military chieftains at the Pentagon because, if the Russians tried to obstruct the column, it would have to use force to break through and that could mean war.*

Denied authorization to bust the Russian ground blockade, Clay insisted it nevertheless had to be immediately defied, before the Kremlin could build up momentum and before pressure on the Allies to abandon Berlin intensified. He consulted with Ernst Reuter who had been elected mayor of Berlin but who had been barred from office by the Russians. Officers of the Soviet Military Administration objected to Reuter for three reasons – he was strong-willed, he was a Social Democrat who refused to take orders from them, and he was a former high-ranking Communist who had turned his back on Communism twenty-five years earlier.

Reuter told Clay that no matter what the circumstances, Berliners did not want the Allies to leave them to the mercies of the Russians and their Communist underlings. He said they were prepared to live on reduced rations rather than give in. Clay was impressed. It was what he wanted to hear. Within forty-eight hours of the commencement of the Berlin blockade, acting without clearance from Washington, he began having essential supplies ferried by air into the city from United States bases in West Germany.

Clay's presumption and impetuousness ruffled many a feather in Washington, where generals are not expected to make political

---

*One former State Department official said, 'The belief in Europe that American generals are warmongers is way wide of the mark. No one wants peace more than they do. People get killed in wars. What most of them want to do is merely get on with their complicated training programmes and play with their expensive toys.'

decisions and are looked upon with suspicion when they do. But when President Truman was advised by senior advisers that, Clay or no Clay, abandoning Berlin was an option that had to be seriously considered, he responded without hesitation. 'There is no discussion on that point,' he said. 'We stay in Berlin – period.' And he gave his blessings for a full-scale airlift to break the blockade. On the same day, British Royal Air Force transports joined in.

When the full dimensions of what Clay had in mind – a round-the-clock service – were grasped at the Pentagon, Air Chief of Staff General Hoyt Vandenberg couldn't help worrying. It would tax America's military transport resources to the limit. Wasn't it a mistake, he asked, to concentrate so much of those resources in one place at a time of international tension? What would he do if the Russians started trouble elsewhere in the world and some of those aircraft were needed to cope with it? No answer was offered, but soon giant transport planes flown in from the Hawaii, Panama, Alaska and US bases elsewhere around the globe were shuttling into West Berlin's Tempelhof, Gatow and Tegel airports (the last built in a hurry during the airlift) right through the day, winging in every pound of food, every ton of coal, clothing, medicine, equipment of all sorts – everything needed to keep West Berlin fed, fuelled and functioning, and the Allied garrisons supplied.

Planes were scheduled to land at three-minute intervals, but there were times at peak periods over the next eleven months when they were arriving every ninety seconds. Tempelhof, in the American Sector, was a nightmare for pilots coming in to land in poor visibility, as they often had to. It was no easy job for them even when weather conditions were satisfactory. The airfield was little more than a grass patch situated right in the middle of the city, in a clearing surrounded by buildings and bombed-out ruins. Pilots would bring their heavily-loaded, giant Skymasters down low over the top of an apartment building and there they suddenly were, at Tempelhof, quickly levelling off and hoping not to overrun the runway, which they sometimes did. Even years later, when the pressure was off and the weather was fine and the airliner you arrived in was not hauling ten tons of coal, landing at Tempelhof was hardly a relaxing experience, for passenger or pilot.

Soviet fighter planes occasionally buzzed American and British transport planes but, though seventy-two lives were lost in ground accidents, no serious Soviet interference was encountered. General Clay had earlier served notice that if such interference did occur, the aircraft would be escorted by armed American jet fighters. The cautious response of the Russians to this warning was taken by Clay as proof that Moscow was prepared to go only so far, and would back off when challenged. It would influence his actions and cause severe palpitations in the White House later on.

There were moments during the blockade winter of 1948–49 when weather conditions grounded the transport aircraft. Sometimes the planes arrived over Berlin only to find they had to turn back because of visibility problems, and then, for the same reason, couldn't land at the West German airfields from which they had taken off. They would then scout around for fields where they could touch down before their fuel ran out. In one case, a Skymaster loaded with coal for freezing Berlin ended up in Marseilles in the sunny south of France.

Essential supplies in the city fell perilously short that winter, and it appeared that the airlift might fail. It was savagely cold. Trees were cut down for firewood. People scavenged for coal dust and other things they could burn to keep warm. Public transport operated on sharply-reduced schedules and came to a dead halt at 6.00 p.m., after which the city was dark and silent. There was electric power for four hours a day, in two two-hour spreads. Dried food products, easier to transport in bulk, featured strongly in the diet of West Berliners.

The Communist press and radio dramatized their hardship and deprivation, and blamed America for it. It was confidently asserted that the West would succumb. Promises were made that relief from the dire conditions would be immediate if Berliners made clear to the western powers that they no longer required their services. It didn't work. At no time during the blockade was there any significant call among West Berliners for a western climb-down or a withdrawal of the western garrisons. On the contrary, the hardships generated a strong spirit of defiance of the Communists. There was a new sense of purpose and a renewed pride in being a Berliner, which defeat in the war and the troubles immediately afterward had done much to obliterate.

While the Russians were trying to lever the West out of Berlin with their blockade, Communist strong-arm mobs were deployed in the city in Soviet-orchestrated bids to regain complete control of the municipal authorities. Council meetings were stormed and outspoken non-Communists were beaten up. Police under Soviet control looked on and did nothing. When such things happened in the Soviet Sector of the city, where the venerable City Hall was located, the Allies, though appalled, could only protest. But elected city councillors could do more, and they did. When the Communists tried to establish a city government which would be their exclusive instrument, non-Communist councillors set up new headquarters for municipal government in the western sectors, where they could operate under Allied protection. The Russians responded to this challenge by formally incorporating the Soviet Sector of four-power Berlin into the Soviet Zone of Germany. Thus, during the blockade, though the barriers hadn't yet gone up and people freely crossed back and forth, the city was divided into East and West.

The Berlin blockade was the overture to the Cold War. It marked the moment when the Russians signalled their readiness to risk direct confrontation with the West in circumstances which could lead to an outbreak of hostilities, and when the West replied in kind. It was then that nostalgia about the wartime East–West alliance finally fizzled out. It was then that most people in the West began thinking of the Russians as adversaries. Though wartime hatreds would linger on in many places for many years, the Germans, having become participants in a common struggle to preserve western values, ceased being the enemy. The western garrisons in Berlin were no longer occupying forces. They were now the forces of the 'protecting powers'.

At the same time, the response to the blockade dramatically confirmed American leadership of the West. The United States government had begun to think in terms of pulling American troops out of Europe by 1952. It was believed that the countries of Western Europe would by then have sufficiently recovered from the war and be united enough to see to their own security, sparing America the expense and responsibility. The blockade changed all that. Not only was it clear to Washington that the Europeans weren't yet anywhere near ready to cope with aggressive Soviet action without the American presence; it was clear to the Europeans as well. The Berlin blockade forged the strategic logic which has kept American troops on European soil ever since.

For Moscow, the Allied ability to resist Soviet efforts to drive them out of their rogue enclave in the middle of Communist territory confirmed the unshakable conviction that the West was determined to destroy the Soviet system. There was no longer any doubt in the Kremlin that, to survive, the Soviet Union would have to become a military superpower. The struggle for Berlin set the stage for the superpower rivalry between Russia and America which was to become the dominant feature in international affairs during the second half of the twentieth century.

For the moment, however, the Russians realized that they had made a mistake and that the situation in Berlin had to be reassessed. With the onset of spring 1949, bad weather no longer disrupted flights from the West. Soviet expectations that the airlift would fail, and that the city in its entirety would be theirs, crumbled. If anything, it was evident that the western powers were more than ever committed to staying in Berlin.

By the beginning of May, the Russians accepted that the blockade had proved counter-productive and had to be called off. The airlift – a staggering total of 276,926 flights, ferrying in more than 2,300,000 tons of supplies – had convinced Soviet leaders that, for the moment at least, they would have to tolerate a western presence in Berlin.

Nothing could disguise the fact that the Soviet Union had suffered an ignominious setback. It had been forced to concede that it was incapable of doing anything about this capitalist outpost maintained in mocking style behind Communist lines. It was not a defeat the Kremlin found easy to digest.

Even worse, the Berlin blockade had accelerated the process the Soviet Union feared most – the establishment of a German nation it could not control. In the spring of 1949, the American, British and French Zones of the country merged to form the Federal Republic of Germany – West Germany. Bonn was to be its 'temporary' capital, substituting for Berlin until Germany could be reunited. In October of that year, five months after the blockade had been lifted, the Russians turned their own zone into the German Democratic Republic – East Germany. Germany was now two rival nations. And Berlin was on its way to becoming two different cities.

East Germany, under Communist rule and with East Berlin as its capital, did not blossom as confidently into existence as West Germany did. How could it when, as everyone in the East knew, life was easier and the rewards greater in the other part of their divided country?

To shield its people from the attractions of West Germany, the East German regime lowered an Iron Curtain along the 858-mile border between the two German states – barbed wire backed up with minefields and other deathstrips, guarded by armed patrols

and scanned from manned watchtowers. Western newspapers
and journals had long been prohibited in East Germany. To keep
people from being led astray by information filtering through
anyway, the Communist press, radio and television assured
people that life in West Germany was disagreeable and hard,
pockmarked with perils of all sorts.

Nevertheless, it could not be concealed that living and working
conditions in East Germany remained backward by comparison.
The dislocations of the war were compounded by the Soviet
stripping of much of the country's industrial base in the years
after the war. Machinery and sometimes whole factories had been
dismantled and shipped back to Russia. Misconceived or fumbling attempts to introduce socialist procedures in agriculture,
manufacturing industries, housing construction and the distribu-
tion of goods made things worse. The result was endless shortages
and recurring bottlenecks. A cloud of discontent settled over East
German workers and professional people. The Communist media
drew a picture of a harmonious, joyful socialist utopia in the
making, but East Germans were abandoning their Democratic
Republic and trekking to West Germany in great numbers.
Virtually all of them were decamping through four-power Berlin
now that the direct route westward had been blocked by the
barrier planted between the two German nations.

Stumbling, fumbling its way, East Germany was becoming a
burden to the Soviet Union, not made easier to shoulder by the
wartime hatred for Germans – all Germans* – still relentlessly
harboured by Russians. The Berlin blockade, launched to give
the East German Communist leadership a more solid footing,
had been a fiasco, which did nothing to enhance that leadership's
standing in the Kremlin. The ceaseless flow of East German
refugees pouring through Berlin was evidence that the Communist regime in East Berlin was not only unable to cope with the
problems it had inherited, but had produced new ones, albeit
under Soviet supervision. What was more, the existence of a

---

*Some Russians preferred dealing with West Germans, who they did not have
to pretend were comrades, to dealing with East Germans, whose leaders
paraded the myth that they had been liberated from the Nazis rather than
vanquished by the Red Army. In East Berlin one day (this was early in 1961),
while walking with a western correspondent, a Soviet diplomat stationed in East
Berlin approached a car he had recently acquired for his personal use. When the
correspondent admired the vehicle, a Mercedes, the Russian conceded it was
not a bad machine. Then he snarled, 'There is just one thing wrong with it,' and
he aimed a kick at the vehicle's East Berlin licence plate.

Communist East German state, whose people were portrayed in the West as practically enslaved, contributed to a fierce anti-Communism in West Germany. That infuriated the Russians, who equated anti-Communism with fascism. It conjured up for them a picture of an aggressive, menacing West Germany. What was more, that German nemesis was allied to the nuclear-armed United States, whose designs and motives the Russians had suspected even when they were fighting alongside them as allies against the Nazis.

A daring way of dealing with the problem was toyed with in the Kremlin. Perhaps agreeing to the reunification of Germany and ending the occupation of Berlin by all four powers would be the right move to make. The West Germans were clamouring for an end to the division of their country. If properly arranged, with firm guarantees that it would remain strictly neutral, a united Germany could serve a dual purpose. It would relieve Moscow of the East German embarrassment. More important, it would block West German involvement in any western military alliance.

For the Russians, such a plan could have even more rewarding consequences. Sooner rather than later, it could lead to the promised withdrawal of American troops from the European continent. There would, however, be a price to be paid. East Germany, as a separate Communist state, would have to be jettisoned. Its Communist leaders would have to be abandoned to the rough-and-tumble of bourgeois democratic politics for which, in Berlin at least, they had shown themselves totally unqualified.

Most dangerously exposed by this kind of thinking in the Kremlin was Walter Ulbricht, the East German Communist leader. Ulbricht had been living dangerously for a long time. After fleeing to France during the 1930s to escape the Nazis, he had gone to live in Moscow. He had managed there to survive Stalin's mindless purges, during which many German Communists who had taken refuge in the mecca of world Communism had been hauled away to oblivion for no reason they could understand. Most were billeted at Moscow's huge Hotel Lux, where the evening raid by the NKVD (as the KGB was then known) and the unexplained disappearance of residents became a terrifying fact of life about which no one dared speak and which no one dared question. People who had devoted their lives to the Communist cause – Hugo Eberlein, a founder of the German Communist Party; Hans Kippenberger, head of the German Communist Party's military wing; and Willy Leow, head of the German League of Communist War Veterans – were picked up, taken away and never heard from again. Four members of the Politburo of the German Communist Party in exile in Moscow – Hermann Remmele, Heinz Neumann, Fritz Schulte and Hermann Schubert – and ten members of its central committee were among the victims, suddenly gone for good. Moscow turned out to be a dangerous place for German Communists. During the period of the Nazi–Soviet non-aggression pact, to their bewilderment and anguish, dozens of German Communists were handed over by the Russians to the Gestapo from which they had fled, as a sign of Soviet goodwill. They were executed or sent to concentration camps, which usually amounted in the end to the same thing.

Ulbricht was spared such a fate. He survived the war years in the Russian capital and returned to Germany with the Red Army, to be installed as head of the civilian administration operating under Soviet supervision. With Soviet backing, he remained the dominant figure in the East German leadership, despite the persistence of the Soviet Zone's problems and despite grumblings among some of his colleagues about the rigid policies he pursued. There was no reason to replace a man who was so reflexively submissive to Russian wishes.

After Yugoslavia's Marshal Tito had presumed to reject Soviet leadership in 1948, the Kremlin was reluctant to encourage feelings of independence among other Communist leaders. This was especially true in East Germany, where some of Ulbricht's independent-minded critics were known to have questioned whether it was right for the Russians to extract such huge reparations from a country they were supposed to have liberated. There were also some who had suggested at the end of the war that abortions be permitted for women raped by Russian soldiers, when the Russians stonily denied that such misbehaviour was taking place. The matter had been raised at a meeting of Communist officials, but Ulbricht, warding off any hint of a suggestion of criticism of the Soviet liberators of East Germany, had quickly and angrily ruled, 'There can be no question of it. I regard the discussion closed.'

Even among the East German Communists who remained scrupulously submissive to Soviet rule, there were some who urged greater flexibility in policy making than Ulbricht, with his Stalinist training, was prepared to allow. They wanted a softer line to raise worker morale and stimulate economic recovery. Their views were shared by some leading figures in the Kremlin who blamed Ulbricht for the dismal contrast between West Germany's economic vitality and East Germany's difficulties.

The Kremlin thought seriously about changing the East German leadership and prepared to put the East German Communist leader out to pasture. Ironically, the failure of his policies saved him from being dumped.

In the late spring of 1953, three months after Stalin died, East Berlin exploded. It was convulsed by the first major anti-Communist uprising ever in a country occupied by Soviet troops. On 17 June, infuriated by newly-promulgated increases in work norms and by the persisting failure of the Communists to improve their standards of living, thousand of East Berliners, led by disgruntled construction workers on the Stalinallee, went on strike and marched through the streets in protest against the regime. The Soviet Sector resounded with catcalls against Ulbricht and the East German regime. Demands were made for the resignation of the government, for free elections and, most daringly of all, for the return from Russia of thousands of German prisoners of war still held there eight years after the end of the war. Youths climbed to the top of the Brandenburg Gate, on the border between the Soviet and British Sectors, and tore down the Communist flag. It was spontaneous, it was devastating and, because it happened in Berlin, the Communist authorities were unable to conceal this violent spasm of discontent from the world.

It started in the Soviet Sector of Berlin, but demonstrations and strikes erupted all over East Germany, in almost every major city and town. Hundreds of thousands of workers were involved. Local security forces couldn't cope with the situation. In places, Vopos openly sympathized with the demonstrators. To their disgust, the Russians had to be called in by the badly-shaken East German leaders. Soviet tanks were sent into the streets of East Berlin to teach the demonstrators revolutionary discipline. Before it was over, 246 East Berliners had been killed. All told, some eight hundred East Germans were reported killed throughout the Soviet Zone before calm was restored. Dozens were sentenced by Soviet military tribunals and East German kangaroo courts to be executed. East German Minister of Justice Max Fechner, who had been unwise enough to concede that the country's constitution guaranteed the right to strike, was arrested and imprisoned.

Publicly, the Communists maintained that the uprising was inspired by the West to sabotage East Germany's march to Communism. But the Kremlin could no longer entertain thoughts of replacing Ulbricht with a more flexible regime. To do so would have been a signal to disgruntled workers in the other Communist-controlled East European lands that public displays of dissatisfaction would not be futile. (Such trouble for the Soviet Union would, in due course, come anyway in Poland, Hungary and Czechoslovakia.) In Moscow, the suggestion that East Germany might be abandoned by the Soviet Union so that a neutral united Germany might be created was hastily consigned to the garbage bin. In view of what had occurred, it would have been an impermissible confession of Communist failure, with unpredictable consequences.

Though the uprisings were dismissed as having been instigated by western agents, both the Russians and the Ulbricht regime had to face up to the continuing, indisputable evidence of popular discontent with prevailing conditions. Given no reason to expect changes for the better at home, and tantalized by reports from friends and relatives in West Germany of the opportunities available there, a steady stream of refugees continued to flood westward through Berlin – 118,000 in 1952; 306,000 in 1953, the year of the abortive East German uprising; 104,000 in 1954; 154,000 in 1955; 156,000 in 1956.

Passage through the four-power city was virtually unrestricted. Tens of thousands of East Berliners had jobs in West Berlin. Family links transcended sector borders – some members lived in one part of the city, others in the other. People went back and forth all day without delay or difficulty. For people wanting to leave East Germany for good, Berlin was an open door. Departing East Germans who did not already live in East Berlin made their way there by train (a simple commuter trip), slipped into West Berlin, and then either settled there or, with help from the West German government, flew on to West Germany where, because of the labour shortage, they were more than welcome.

By 1957, the relentless human leakage had so damagingly compounded an already serious labour shortage in the East that East German leaders listed a new offence in their criminal code – *Republikflucht* (Fleeing the Republic). It was punishable by imprisonment if the flight was foiled. But only rarely was it foiled in Berlin. If simple discretion was practised, departure was as simple as crossing the street or taking a train on the subway (*U Bahn*) or elevated line (*S Bahn*) to the next stop.

As the drain away of workers continued unabated, increasingly tough measures were introduced to make good lost production. Workers in mines and factories were urged to emulate heroes of labour who, for the glory of the Socialist Fatherland, were said to

have fulfilled their work quotas many times over. When this
failed to draw the desired response, work discipline was enforced
– and still more workers hurried westward through Berlin.

For the Russians, West Berlin, and the escape route it provided
for those who rejected the realities of Communist rule, was an
insult and an embarrassment. The corrupting influences – the
glitter, the western propaganda, the capitalist enticements –
radiating through a city for which their troops had shed so much
blood were doubly outrageous because they undermined Soviet
plans to build a stable, reliable Communist nation in East
Germany. That nation was meant to serve as a buffer for the rest
of Communist East Europe against the military and economic
threat a revenge-seeking West German state might one day pose.
Instead, it was being humbled by the Berlin blot on the
Communist landscape. Once more, the Russians decided that
blot would have to be soaked up.

4

Ultimatums and Departures

Soviet Prime Minister, Nikita Khrushchev – a shrewd, articulate man – habitually went far beyond official Kremlin policy in his public utterances. It was a ploy which enabled him to seize an advantage if one was available, or to back away without damage if it got him nowhere. This device of his was well known, so not a great deal of attention was paid when, at a Moscow reception on 10 November 1958, Khrushchev took the opening step in the next Soviet campaign to boot the West out of Berlin. He declared that the time had come for the occupation of Germany to be ended, and for the western powers to deal with the government of East Germany on all questions concerning Berlin, on whose territory the four-power city was situated. That the West did not recognize the East German regime which claimed sovereignty over West Berlin, and did not intend to recognize it, was not a factor Khrushchev was prepared to take into account.

The statement by the Soviet leader was dismissed by the United States as just another fishing expedition. When questioned at a press conference, Secretary of State John Foster Dulles drawled, 'The international Communist movement is disposed periodically to try to probe in different areas of the world to develop, if possible, weak spots.' Dulles gave assurances that Moscow would find no weak spot in Berlin and he forecast that its probing would then cease.

However, two weeks later, the Soviet foreign ministry turned Khrushchev's off-the-cuff remarks into a formal ultimatum. 'It should be clear to anyone with common sense,' it said in a message to the governments of the United States, Britain and

41

France, 'that the Soviet Union cannot tolerate a situation in West Berlin that is detrimental to its lawful interests, its security, and the security of other Socialist countries.' It demanded that the western powers remove their garrisons from the city. They were given six months in which to do so. If they did not get out, the Russians would unilaterally sign a peace treaty with East Germany. That, they said, would end the post-war occupation of Berlin which would then become a 'free city'.

Moscow's call for a peace treaty was to be made repeatedly as the crisis built up. It sounded logical and innocent enough to people persuaded that its only purpose was to bring about an overdue formal conclusion to the Second World War. But, if implemented, such a treaty would have a wider significance: it would put paid to any legal justification for the presence of the western garrisons in Berlin; it would endanger the access routes from West Germany by which those garrisons were supplied; and it would leave West Berlin open to a Communist take-over. As a 'free city' located within Communist East Germany, shorn of Allied protection, West Berlin would not be 'free' very long.

The Russian ultimatum was backed by an implied threat. 'Only madmen,' it said, 'can go to the length of unleashing another world war over the preservation of occupation privileges in West Berlin.' Unwittingly implied in that observation was the converse – only madmen would unleash a world war to *end* the occupation.

No matter how unconventional his behaviour from time to time, Khrushchev was no madman. When the West responded to the Soviet ultimatum with firm assurances to the people of West Berlin that they would not be abandoned to the Communists, the Russians backed off. Harassment of the western access routes through East Germany to Berlin continued sporadically as they contemplated their next move. But they passed word along that they hadn't really meant to set a six-month deadline; it was only to stimulate four-power talks to find a Berlin solution – and that it did.

At the four-power foreign ministers conference duly held in Geneva in the summer of 1959, the western powers hoped to defuse the situation before the climate of East–West relations was completely soured. But Soviet Foreign Minister Andrei Gromyko's stoney-faced hard line indicated that the Russians remained determined to terminate the western presence in Berlin. The gathering ended without agreement.

Nevertheless, the Russians, their eyes focused as always on long-term results, were left with the impression that the West, alarmed by the danger of war, would give ground if Soviet pressure was maintained. If properly prodded, western officials would meet among themselves to discuss and debate how to save the world from catastrophe by making concessions. And few world leaders were more skilled than Nikita Khrushchev in sending westerners into a frenzy of hurried conferences and consultations to decipher the significance of his repeated, menacing, off-the-cuff pronouncements. Discussing Berlin with veteran diplomat Averell Harriman, Khrushchev suddenly shouted at him, 'If you want war, you can have it. But remember, it will be your war. Our rockets will fly automatically.' Did that mean Russia was already on a war footing? Did that mean he would send those rockets off if he didn't get his way?

However, a visit by Khrushchev to the United States in the late summer of 1959, during which he made repeated references to 'peaceful coexistence', left a different impression. He conferred congenially with President Eisenhower at the Camp David presidential retreat in the mountains of Maryland, spoke to the American people on television, was made a fuss over in Hollywood, and visited a cornfield in Iowa. The agreeable tone of his American tour and the cordiality shown by all concerned seemed to signal that peaceful coexistence was indeed possible, and that some sort of mutually acceptable Berlin solution could be worked out. It was decided that the situation would be discussed the following spring at a four-power summit in Paris.

Khrushchev made it clear that he expected movement there towards western diplomatic recognition of East Germany and the creation finally of 'a normal situation' in Berlin. Eisenhower agreed with him that the situation in the city was 'abnormal'. Though it wasn't what the President intended, his comment seemed to imply that the Berlin situation needed changing and confirmed the belief in the Kremlin's America-watchers that the process of attrition was indeed working. It was only a matter of time and persistence before the 'abnormality' of West Berlin would be rectified.

They weren't alone in believing that an American climb-down at the forthcoming summit was a distinct possibility. When, to keep the pot boiling, the Russians resumed their public demands that the Berlin situation be 'normalized' without delay, West German Chancellor Konrad Adenauer did not conceal his anxiety. Adenauer warned the White House that an irredeemable mistake, with catastrophic consequences, would be made if America permitted itself to be manoeuvred by Khrushchev into negotiating over Berlin while ignoring the bigger problem of German reunification, in which the Russians were no longer interested.* West Berlin Mayor Willy Brandt also feared that the West was tiring of the protracted Berlin hassle and might be preparing to succumb to Soviet perseverance.

Though reluctant to engage in a war of words prior to the summit conference, the White House and the State Department came to realize that a lot of people, including the Russians, were getting the wrong impression. The record had to be set straight. As expressions of concern, both abroad and in the United States, accumulated about how things seemed to be drifting, the American government set about offering assurances that the United States would not be found wanting in defending the cause of freedom. In a speech carefully drafted so that no one would misunderstand, Under Secretary of State Douglas Dillon declared that 'No nation could preserve its faith in collective security if we permitted the courageous people of West Berlin to be sold into slavery.'

Washington recognized that West Berlin remained a militarily exposed diplomatic trouble spot, the place where the Soviet Union could stir the cauldron of mischief whenever it wished to subject the United States to pressure. Khrushchev knew that West Berlin was 'the sore blister' on the American foot in Europe, to be stepped on 'any time we wanted to . . . make them feel pain'. But recollections were dusted off in the White House of how Stalin's Berlin blockade had been foiled by American defiance when things had looked grim. President Eisenhower, who had long been stung by criticism of his failure to capture the city during the war, served notice that the United States would not surrender 'the rights we have' in Berlin. As the date for the summit conference in Paris approached and the American position on Berlin publicly hardened, the Russians realized that their expectations of gaining western concessions there had no chance whatsoever of being fulfilled.

Khrushchev was now under growing pressure at home. His colleagues in the Kremlin recognized that, despite the hullabaloo over his visit to America and the forthcoming summit, no

*Yugoslav Ambassador in Moscow Veljko Micunovic recounted a choice bit of Khrushchevian ribaldry on that point: 'If you strip Adenauer naked,' he quoted Khrushchev as saying, 'and look at him from the rear, then you can see clearly that Germany is divided into two parts. But if you look at Adenauer from the front, then it is equally clear that his view of the German question never did stand up, doesn't stand up, and never will stand up.'

progress was being made over Berlin. The western garrisons showed no signs of packing up and pulling out. The only tangible result so far of Khrushchev's ultimatums and threats was a sizable increase in the number of refugees streaming out of East Germany and into West Berlin. East German Communist leaders were whining and moaning about the desperate situation in which they found themselves and begging the Kremlin to do something about finally driving the West out of the city.

The Paris summit in the spring of 1960 was the place where Khrushchev expected to start that process. But with the United States publicly standing firm over Berlin, the Soviet leader realized that he now had nothing to gain and much face to lose from the forthcoming summit conclave. His foreign ministry told him that Soviet ambassadors in Washington, London and Paris were reporting that the western powers would not be in a generous mood in Paris. He would be left with the stark choice of making a fool of himself by emerging from the conference hall empty-handed, or escalating the confrontation with America, with the danger that it might career out of control. He had no wish to do either.

For a long time before they could do anything about it, the Russians knew that high altitude American reconnaissance planes were overflying Soviet territory. They had made no fuss about them because to do so would have been an embarrassing admission that the Americans possessed far more sophisticated technological wizardry than they did, and that they were helpless to do anything about it. But by the spring of 1960, they had developed the means to deal with those spy planes.

Just after dawn on 1 May, an American U-2 reconnaissance plane, equipped with highly sophisticated, ground-scanning cameras, took off from a base in Pakistan and entered Soviet air space at a height of more than 65,000 feet. It was to cross the Soviet Union, making a photographic record of security installations, and land at a base in Norway.

But over the city of Sverdlovsk in the Ural Mountains, the U-2 was hit by a ground-to-air missile and brought down. Its pilot, American CIA agent Francis Gary Powers, parachuted down and was captured alive. The incident was to give Khrushchev the excuse he needed to break up a summit that clearly would earn him nothing but trouble.

Though Soviet espionage operations in the United States were extensive and highly successful – gaining for the Russians, among other things, important information for the development of nuclear weapons – after arriving in Paris, Khrushchev demanded that Eisenhower publicly apologize for the U-2 flight. He also insisted that the President dismiss all Americans who had been involved in the spying mission. As Khrushchev knew, the President could not, and would not, comply with those demands. When he did not, the Soviet leader announced that under the circumstances he could not possibly engage in the friendly talks which had been planned and stalked out of the conference.

As Henry Kissinger has said, 'The Soviets choose when to be insulted.' It solved the immediate problem of how Khrushchev was going to extricate himself from the summit he no longer wanted. But it left the Berlin situation, which the Russians still found intolerable, exactly where it had been earlier. It would not stay there very long.

By early 1960, with the crunch still to come, Berlin was already far more conspicuously bisected than any city had ever been before. It remained a single geographical entity, but it was evident, even to a newcomer like myself, that West Berlin was one place, while East Berlin was unmistakably someplace else. And it was not only the ideological divide, and the Vopos at the Brandenburg Gate checking western cars going in and out of East Berlin for subversive literature and contraband, that made them places apart.

West Berlin – the dividing lines between the three western sectors in it were, for all practical purposes, irrelevant – was a bustling place, very much on the move, very much up-to-date, even in its outcroppings of nostalgia here and there. Crossing into East Berlin was a curious experience in contrasts. Notwithstanding the huge banners strung up in public places exhorting the populace to work energetically to build socialism, it seemed drowsy and old fashioned, a touch Ruritanian with a big city overlay.

Whatever the overlay, Berlin was a metropolis, a sprawling urban realm with boulevards and backstreets, tenements and trolley tracks, parks and parades, museums and mass-circulation newspapers, two rivers and a couple of canals meandering through it. A network of subway and elevated train lines covered the city, reaching out almost as far as the thick forests and sleepy lakes on its fringes.

Berlin also had a magic that was distinctively its own. In no other city was the contest between two dynamic world philosophies so visibly played out. Berlin also had a fascinating history, part horrific, part seductive. During the hysterical obscenity of Nazi times, here was the heart of a gruesome political organism in which men who loved music and children and toyed with ethical vegetarianism had millions of people systematically tortured and slaughtered.

But before the Nazis ruled Berlin, and ultimately brought it destruction and ruin, the city was something else altogether. If Paris had been the City of Light in the early part of the twentieth century, Berlin had been the City of Depth and Imagination. It was here that Bertolt Brecht had contrived savage caricatures on the stage, where the Bauhaus architectural experimenters had uniquely blended art with craftsmanship, where restless movements among artists had created one 'secession' after another from the mainstream, where new ideas had been endlessly in the air, endlessly growing and changing.

In 1960, Berlin was living in the shadow of its past and, most pressingly, in the shadow of the facts which had made it two places instead of one. In the West, the rubble of the war had been mostly cleared away or tucked out of sight, but the tower of the Kaiser Wilhelm Memorial Church in the heart of the city was left as a standing ruin, a reminder for all to see of what Hitler had done to Germany. However, consistent with its Bauhaus past, Berlin – at least its western sectors – had again become something of a playground for experimental architects. Some of the buildings which had sprung up from the wreckage of bombing and battle were daring, almost whimsical in concept and design. Not for nothing did Berliners call the new Congress Hall 'The Pregnant Oyster'.

Whimsy could sometimes also be detected in the vision of a new breed of artists who had turned parts of the Kreuzberg district of West Berlin into a miniature Montparnasse. But they tended to be a serious lot and their work generally ranged from the aesthetically sensitive to deeply paranoid, the two not always being mutually exclusive. Variety was very much a part of the city. The glum, tenement-lined streets of Kreuzberg and Neukoelln, which had been recreated in many of the weird, surreal pre-Nazi Berlin movies, were, in mood, a world away from the serene atmosphere of the Dahlem district, with its tidy, single-family homes, as antiseptic a residential quarter as one could expect to find so close to the centre of a big city anywhere, and even further remote from the rural tranquillity of Lubars, a country village tacked on to Berlin, as if by mistake.

The Kurfürstendamm ('Ku'damm'), which was lit up brightly

at night, offered still another aspect of this unique frontier outpost. This broad boulevard, West Berlin's main thoroughfare, Fifth Avenue (as it once was) and the Champs Élysées rolled into one, had originally, in the sixteenth century, been hewn out of countryside to provide local nabobs with a direct path to their hunting haunts in the Grunewald Forest. Now it was flanked part of the way, before its further reaches fizzled into urban ordinariness, by elegant shops flaunting the latest fashions and chic travel goods, and by cafés blending old world *gemütlichkeit* with state-of-the-art ambience. The finest ice cream sundaes on the far side of the Atlantic were to be had at Kempinski's, though many who lounged in the sun on its Ku'damm patio generally indulged instead in lush slabs of hazelnut torte capped with outsized dollops of snowy, outrageously rich *schlagsahne*. Down the street, the dignified Kranzler Café had become a meeting place for people of discrimination who preferred to shun the newer, more pedestrian, more up-to-date comforts of one of the first Hilton hotels in Europe, which had risen like a shrine to the American presence in Berlin.

West Berlin – with a population of a little more than two million, twice that of East Berlin – was an intricate complex of moods and images, sensations and experiences, all compounded by politically charged headlines and the presence of foreign soldiers. The troops – 5,000 American, 4,000 British, and 2,000 French – were mostly out of sight except near their quarters, but the huge American establishment around Clayallee was practically a village of its own, equipped with a sizable PX, bank, post office, cafeteria, dry cleaning service, movie house, radio station, bus stops and 'No Littering' signs. The British and the French, with much smaller military, diplomatic and support contingents, offered their personnel various home-style services as well, though on a more modest scale. Similarly, in the Karlshorst district of East Berlin where the Soviet garrison and civilian personnel were quartered under tight security, there were facilities to buy goods with rubles and see Soviet movies.

There was mystery behind the scenes in both East and West Berlin. Foreign correspondents and their German stringers debated among themselves about which of their colleagues, and others they encountered in the course of the day's work, were 'spooks', employed by one espionage organization or another, or perhaps by more than one. It added to the peculiar magic of the two-part metropolis, as did the Soviet military sedans which cruised daily through West Berlin, counterparts of the American,

British and French 'flag-showing' vehicles which, by agreement, did the same in the Soviet Sector.

For a place that was supposed to be a showcase of westen lifestyles, cultural life in West Berlin was suitably stimulating. Theatre, opera and concert halls drew large and appreciative audiences, hungry especially for cultural imports from abroad. Aside from the aesthetic pleasures which might or might not be involved, such imports lent a cultural solidarity which eased the distinct sense of isolation felt in this frontier outpost of the western world.

It wasn't easy getting a ticket to the German-language rendition of *Kiss Me Kate*, or even to the English-language production by a visiting American company of *The Miracle Worker*. To underscore the western presence, the Allies sponsored and ferried in a parade of visiting performers, entertainers and educators, sometimes to the befuddlement of the Russians in the East. After a performance by an American troupe of an experimental drama which agonizingly portrayed the lives and ways of a group of wretched New York junkies, a Russian diplomat who had been invited to the premier confided that he was baffled by the American government's promotion of such a play, since 'no society in which such things not only happen but are also glorified can long survive'. Movie houses, showing American, British, French and Italian as well as German films, were full on weekends and didn't do badly during the week either.

As befitted its cosmopolitan aspirations, West Berlin boasted nightclubs – Charly's, Cherchez la Femme, Chez Nous – which promised programmes of entertainment by distinguished artistes. Prohibitively expensive by local standards, these tended at the time to be frequented by visitors to the city or resident foreigners. For a convivial night out with friends, native Berliners preferred leisurely dining out, either in the *gasthaus* around the corner where the *goulaschsuppe* and *sauerbraten* could generally be relied upon, or in such atmospheric city-centre hangouts as Hartke's on Meinekestrasse, where the house-made *wursts* were highly commendable (and which served as the regular venue for a lunchtime round-table of American correspondents in Berlin). It was generally only foreigners or well-heeled local professionals who converged on such up-market establishments as the Ritz, where the wild boar with *spaetzle* was something truly unique.

The *Stachelschwein* (Porcupine), a popular cabaret, had brought clever irreverence back to the Berlin stage, mocking all aspects of politics and society, though it generally found ridiculing developments in East Germany too easy a target. It was particularly biting about the unstoppable surge of West German consumerism which had spilled over into West Berlin. Acquiring a television set and a washing machine had become the prime goal of many of the same people who had dug through the ruins of their city for a potato or a lump of coal a mere fifteen years before. While foreigners and less sophisticated natives might consider Germany to be the setting of major developments affecting the fate of the world, performers at the *Stachelschwein* found the country vacuous and boring. Recalling the patriotic slogan 'Think of Germany!', they sneered, 'We do think of Germany. That's what puts us to sleep at night.' And the audience roared with laughter.

For those in West Berlin who could not fall asleep so easily, there was also a handful of creepy dives where the legendary degeneracy of 1920s Berlin was squalidly revived. There was one where a swarthy, unhappy man with sleeked down hair, stripped to the waist, tried (and mostly failed) to whip a cigarette from the mouth of a worn, vast-bosomed blonde well past her prime, while people sitting at small tables, drinking an overpriced excuse for *sekt*, maintained a mask of apathy, barely managing meagre applause when the cigarette was finally whipped to the ground. It attracted the scrutiny of scholars at the recently established Free University, which was already turning into one of central Europe's main centres of intellectual probing and controversy.

There were two or three biggish, shadowy dance-hall pick-up joints which tended to be packed on weekend nights and the venerable Resi (situated a long time before in what was now East Berlin), where dance or table partners were contacted, or mere flirtations were conducted through table telephones.

But West Berlin was also very much an out-of-doors city. On weekend afternoons, people flocked to the patios of mock-rural tea houses in its leafy suburbs and sat there nursing pastries and glasses of tea until they grew weary of defending them from the bees which buzzed around in great but harmless numbers. Sailboats drifted lazily across the Wannsee and campers, pretending to be miles from civilization, pitched tents in the Grunewald Forest and lived in them for days and sometimes weeks on end. With springtime, the fierce Siberian wind which swept across Berlin in winter and could send thermometers plummetting to below the zero fahrenheit mark was forgotten. East Berlin, however, had been living with a Russian import of a more pervasive kind since the end of the Second World War.

Someone entering East Berlin for the first time during that spring of 1960 by driving from West Berlin through the Brandenburg Gate might easily have felt he was passing through that majestic portal into a realm of enigmatic dreams. Leading up from the gate, which was modelled on the Propylaea in Athens, was the broad avenue of Unter den Linden (Under the Lime Trees.) Well before Nazi battalions had goosestepped along it, it had been the main thoroughfare of a proud metropolis. Heinrich Heine had lived here; Goethe had stayed here. Still an elegant boulevard, it was flanked part of the way by stately facades of bygone days, or the stately remains of them.

But this famous street, once the centre of greater Berlin, was virtually deserted. A few Vopos stood outside the huge, new Soviet embassy building, built on the site of the old Russian imperial embassy. Two or three pedestrians were in motion here and there. One or two cars crossed from side streets. But for a driver new to the scene, there was a sense at first of cruising through a void, backed by an imposing but desolate facade.

Further into East Berlin, along Friedrichstrasse and at Alexanderplatz, that desolate sensation was overcome. The stately architectural remains were no more to be seen, but people were finally there, going about their business. There was a different dimension of strangeness here. Unlike West Berlin, there seemed to be no bustle, no sense of time passing, no urgency. The urgent exhortations of the massive Communist street placards – BUILD THE SOCIALIST FATHERLAND; FOR PEACE AND PROGRESS – were the only visible signs of direction, and they seemed ironic rather than purposeful. It seemed very calm, aimless, relaxing.

That feeling was soon overlaid by another. There was a sense of poor-but-honest about the place which evoked sympathy and admiration. Men and women were dowdily attired but not undignified. The men, mostly clutching well-worn leather brief-cases, wore dark-hued, rough woollen trousers and jackets – the jackets often slightly ill-fitting, the trousers usually baggy at the knees. Many of the women were in dresses or blouses and skirts they had apparently tailored themselves, with some tailoring skill but not always with much flair for design or colour sense. On first sight (and last) there was not much to disabuse an outsider of the belief that this was truly a place of straightened circumstances, as indeed it was.

Denied the kind of investment that was pouring into West Berlin from West Germany and western countries (the Russians had taken out rather than put in), the Soviet Sector of the city was still dotted with countless mementoes of the Second World War. Even in the centre of old Berlin, the precinct that had once been called *Mitte* (Middle), rusting, twisted girders and rubble marked the spots where buildings had been bombed by American and British aircraft or battered by Soviet artillery more than a decade and a half before. Empty lots which had been cleared of rubble were overrun with weeds.

The East Berlin authorities had made a strenuous effort to deal with the serious housing shortage they had inherited from the war. But the new buildings they had constructed tended to be humdrum, box-like edifices with frontages of bathroom yellow tile. It was the kind of structure that passed for modern housing wherever the Stalinist imagination and a shortage of resources, investment and labour converged. Pre-war edifices which still stood were more substantial in mood and feeling, but were invariably chipped and pockmarked where bullets or shrapnel had left their mark.

The buildings along the mile-long Karl-Marx-Allee – as Stalinallee had been renamed after Khrushchev had denounced Russia's wartime leader – were new, tall, glistening, and largely unadorned with gimmicks. But they looked like magnified versions of tinker toy contrivances, minus the charm, minus the flair. To squeeze in as many accommodation units as possible, planners had decreed that the apartments in the new buildings be basic, often consisting only of one or two rooms with kitchen alcove and toilet. Under the circumstances, in some new buildings, bathtubs were deemed a luxury people could manage without. They could attend clean, accessible neighbourhood public bath houses.

The needs and wishes of East German consumers had to be sacrificed to the greater good. The country was desperate for export markets in which hard currency could be earned. As a consequence, not only bathtubs were hard to come by. Many types of manufactured goods were not released onto the domestic market and those that were available were often of poor material, shoddily manufactured and, to make matters worse, in short supply.

An East German who could afford a refrigerator had to spend a year working his way down the waiting list before he could buy one. There was a two-year wait for a washing machine. To own a car was a long-term ambition few could realize, no matter how hard they worked. At night, especially at weekends, there was sometimes heavy traffic on main streets in *Berlin Mitte.* But virtually all the cars bore West Berlin licence plates. At that stage, people could drive in and out of East Berlin with a minimum of formalities.

Restaurants tended to be crowded at night, again mostly at weekends. But that was partly because, again, many of the diners were people from West Berlin – visiting family, taking in the opera or theatre, taking advantage of the favourable exchange rate, or just slumming. The East Berliners to be found in the restaurants were generally higher-paid professionals, managers, specialists and others who had few other places to spend their earnings unless they went over to West Berlin. But in the West their East German marks were worth only one-fifth of their face value, so spending sprees for East Berliners on the far side of the sector boundary were infrequent. As for East Berliners buying goods in the West, East German customs police at the sector crossings confiscated appliances and other largish items people might try to cart home with them.

However, people with East Berlin identity cards were able to buy cut-rate theatre, concert and movie tickets in West Berlin with their own currency. They were not to be denied the pleasures of this part of their city simply because they lived in the other part. In 1960, the year before the practice came to a sudden, enforced halt by the building of the Wall, ten million East Berliner admissions to movie houses in West Berlin were subsidized by the West German government. At weekends, while movie houses in East Berlin, strong on propaganda and/or culture, were half full, East Berliners jammed with West Berliners into those on the other side of the border to see the likes of Marilyn Monroe, Marlon Brando, and Brigitte Bardot.

There was, however, no cut-rate food in West Berlin for people from the Soviet Sector. So except for the occasional luxury – coffee and sometimes butter – East Berliners did their food shopping back east, which was usually a dreary experience. The smaller groceries were now marked by un-German signs of neglect. The shelves of what had been the proverbial shop-around-the-corner were half empty and the fresh foods they displayed did not look overly appetizing. Other, newer, state-run stores were scrubbed spotless and displayed neat shelves lined with brightly-labelled cans and bottles. But the canned beets from Bulgaria, canned pineapple from Cuba, bottled pickles from Poland, and other such stuff seemed largely untouched. People emerged from those stores carrying small string sacks, or those omnipresent briefcases, into which only one or two purchased items had been squeezed.

There was enough food to go around if people weren't fussy. But East Germany had traditionally been the breadbasket of all of Germany and much of the surrounding region. Hearty eating, suspended during the war and immediate post-war years, had, however, not been revived here, except for those who could afford to patronize the Budapest, Warschau, or other up-market restaurants.

Some foodstuffs were still rationed. The size of the ration depended on where a person lived – 200 grams of butter per person per week in Frankfurt am Oder, 150 grams in Leipzig, only 90 grams in Potsdam. East German housewives complained that the different authorized grades of margarine they were offered were exactly the same, except for the different packaging which was supposed to distinguish the higher-priced ones from those of inferior quality.

At butcher shops, more often than not, everything but sausage meat was sold out by mid-morning. Coffee, when it was available, cost four times what it cost in West Berlin. Despite all of this, when crates were unloaded, people reflexively lined up outside food stores in the Soviet Sector on the odd chance that there might be something that would help make a tasty meal. Young Englishwoman Mary Kellett-Long who, with her Reuters correspondent husband, Adam Kellett-Long, lived in East Berlin at the time, vividly described the prevailing circumstances in her diary:

> I walked past the open door of a greengrocer's shop and saw a queue of about twenty-five people. My already well-trained nose smelt an air of expectancy among the patiently waiting people so I faithfully joined the queue only to find that when my goal was in sight, I had been waiting twenty minutes for nothing other than that, to Western ideas, very ordinary commodity of potatoes! It is incredible I am sure to an English or any other Western housewife to imagine standing in a long queue in the rain in order to be able to give your family potatoes for dinner, but it is not an out of the ordinary occurrence here in East Berlin . . . Meat is rather limited and the most usually found sorts are pork and beef, although if you are lucky you may have the occasional treat of a piece of rather tough veal or a scraggy chicken or goose . . . The English habit of having meat twice a day is regarded here with amazement. Butter at the moment is rationed to a half-pound per head per week . . . East German margarine is, in my opinion, almost uneatable. We are back to the post-war habit of thinking whether we must keep

the butter for when we have guests. Often too in the summer months, butter and milk are 'off' before you have them home as very few shops have refrigerators . . . The clothes for women can only be described as shapeless and the majority of East Berlin girls and young women owe their good shoes and short pleated skirts to the West Berlin shops being only too willing to take East Marks at the rate of 5:1 [rather than the artificial 1:1 rate insisted upon by the East German authorities]. Seamless stockings are also unobtainable here and the West Berlin shops must take more money from the East Berliners for stockings than for anything else. When buying shoes in West Berlin, the girls, women too, wear an old pair of shoes to go over in and leave them in the shop and come back wearing the new ones, in this way avoiding the eyes of the Customs men who are apt to pounce on people carrying bulky bags or parcels.

Life in East Berlin was, however, not without its compensations. While only high-ranking party and government officials, senior managers of industrial enterprises and some key professional personnel could command spacious, well-appointed accommodation, rents for everyone were very modest and though there was no great choice or excitement in the variety of foods available in the stores, food prices, except for imported items, were kept very low by government decree.

For those repelled by the more hectic pace of life in the West, East Berlin had distinct attractions. But workers were required to attend regular indoctrination sessions and lectures at their factories and offices. They were also expected to turn out for frequent public demonstrations of support for the government, arranged by the party. Party membership or conspicuous co-operation with party cadre was the path to promotion and to better housing, when it became available. But though a person could be jailed for open expressions of dissent from party policy, no one could be fired from his job.

The dismay of the Communists at their inability to control all of Berlin verged at times on hysteria. They called West Berlin a centre of slanderous propaganda and psychological warfare against East Germany, which it was, though similar charges could be made about their activities against West Berlin and West Germany. They said that cheap novels and all sorts of militaristic and anti-Communist publications were brought by the planeload into West Berlin and then smuggled into the East. It was charged that the movies, the press, television and radio in the western sectors had been 'enlisted for service in the cold war'. It was said that the authorities in West Berlin had resorted to devious means to damage the East German economy and keep the East German mark at a low rate against the West German mark. It was claimed that more than ninety western espionage and intelligence agencies and organizations in West Berlin were engaged in trying to undermine the German Democratic Republic.*

Whatever its drawbacks, East Berlin was a fascinating place to visit. The contrast with West Berlin was extraordinary and intriguing. Opera there was superb, particularly at the revived *Komische Oper* under the direction of Walter Felsenstein (who preferred to live in West Berlin, and was allowed to). The Berliner Ensemble Theatre was still a shrine to the memory of Bertolt Brecht. Under the direction of Brecht's widow, Helene Weigel, it offered regular, entrancing revivals of *Gallileo*, *Arturo Ui* and Brecht's other dramatic masterpieces. The ancient Greek altar, set out in all its glory at the Pergamon Museum, was (and remains) a breathtaking vision. The outlying regions of East Berlin, even better endowed than those of West Berlin with forests, lakes and bucolic patches, were excellent for excursions away from the urban swirl.

But East Berlin had no urban swirl. It seemed curiously provincial, an impression reinforced by its newspapers – mostly tiresome publications endlessly glutted with verbatim accounts of documents and speeches emanating from government or party sources or from government or party organizations in the other Communist countries. The effect was stultifying.

For a working correspondent from the West, dealing with the East German authorities in East Berlin was generally a frustrating waste of time. Their official spokesmen, usually hard to track down, rarely had anything to say that might make the effort to see them worthwhile. A visit to the House of Ministries could entail an hour's wait in the huge, eerily silent reception hall and then earn you either regrets that the official you had come to see was unavailable at the moment, or a paraphrased recital of a speech or document printed that morning in *Neues Deutschland*, the official party daily.

*The Russians were particularly well versed in Allied espionage operations as a result of the activities of George Blake. Blake had been deputy director of technical operations for the British MI6 intelligence service in West Berlin before being arrested early in 1961 as a Soviet agent. He was convicted and sentenced to forty-two years in prison because of the damage he had done to British intelligence efforts, but the KGB soon had him spirited away from behind bars in England and safely into Russia.

Contacting the Russians in East Berlin was sometimes more rewarding, though it was startling to observe that a Soviet spokesman at the embassy, Ivan Shishkin by name, appeared to be such a lightweight. Judging from his attitudes and responses, Shishkin understood very little of the Berlin situation. It was remarkable that the Russians could have put a man like that in so delicate a post. He was, of course, putting it on. It turned out that he was a very high-ranking KGB official, one of the most senior Soviet intelligence officers in that part of the world, and someone who, it later became apparent, was very keenly aware of just about everything happening in every corner of that schizophrenic metropolis.

Among other things, Shishkin and his colleagues must have reported back to Moscow that the promise the East German leaders had given five years earlier that East Germany would soon surpass West Germany economically was an absurd fantasy. The two parts of the German nation had been locked in competition for fifteen years and no one – not even dedicated Communists – could pretend that the East was anywhere near catching up with West. If anything, as a place to live, the West was growing ever more attractive to people in the East. That wasn't merely a matter of opinion. It was a provable fact.

Bertolt Brecht was, of course, being ironic when he suggested after Russian tanks were called out to crush the 1953 workers' uprising that, if the East German regime could not gain the confidence of the people, it should dissolve the people and elect a new one. However, by the spring of 1961, it looked as though, as a people, the East Germans were bent on dissolving themselves.

In the period since the end of the Second World War in 1945, some four million of them had left East Germany, trekking westward. It was the most concentrated mass migration ever in a highly-developed industrial society. Between 1949, when the German Democratic Republic was founded, and 1961, 2,800,000 people, one in every six, abandoned East Germany for the West, a total greater than the remaining populations of the dozen largest East German cities.

The Soviet occupation of East Germany was partly responsible. People in that part of the country had long feared and mistrusted their Slavic neighbours to the east. Their folk literature was rich in tales and legends of ancient, heroic battles fought against them, even before Charlemagne (*Karl der Grosse*) subdued the Slavs in eastern Germany in the eighth century and long before those 'barbarians' were pushed back across the Oder

River four centuries later. For many Germans, the racial rantings of the Nazis, either evoking superstitious fear – Hitler once described them as frogs living in a swamp – or portraying Russians as subhuman creatures who slaughtered indiscriminately, raped and looted, had turned those prejudices into almost pathological terror as the war ended and the Russian armies advanced relentlessly. Some outnumbered and outgunned German army units had fought on fiercely to the end in the belief they would be slaughtered anyway if they surrendered. An epidemic of raping and looting actually perpetrated by Russian troops during the early days of their occupation of the Soviet Zone did nothing to alleviate German fears. As the end-of-war cruelties, as well as the hardships and austerity, set in, hundreds of thousands of people headed westward, seeking sanctuary. Included among them were many who had been driven out of former German provinces which were 'cleansed' of Germans and annexed by Poland as compensation for Nazi atrocities, and to make up for the Soviet annexation of a chunk of eastern Poland.

By 1961, though some Germans still pined for the return of the eastern provinces (a few still do), for practical purposes that transaction was past history. However, the westward migration across Germany was by then greater than before, amounting to a ceaseless cascade of refugees streaming away from the Russians and their East German Communist subordinates. Individuals were on the move: married couples, whole families, groups of friends. Terror was no longer the reason for the continuing exodus; nor was the impetus even essentially political. As the years had passed, more and more people had simply grown fed up with the failure of the Soviet-sponsored government of East Germany to create for the people, or permit them to create for themselves, an acceptable standard of living and way of life.

Some workers were going over merely to sell their labour to a higher bidder. But many had grown weary of endless shortages and rationing, oppressive work conditions, unfulfilled promises by their leaders, police controls, and the snooping of *obleute* (party-appointed block wardens). Workers were fed up with being herded to factory meetings after work hours to be shouted at and harangued by party activists. They were tired of incessant, sometimes idiotic political hectoring. (Children in the city of Halle were, for example, warned that reading Mickey Mouse comics, available in German, could lead them astray.) They were soured by the drabness of life generally in the Soviet Zone and the Soviet Sector of Berlin, while their friends and relatives in West Germany and West Berlin were beginning to tap what seemed like the good life – spacious homes, cars, holidays abroad, career advancement. They were angered by being told off and threatened by party toughs for complaining that they hadn't seen an orange in weeks and that potatoes were harder to come by than they should have been. Farmers, many of whose families had claimed title to their patches of land for generations, were angry at being forced into agricultural collectives which, they muttered bitterly, were similar to atomic bombs in that they both laid waste to the land.

The migrants came from all elements and strata of East German life and society. There were men and women, skilled and unskilled workers, agricultural labourers as well as farmers, scientists, professional people, academics, civil servants, writers and artists. More than 16,000 of those who fled were trained engineers. In one industrial plant, the seventeen key engineers absconded, taking with them the plant's blueprints, either out of pique or to help them find good jobs in West Germany. There were more than 5,000 doctors, dentists and veterinarians among the refugees, including such senior men as the chief physician at Potsdam's St Joseph's Hospital. The medical director of the surgical clinic at Leipzig University fled. The man appointed to succeed him followed shortly afterwards.

Almost a thousand university professors and lecturers (including the entire law faculty of the University of Leipzig) joined the exodus, more than 15,000 high-school and elementary-school teachers, and some 30,000 students, many of them waiting to receive their graduation diplomas before departing. A West Berlin television executive says that out of his high-school class of twenty-five in a small town outside Erfurt, twenty-two ultimately made their way to the West. More than half the refugees were under twenty-five years of age. Three out of four were younger than forty-five. These were the people the East German Communist leaders were counting on to build the first German socialist state, but who had decided they'd rather not, though older people, on state pensions, generally preferred not to shift to new surroundings so late in life.

The refugees came from all parts of East Germany – from near the new Polish border in the East and from within sight of the West German border in the West, from the countryside in Thuringia and Saxony and the shores of the Baltic Sea in Pomerania. They came from such industrial hubs as Karl Marx

Stadt and Cottbus, and from historic cultural centres like Dresden and Potsdam, and most of all from East Berlin itself.

Nor did a refugee have to fear that in abandoning his home in the East he was plunging into circumstances in which he and his family might be stranded in strange surroundings, without help, without resources, and without any way of knowing what awaited him. Refugee half-way houses had been established in West Berlin. Most were accommodated at the huge, barracks-like reception centre at Marienfelde, where people were fed (the United States Army chipped in with up to 2,500 field rations daily), processed and sheltered (the British Army set up tents to house the overflow) before being flown out, if they wished, to West Germany – all at the expense of the West German government. After being interviewed and screened, which could take several days, they were assigned available seats on scheduled Pan American, British European Airways and Air France flights, with extra flights chartered if needed. Political refugees who had reason to fear for their personal safety in Berlin and unmarried young men who could be quickly slotted into jobs were flown out without delay. In West Germany, the refugees were bussed to one of fifty regional reception centres where they were helped to find homes and suitable jobs.

It was highly organized and very efficient. For people soured by increased work quotas at the factory, the persistence of food rationing, and having to glance over their shoulder whenever uttering unauthorized opinions, it was exceedingly tempting. It was joked at the time that the first three words an East German baby learned were 'mama', 'papa', and 'Marienfelde'.

At the refugee reception centre, lines of refugees waited every day, often in the rain, to file indoors and be processed. Many were surprised at Marienfelde to meet friends, neighbours or workmates from whom they had carefully concealed their own escape intentions and plans. In one case, seven coalminers who worked in the same mine found themselves waiting on the same line, and none had known that any of the others was heading West.

Aside from the obvious general reasons why the refugees had pulled up roots and bolted, there was a variety of specific impulses which had propelled them westward. One man, ambitious for himself and his family, said they saw no future for themselves in East Germany. A woman feared that people would be given identity cards which would confine them to living, working and travelling in certain restricted areas of the country which, she understood, was the way the Russians did things. One man had fled west because he had been instructed by the police to spy on another man who was believed to be contemplating departure.

Some had fled disagreeable work conditions – a car mechanic, for whom there were no cars to repair, had been dispatched to work instead on a collective farm. A farmer who had fled from such a farm spoke with derision of party functionaries put in charge who couldn't tell a hoe from a hockey stick, and who were enraged when the farmers took seriously the promise that they would have to work only an eight-hour-day once they had given up their private holdings. Some people said they had had enough of shortages – with soap unavailable one day, cheese the next, nails the third, sewing needles, light bulbs, fresh vegetables, sometimes even bread. One young man had left because, considered unreliable by the local police, he had been refused permission to buy a motorcycle with his savings.

But resettlement assistance was extended at Marienfelde only to those who said they were fleeing political persecution in the East. Those believed by the interviewers to have flimsy reasons for fleeing, or merely to be after a better job and higher pay, were not denied permission to stay in the West, but were told they would have to fend for themselves. Though work was easy enough to come by in West Germany – where a half-million jobs were going begging – as well as in West Berlin, the refugee grapevine quickly spread the word of what was required, and soon few people arriving at the reception centre claimed to be seeking anything but political asylum.

The effect on the life and economy of East Germany of these mass departures was momentous. There was no telling who would be missing from work, and when. People left their jobs or offices after work one evening and, without offering hint or suggestion, simply did not show up the following morning. Only the closest of intimates was trusted, and sometimes not even those – to give advance notice would have been an invitation to be hauled in by the police for questioning and worse. As a result, no prior arrangements could be made for the work done by those departing to be taken on by others, even when those others might have been available, which increasingly they were not.

When a clutch of bus drivers employed by the public transport system of an East German city turned up at the Marienfelde centre rather than at their depot one day, the city's bus schedule was thrown into chaos. The entire workforce of a small rope-making factory went west en masse. People entered stores to find there was no one there to serve them. They went to offices to find that those with whom they had made appointments were no longer to be found. Plumbers, carpenters and other skilled workers were becoming vanishing species. A bottleneck resulting from a missing factory assembly line hand would be resolved with difficulty one morning, only to recur the next morning when someone else failed to appear. People often didn't know whether to say good night or goodbye to their workmates and colleagues at the end of each day.

More and more housewives were drawn into the labour market to fill the gaps left by the refugees. Crèches, attended by elderly 'grandmothers', were established at factories to care for their children during the work day. Shock brigades of women workers were formed, to be shunted around where needed. Retired people were urged to return to part-time work. Full-time employees were asked to work longer hours. The five-day working week was dismissed by the East German authorities as a western conspiracy. These were desperate measures. Unskilled people often found themselves expected to handle skilled tasks – it served only to complicate the situation. To East German economic analysts the long-term economic outlook appeared bleak, and totally unpredictable (in a country where everything was done by plan) unless the outflow of workers was halted.

But warnings, threats and jail sentences imposed on would-be fugitives caught in the act had no noticeable effect on the numbers departing, except sometimes to increase those numbers. Included among the refugees were men with criminal tendencies, work-shy individuals and other anti-social elements, and that was no doubt welcomed by the local authorities, but it was a very small compensation for the greater loss East Germany was suffering.

World attention focused on this extraordinary mass procession. Each new headlined departure – a distinguished jurist, a famous doctor, a colourful chimney sweep, a pair of honeymooners – seemed more embarrassing than the last, whether it was the disclosure that among the near 200,000 refugees who had passed through the Marienfelde Reception Centre in 1960 were 4,000 card-carrying members of the Walter Ulbricht's own Socialist Unity Party, or the fact that the twenty-one-year-old statuesque blonde beauty who was crowned Miss Universe at Miami Beach in 1961 was an East German refugee.

Aside from the damage done to the country and the fury of the

Soviet Union at this humiliating spectacle, other East European Communist regimes protested that, though not in great numbers, they too were losing people through West Berlin. Communist bloc meetings and conferences held in East Berlin were attended by delegates from Poland, Bulgaria, Czechoslovakia and the other Communist countries who otherwise rarely had access to the West. Several of those delegates had seized the opportunity to slip away into West Berlin and apply for political asylum. An American military officer, out shopping one afternoon, parked his car – identifiable from its American military forces licence plate – on the Ku'damm. When he returned, he found a high-ranking Hungarian official waiting for him to ask how he could make contact with American intelligence. It became a joke among western intelligence circles in West Berlin that the best way to make contact with would-be defectors from Eastern Europe was to park on the Ku'damm.

Then there were the *grenzgängers* (border-crossers). These were people who lived in East Berlin but had regular jobs in West Berlin to which they went every day. Some 50,000 of these commuters were registered with the West Berlin authorities; thousands more were unregistered. By choosing to work in West Berlin, the *grenzgängers* deprived East Germany of their badly-needed services and thus contributed to the country's economic shambles. They were also an additional embarrassment to the Communist authorities, disregarding, as they so blatantly did, the urgings that the good people of the Fatherland should strive to build a socialist future.

There was, however, nothing ideological in their choice. The simple fact was they were better paid in the West than they would be in the East. They were also able to change some of their west mark earnings into east marks at black-market rates (change booths were everywhere in downtown West Berlin), which meant that even the lower-paid among them ended up with considerably more money at their disposal than their neighbours and friends who worked in the East.

A woman who cleaned offices in West Berlin might earn a standard wage for the job of two hundred west marks a month. If she was registered as an East Berlin resident, she would get forty percent of her wages in west marks, the rest in east marks. Her monthly eighty west marks could be exchanged at a currency exchange booth for 400 east marks, giving her a final salary of 520 east marks. That was a good deal more than even a skilled worker earned in the East. That skilled worker was, of course, deeply offended and envious. So was the office cleaner who worked in East Berlin and who had no opportunity of converting her meagre earnings into a fat wad of cash.

These *grenzgängers* were reviled in the East German media as freeloaders and swindlers, and were often harassed by Vopos at the border crossings. Nor were they highly regarded by West Berliners, because they were exploiting the situation in a not altogether wholesome fashion. Freedom of movement throughout Berlin was guaranteed by treaty and the *grenzgängers* had a legal right to do what they were doing. But it was widely felt that there was something shabby in the currency-exchange advantage which came with their situation, and that it would have been more appropriate for them to shift over to West Berlin lock, stock and barrel, forsaking the cheaper housing and cheap groceries at their disposal at home in the Soviet Sector.

Nevertheless, these commuters contributed to the economic vigour of West Berlin. The border-crossing office cleaners, hotel housekeeping personnel and sanitation workers served eminently useful functions. Even more useful were the engineers, mechanics, and other skilled personnel who crossed over each day, infuriating the Communist authorities who saw the border-crossers not only as traitors, but also as badly-needed numbers extracted from East Germany's shrinking labour force. Despite pleas from Ulbricht, the Russians declined to permit a crackdown on the *grenzgängers*. They considered the problem they presented peripheral to the bigger Berlin issues with which they would soon have to cope.

Following the collapse of the Paris summit conference in May 1960 over the U-2 incident, Khrushchev was advised by his foreign ministry to play down the Berlin controversy until after the American elections in November of that year. He was told that to challenge the Americans before then would only induce the rival candidates, Richard Nixon and John Fitzgerald Kennedy, to outbid each in taking a vote-winning hard line from which they might not be able to disentangle themselves once elected. It was best to tone things down until a new man, with perhaps a new approach, had moved into the White House.

This waiting game was agonizing for East German leaders. Incapable of stemming the refugee tide themselves, unable to prod Moscow into the promised action to slam the West Berlin escape hatch closed, they were faced with a collapse of morale in the Socialist Unity Party. Reports kept coming in to party headquarters in East Berlin of questions being asked by cadre in the provinces, and in East Berlin itself, about how socialism could possibly be built without the people to build it, and telling of despair permeating party ranks. Party leaders and officials of the regime felt obliged to make repeated public assertions that vigorous steps were about to be taken to guarantee the safety and wellbeing of the German Democratic Republic. They also tried repeatedly to impress the Russians with the urgency of the situation.

They were not without advocates in the Soviet hierarchy. Just as there were people in Washington who were certain the Soviets were bluffing in their threats, so there were people in Moscow who were convinced the United States would not risk a war over Berlin. And, like Khrushchev, they were outraged at the continued alien presence on what they held to be Communist territory.

In March 1961, as John F. Kennedy was settling in at the White House in Washington, a meeting of Warsaw Pact leaders was convened in Moscow, at which the Berlin situation was closely reviewed. Despairing of any immediate Soviet move to give him control of the access routes between West Germany and West Berlin, Ulbricht revived a plan to end the refugee flow that had been on file since 1958. It involved sealing the border between East Berlin and West Berlin. Barbed wire would be stretched between the Soviet and western sectors. The barrier would be heavily patrolled and the few border points that remained open for pedestrian or vehicular traffic would be tightly controlled. Thus, Ulbricht said, would the imperialist efforts to destroy the first ever German workers' state be thwarted, pending the signing of a peace treaty to end the occupation of West Berlin.

Ulbricht's plan aroused more anxiety than sympathy from his fellow Communist leaders. Some feared this proposed violation of four-power agreements, ending the right of unrestricted passage throughout Berlin, entailed a risk of war. Others said that the proposed barbed wire barrier, in the middle of a big city, would be a poor advertisement for Communism. But they agreed that, sooner or later, something had to be done about the refugees and that there would be no harm in preparing to take drastic steps, along the lines Ulbricht suggested, should the situation deteriorate further.

The task of laying the groundwork for the building of what was to be the Berlin Wall fell to Erich Honecker, a resourceful Ulbricht protégé and SED Central Committee member (later to be East German leader and party chief himself). In deepest secrecy, Honecker set to work gathering the staff and the materials that would be needed and making the plans that would be implemented on a hot summer's night five months later.

Khrushchev had raised no objection at the Warsaw Pact meeting to such preparations being made. But dividing Berlin was not his idea of an acceptable solution. He wanted the West out of the city, not quarantined within it. Arrangements were already in the works for a face-to-face meeting with the new American President, at which the Soviet leader intended to drive that point home and finally get the results he wanted.

5

Collision in Vienna

THE SPRING of 1961 should have been a time of jubilation for John Kennedy. He had just become President of the United States, the youngest man and first Catholic ever to attain that office. But his triumph over Richard Nixon in the presidential elections had been very narrow. Of the 69,000,000 votes cast, his victory margin had been a mere 100,000, which meant there were an awful lot of Americans still to be convinced that he was made of the stuff of which the nation's leaders ideally should be made.

Kennedy's youthfulness, good looks, articulateness, quick wit and charm did much to persuade many sceptics that he might be worthy of the job. Patriotic pride had been stirred when, in his January inauguration address, he had told the world, 'Let every nation know . . . that we shall pay any price, bear any burden, meet any hardship, support any friend, oppose any foe to assure the survival and the success of liberty.'

That was good old American 'can do' talk and the people loved it. But those brave inaugural words turned hollow and mocking when, a mere ninety days later, 1,400 anti-Castro Cubans, trained and supplied by the Central Intelligence Agency, were left to fend for themselves under withering gunfire on the beach at the Bay of Pigs in Cuba. Kennedy had been assured by the CIA that this bid to infiltrate men into Cuba to overthrow Castro and his Communist regime would succeed without recognizable direct American military intervention, and that assurance had not been challenged by the Joint Chiefs of Staff. Nevertheless, after the Cuban rebels were on the beach, and it had become apparent that the entire adventure, as planned, had been misconceived and doomed to failure from the very start, he was asked to authorize such intervention. It would have meant the United States openly joining in an armed invasion of a small country, an act that would have outraged world opinion, and much public opinion in the United States as well. Furious because of the way he had been backed into this corner by his military and intelligence advisers, Kennedy said no. The United States government could not be put in such a position. As a result, the Cuban rebels were left to die on the beach or be captured by Castro's forces.

Though the operation had been approved and was well into its planning stage before he became President, and though he had relied on the judgment of his military and intelligence experts, Kennedy publicly accepted full responsibility for the fiasco. Privately he muttered to his intimates, 'How could I have been so stupid to let them go ahead?' With good reason, many people, abroad as well as at home, both hawks and doves, agreed that he had badly botched the first major challenge he had faced as President. Former Secretary of State Dean Acheson, who had been in Europe at the time, reported that America's allies, assessing Kennedy's performance in the Bay of Pigs affair, felt as if they had been 'watching a gifted young amateur practise with a boomerang when they saw to their horror that he had knocked himself out'. That 'gifted young amateur' knew very well what impression he had made. It would colour his response to the Berlin crisis the Kremlin was brewing for him.

As a member of the Senate Foreign Affairs committee, Kennedy had known even before he was elected President that Berlin meant trouble. He was well aware of the Khrushchev ultimatum and of the harassment of American convoys on the Berlin access routes. Shortly after he moved into the White House, he had asked Acheson to undertake an up-to-date analysis of what was happening and likely to happen in the city, and to assess the views of America's allies. At first, however, neither Kennedy nor his chief aides devoted much attention to the subject. Although the Russians continued to make noises about Berlin, they had blown hot and cold over the fate of the city for more than a decade, ever since the blockade, without posing any tangible threat there. More pressing matters concerned the President as he came to grips with foreign policy problems – Cuba, a Communist take-over bid in Laos, and possibilities for working out an East–West disarmament agreement.

All of these involved establishing an improved line of communication with the Kremlin. Kennedy did not for a moment believe that Russia's aspirations coincided with those of the United

States; but he was convinced that friction between the two countries could be kept within manageable bounds if both better understood what the other was up to. As far as he was concerned, that was the purpose of the forthcoming summit meeting with Khrushchev, at which he and the Soviet leader would size each other up and decide how to proceed.

Berlin would undoubtedly come up at the summit. Khrushchev had only recently sworn to 'remove this splinter from the heart of Europe'. The Soviet leader had issued such threats before, but Llewellyn Thompson, the American ambassador to Moscow, now believed a showdown with the Russians over the city was likely later in the year. He thought it would probably come after the West German elections in the autumn, which the Russians did not want to influence adversely by premature pressure. At least one White House adviser, Henry Owen, believed that, 'Of all the problems the Administration faces, Berlin seems . . . the most pregnant with disaster.'

Accordingly, during the weeks before his departure for Europe, Kennedy had himself thoroughly briefed on Berlin, as well as on the other issues likely to come up at the summit. Trimming other activities and duties to a minimum, having visitors he felt obliged to see ushered in and out of the Oval Office practically as if they were in a revolving door, he pored over scores of intelligence reports. He studied position papers and minutes of previous meetings between Khrushchev and American dignitaries; he was provided with a thorough analysis of Khrushchev's personality and mannerisms; he was warned not to be rattled by the Soviet leader's often unconventional behaviour, or his unpredictability; he was told that it was not uncommon for Khrushchev to trade pleasantries, laughing and joking one instant, and then to erupt with furious accusations and outrageous demands the next – it could be unnerving and even intimidating for those not prepared for his more spectacular outbursts. Khrushchev was, after all, the man who, to the chagrin of the regular Soviet United Nations delegation, had taken off his shoe at a meeting of the UN General Assembly and banged it on the table to signify his disapproval of a speech being made from the rostrum.

Kennedy was advised to stand his ground on matters of policy without responding in kind to whatever explosions of anger (sometimes genuine, sometimes fabricated) the Soviet leader might subject him to. Veteran diplomatic trouble-shooter Averell Harriman told the President that Khrushchev's style in negotiations was to go on the attack rather than to present his arguments in a reasoned fashion. It was a ploy, a negotiating device. Kennedy was urged by Harriman to rise above such provocations, to take things easy and enjoy himself.

It was easier to say that to do. After the mess that had been made of the Bay of Pigs episode, Kennedy knew well enough that a gut fighter like Khrushchev would use the summit encounter to test his firmness and resolve. It would be a challenge, but the prospect did not faze him. Instead he saw the Vienna summit as an opportunity to redeem himself after the Cuba fiasco and establish his credentials as an international statesman.

If the two-day encounter in Vienna at the beginning of June 1961 was to be a moment of truth for the American President, it was meant to be a moment of triumph for Nikita Khrushchev. By then, the Soviet premier and chairman of the Communist Party of the Soviet Union had been the dominant figure in the Kremlin for the better part of eight years. He was a crafty, intelligent man, profoundly patriotic, with an almost religious belief in the fundamental greatness of Mother Russia. The fact that the Soviet Union lagged far behind the United States in material living standards, technological innovation, and industrial efficiency deeply distressed him. He repeatedly promised that Russia would soon catch up and surpass America ('We will bury you!') and tried to do what he could to make good that promise. The Soviet leader was a devout Communist who believed in the historic inevitability of the collapse of capitalism and the triumph of Communism. He was also, as Kennedy had been warned, impulsive, emotional and mercurial.

Khrushchev's ascendancy had been marked by major achievements by the Soviet Union. It was first in space, having launched the pioneering earth-orbiting satellite in 1957. That same year, the Russians successfully tested an intercontinental ballistic missile and boasted that they could now finally match the Americans in being able to dispatch weapons of destruction to any corner of the globe. Russia's claim to superpower status had thus been authenticated. The Russians did not, of course, reveal that they had far fewer of those missiles than the United States, but over the years they had so substantially increased their military might that Kennedy's misleading claim during the presidential election campaign that they had a missile lead over America did seem credible at the time.

The Soviet Union was still heavily burdened by economic troubles and travails, but most Soviet citizens, proud of their country's post-war achievements, believed that, despite the denial of comforts and conveniences enjoyed by people in the West, their country was marching towards a sublime Communist future. Their access to information and informed opinion carefully controlled by the authorities, few Russians doubted that Khrushchev was briskly shepherding them along that glory road.

Nevertheless, there were those in Moscow, and even in the Kremlin, who would not have mourned his passing from the scene. The military, ever jealous of its privileges, resented the cuts the Soviet leader had made in the non-nuclear military budget in order to earmark greater funds to stimulate the country's stagnating civilian economy. Colonel Oleg Penkovsky, a Soviet military intelligence officer spying in Moscow for the West, said, 'All officers, especially marshals and generals, were quite unhappy when Khrushchev cut their pay and took away many of the privileges they had enjoyed under Stalin.' The pensions of retired senior officers were also slashed.

Some Soviet officials responsible for implementing government programmes resented Khrushchev's haphazard and unpredictable approach to problem-solving. They were increasingly, if quietly, exasperated by not knowing what he was going to do next. In addition, old Bolsheviks, like Molotov and Kaganovich, and other senior figures elbowed aside by him in his rise to power retained resentful cronies in the government and party machinery. Aware of these resentments and backbitings, Khrushchev was continually playing factions off against each other. He strove to prevent his adversaries, who knew enough to keep their heads down, from becoming bolder and grouping together to lever him out of the way (as they finally managed to do three years later).

There was also the Stalin factor. Russians still thought of Joseph Stalin as their wartime leader and hero. Many had been perplexed by Khrushchev's widely-publicized exposure of Stalin's crimes against the Soviet people in 1956. It also presented difficulties in Soviet-dominated East Europe, where Communist leaders had obediently Stalinized their countries and had then felt obliged to de-Stalinize them.

The pace and direction of events in those countries was not altogether to Moscow's advantage, and not only in East Germany. The army had been needed to put down anti-government riots in Poland. Still restive, the Polish people no longer bothered to conceal their anti-Russian sentiments. It had been necessary to send in Soviet forces to crush an anti-Communist uprising in Hungary. What was more, the sluggish economies of the East

European countries were hardly testimony to the success of the socialist systems those countries had adopted and, unlike the United States, the Soviet Union was in no position to render them meaningful economic assistance.

There had also been setbacks for Khrushchev in foreign affairs elsewhere. He badly needed a success to balance them off. The drive to spread Soviet influence around the world had bogged down. In the Middle East, the United States was unquestionably the dominant superpower, with the Russians reduced to looking on from the sidelines. Relations with Egypt were strained and Iraq, ostensibly allied to the Russians, was busily rounding up its Communists and executing them. Patrice Lumumba, the leader the Russians had counted on to help spread Soviet influence in what had been the Belgian Congo and in the rest of black Africa, had been murdered and rivals with closer links to the western powers were in command.

These setbacks were dwarfed by a much more serious Kremlin foreign policy concern. In the early 1960s, China, previously considered Russia's junior partner in the international revolutionary movement, featured far more prominently in Moscow's calculations than any of those other countries or regions. Chinese Communist leaders were presuming to challenge the Russians for ideological leadership of the Communist world. From Peking came accusations that Khrushchev was a paper tiger, making growling noises but actually kow-towing to the evil Americans when they should be locked with them in the knock-down/drag-out struggle that would truly herald a worldwide Communist future. In East Berlin, diplomats from Peking went around telling frustrated East German officials, watching the refugee numbers mount, how different the situation would be if the genuinely revolutionary Chinese rather than the craven Russians were running the show.

Though infuriated, the Russians sought to derive advantage from that kind of talk. Before the Sino–Soviet split flared into the open, an East European journalist, based in East Berlin and suspected of having KGB links, confided practically in a whisper over lunch that the Americans were really lucky to have a chance to negotiate with the Russians. The Russians, he said, were reasonable people, unlike the Chinese who were reckless and who, with their hundreds of millions of people, really didn't care if a nuclear confrontation incinerated ten, twenty, thirty million or so. It soon became apparent that this 'confidence' was being entrusted by East European journalists and officials to many western correspondents in Berlin and elsewhere. The Soviet campaign to negotiate the West out of Berlin was beginning in earnest.

Although Khrushchev hoped to benefit from western fears of a nuclear holocaust, he was, in fact, deeply worried that such a catastrophe might take place. He fully understood the extent of the devastation that would result from a nuclear exchange. He said, and believed, that 'after a nuclear war, the living would envy the dead'.

Nevertheless, he had to do something about Berlin. There was great pressure on him to disprove Chinese charges of Soviet revolutionary impotence. More important, the western presence in Berlin, that gaping capitalist hole in Communist East Europe – with its glitter, glamour and more pedestrian attractions – made a mockery of Soviet boasts about Communist achievements. As Khrushchev declared repeatedly, dredging up one vivid metaphor after another, Berlin was for the Russians 'a bone stuck in the throat which had to be disgorged', 'a splinter that had to be extricated', 'a cancer that had to be carved out', 'a rotten tooth that had to be extracted'. No matter what public pronouncements the Americans made about their rights in Berlin, Khrushchev headed for the summit in Vienna with the intention of finally forcing the United States to give way.

He was confident he would succeed. He needed no position papers to believe that Kennedy lacked the determination and daring to face up to the Soviet Union in Soviet-dominated East Europe. He had heard the American President's defiant talk about paying any price and bearing any burden to assure the survival of liberty but, more convincingly, he had seen Kennedy in action (rather, as he saw it, at rest) at the Bay of Pigs; he was not impressed.

Khrushchev had dealt with a comparable problem in a different way. Scorning outraged public opinion in the West and ignoring United Nations condemnation, he had, without qualms or hesitation, sent Soviet tanks in to crush the Hungarian anti-Communist uprising. It seemed obvious to Khrushchev that Kennedy wasn't up to making that sort of decision: if the American President couldn't cope with trouble at his doorstep, how would he be able to handle a showdown thousands of miles from home on territory ringed by twenty Soviet divisions? He had decided that 'the time had come to lance the blister of West Berlin. It was no longer possible to avoid using the surgeon's knife, but we wanted to conduct the surgical operation under anaesthesia.' He was going to the Vienna meeting to administer the anaesthetic in his own, inimitable fashion.

Both Kennedy and Khrushchev were strong believers in the impact of their personalities. Each was convinced that direct contact between them would serve much more effectively than the efforts of intermediaries to eliminate the possibility of misunderstanding or miscalculation. Khrushchev wanted to terrify Kennedy into abandoning Berlin without too much hassle, something that could not be done by the Soviet ambassador in Washington. Kennedy wanted to make America's determination not to abandon Berlin absolutely clear in this face-to-face encounter. But at the same time he was more concerned about prospects for disarmament.

Not all of Kennedy's advisers liked the idea of the summit, which was not to have a carefully prepared agenda. Secretary of State Dean Rusk, a firm believer in low-keyed diplomacy, tended to be suspicious of top-level free-for-alls. Rusk felt that 'though you really can't reach substantial agreement on big issues in just two days, Americans have been conditioned to expect a lot from summit meetings . . .' by the legions of reporters who cover such events. Thirteen hundred newsmen and women converged on Vienna for the Kennedy–Khrushchev encounter. Many were under pressure to justify their expensive presence in the Austrian capital by probing diligently behind bland official press handouts to file exciting headline stories.

The meeting – the first day at the American Ambassador's Vienna residence, the second at the Soviet embassy – began satisfactorily enough with an exploratory exchange of views on fundamental differences. To Kennedy's surprise, Khrushchev quickly agreed that greater efforts should be made to arrange a ceasefire in Laos, where a civil war between Communist and non-Communist forces threatened to intensify. They then proceeded to a discussion of a possible nuclear test ban treaty, but could find no common ground there. However, it wasn't till the second day of the conference, when they turned to the Berlin situation, that it became apparent that public forecasts the Russians had made that it would be an amicable and fruitful meeting were decidedly premature. By the time they said their goodbyes, Khrushchev had convinced Kennedy that the world trembled on the brink of catastrophe.

Having kept Berlin quietly simmering on the back-burner for so long – more than two years had passed since his 1958 ultimatum – Khrushchev seized the occasion to return to the

offensive. It was ultimatum time once more. The Soviet leader
told Kennedy that unless the West agreed to a German peace
treaty before the year was out, the Soviet Union would sign a
separate peace treaty with East Germany which would 'normal-
ize' the situation in Berlin, leaving no reason for Allied garrisons
to remain there. Khrushchev said West Berlin would have to be
'strictly neutral':

> It must not be tolerated . . . that West Berlin be used further
> as a base for provocative hostile activity against the USSR, the
> German Democratic Republic or any other state or that it continue
> to remain a dangerous seat of tension and international conflict.

Berlin would have to become a 'free city'. The western powers
would no longer be able to cross East German territory without
the permission of the East Germans. The Russians would view
any violation of East German sovereignty as an act of aggression,
and the aggressor would be responsible for the consequences.
The United States and the other western powers would have no
special legal rights in West Berlin after the peace treaty had been
signed.

The Americans, said Khrushchev, would have to realize that
the situation was changed. Time had passed. The occupation days
were gone forever. America would have to face up to realities.
There was no going back. To salvage American prestige,
Khrushchev allowed that the change in Berlin's status did not
have to happen overnight; there could be a delay – but the two-
thousand-word declaration of intent he handed Kennedy insisted,
'It is necessary to establish deadlines. The Soviet government
regards a period not exceeding six months as adequate.'

Kennedy was caught completely off guard. His pre-summit
briefings had led him to expect Khrushchev to press for renewed
Berlin negotiations, not an American cave-in. But the President
declined to be intimidated by the Soviet leader's uncompromising
stance. He refused to accept that the Soviet Union could either
make the changes it proposed or hand the United States such an
ultimatum. He told the Soviet leader that America considered its
national security to be directly linked to Berlin. He said that the
United States was not in the city by courtesy of the Russians.
Stretching facts a bit, he told Khrushchev, 'We fought our way
there' and, through international agreement, had established the
right to remain there until all parties concerned, including the
United States, decided otherwise.

Khrushchev responded with a threat, a warning and his six-month deadline. Dismissing western rights to the city as old hat, he said the United States was crazy if it wanted to go to war over a patch of land in the middle of East Germany, but war, he told Kennedy, would result from any interference with the Soviet plan.

Despite all his preliminary briefings, despite the warnings that Khrushchev talked tough, Kennedy had never imagined that, even before he had settled in properly at the White House, he would emerge from the Vienna meeting facing the possibility of a nuclear cataclysm. Never before had an American President been spoken to the way he had that day. He was badly shaken by it. Khrushchev later recalled:

> He looked not only anxious, but deeply upset. . . . I couldn't help feeling a bit sorry and somewhat upset myself . . . But there was nothing I could do to help him . . . Politics is a merciless business, but that realization didn't keep me from feeling sorry for Kennedy.

Both men looked sombre and weary as they went through the ritual of shaking hands for the press photographers when Kennedy left the Soviet embassy at the end of their meeting. The handshake was clipped and neither of them smiled. The final communiqué issued jointly by Kennedy's press secretary, Pierre Salinger, and Khrushchev's press secretary, Mikhail Kharlamov, revealed nothing of what had transpired between the two leaders. It said little more than that, 'The President and the Chairman have agreed to maintain contact on all questions of interest to the two countries and for the whole world.' Correspondents were told that the talks had been 'frank [which sounded like trouble], courteous and wide-ranging.'

Privately, Russian spokesmen said that a great deal had been accomplished and the meeting had gone off very well. But correspondents probing for details were advised by White House spokesmen that it might be wise to refrain from optimistic speculation. Word spread that Austrian Foreign Minister Bruno Kreisky had told Khrushchev that Kennedy looked gloomy when seen off from Vienna. Only later was it learned that Kennedy, in a parting remark to Khrushchev, had said it looked like it was going to be a cold winter. As it happened, the political climate was to turn nasty well before winter set in.

John Kennedy returned to Washington from his Vienna meeting with Nikita Khrushchev badly jolted. While not wishing to underestimate the seriousness of the situation, the American ambassador to Russia, Llewellyn Thompson, who had himself weathered a fair share of threats and scoldings in Moscow, tried to reassure him about Khrushchev's daunting fulminations – 'About par for the course,' he called them.

Though Kennedy was confident that he had stood up well enough to the demands and threats to which he had been exposed, he had been genuinely shocked by the Soviet leader's attempt to intimidate him. Despite the pre-summit warning of Khrushchev's propensity for bluster and table-thumping, he was startled and outraged that the Soviet leader had presumed to talk to the President of the United States that way. *New York Times* correspondent James Reston, who saw Kennedy a few minutes after he and Khrushchev had taken leave of each other, described him as 'shaken and angry'.

British Prime Minister Harold Macmillan, whom the President stopped off to see in London on his way home from Vienna, said he 'seemed rather stunned – baffled, would perhaps be fairer'. Macmillan said that, for Kennedy, meeting Khrushchev had been 'rather like somebody meeting Napoleon at the height of his power for the first time'.

Chicago Daily News correspondent Peter Lisagor, who was on the plane which carried the President to Britain, said, 'Kennedy looked kind of tired and a bit used up when we went into London.' Columnist Joseph Alsop, who encountered the President on a social occasion during that London stop-over, was baffled to hear him say, 'I just want you to know, Joe, I don't care what happens. I won't give way, I won't give up and I'll do whatever's necessary.' Not privy to what had transpired at the summit, Alsop wasn't sure what he was talking about.

The President was stricken by a sense of foreboding, a fear that, even if Khrushchev was bluffing, things could be slipping out of control. To his friend and appointments secretary Kenneth O'Donnell he said grimly, 'If we're going to have to start a nuclear war, we'll have to fix things so it will be started by the President of the United States and nobody else. Not by a trigger-happy sergeant on a truck convoy at a checkpoint in East Germany.' On becoming President a few months earlier, Kennedy had promised Americans they would cross a 'new frontier'. Could that new frontier turn out to be one of war, death, grief and destruction?

On his way back to Washington, the President pored over notes on his exchanges with Khrushchev to find something he might have missed. Despite his aggressive manner and angry words, the Soviet leader might have dropped a hint that it was really only talk. But Kennedy could find no peg on which to hang that hope. The only relieving aspect of Khrushchev's Vienna warning was the indication that there was no absolute immediacy involved.

Khrushchev had spoken of taking action by the end of the year if his demands were not met. That seemed to confirm the view that whatever he intended to do would not be attempted until after the German elections in September, as Ambassador Thompson had suggested, and perhaps even not until after the Soviet Communist Party Congress in Moscow in October.

Nevertheless, October was only four months off; and even if the Russians held off for the full six months of the deadline period, there wasn't much time to get ready. Up to that moment, Berlin had not been a high-priority consideration for the US administration. Now it was *the* priority consideration. What were the Pentagon and NATO doing to prepare for all eventualities? What shape was the West Berlin garrison in? What was the State Department's thinking on what should happen next? What about Dean Acheson's Berlin review? What does the American public know, think and care about the situation?

First of all, Americans had to be prepared for any serious steps the administration would take to meet Khrushchev's challenge. At the same time, it had to be reassured that war was not about to break out. The American press, fed only meagre bits and pieces of hard fact by the White House and the State Department, was only beginning to appreciate the serious turn the situation had taken.

The Russian media were telling a different story. In an apparent bid to hold the United States responsible when things went publicly sour, the Russians were reporting that the Vienna get-together had been a totally successful affair, 'a good beginning', a step on the road to peace and international amity. They were publicly suggesting that the two leaders had not found Berlin a major cause for concern. Kennedy realized that the American public had to be told at once that, whatever the Russians were saying, there was little to cheer about.

His report to the nation on his Vienna encounter was drafted on board the plane back to Washington and tidied up at the White House for delivery on the night of the President's return home. Kennedy did not tell the American people the full story of what had taken place in Vienna, and what he did say was not completely accurate. But there was no complacency in it:

> I will tell you now that it was a very sober two days. There was no discourtesy, no loss of temper, no threats or ultimatums by either side; no advantage or concession was either gained or given; no major decision was either achieved or pretended . . . Our views contrasted sharply but at least we knew better at the end where we both stood . . . At least the channels of communication were opened more fully . . . I made it clear to Mr Khrushchev that the security of western Europe, and therefore our own security, are deeply involved in our presence and our access right to West Berlin, that those rights are based on law and not on sufferance, and that we are determined to maintain those rights at any risk.

Kennedy made it clear with both words and tone that things could very well get worse before they got any better. At the same time, in view of bellicose warnings that had emanated from Moscow prior to the summit, he sought to reassure the American public that the guns were not about to go off, nor were the bombs about to drop.

He did not broadcast the fact that senior personnel at the National Security Council, State Department, the Pentagon and the CIA had been ordered to immerse themselves immediately in a detailed review of the Berlin situation and American policy with regard to it, and that he himself was about to do the same. The President had no intention of being caught unprepared or ill-advised again. One Bay of Pigs was enough for him. He intended to remain on top of this brawl as it slithered inexorably towards a climax.

The strain of dealing with the Berlin situation did the President's health no good. Even before his Vienna excursion, he had been troubled by renewed back pain. On a visit to Canada in May, he had strained his back while ceremonially shifting three shovelsful of earth to plant a red oak in front of Government House in Ottawa. Despite the steel corset he donned, his back had continued to trouble him. He was in pain before his trip to Vienna. He was in pain during his meeting with Khrushchev. And as he began facing up to the difficult decisions he would have to make, decisions which he believed could affect the lives of many millions of people and the future security of the United States, that pain became more intense.

Under pressure from the White House press corps and to prepare the public for a planned public appearance of Kennedy on crutches, the President's physician, Dr Janet Travell, was authorized to give the press details. She said the President's problem was lumbosacrial strain, a common cause of low-back pain. It was revealed that at times he used crutches to relieve the pain while getting about when he was out of the public eye. He was also being treated with novocaine injections and hot packs.

To unwind, relax and rest his back, Kennedy went off to Palm Beach, Florida, to stay at the home of his long-time friend LeMoyne Billings. But the intense pain persisted and a week after his return from Vienna it was disclosed that an orthopaedic specialist, Dr Preston Wade, had been called in to examine the President and consult with Dr Travell. Inevitably, stories of the President's earlier back problems were revived and publicized – a football injury while he was at Harvard, followed by the damage done to his back when his PT boat was in collision with a Japanese destroyer during the Second World War. It was also publicly revealed for the first time that, seven years earlier, he had spent months in hospital and had undergone a dangerous lumbar fusion operation, during which a steel plate had been inserted in his spine. After he had almost died – last rites had, in fact, been administered – he underwent another operation to have it removed. Kennedy also suffered from a form of Addison's Disease and lived much of his adult life believing it would kill him by the time he was forty-five. After his assassination in 1963, his brother, Robert Kennedy, said, 'At least one half of the days he spent on this earth were days of intense physical pain.'

Though Kennedy was used to pain, the American people weren't used to the image of their President on crutches, particularly since his youthful sprightliness had charmed many into voting for him. To ease his discomfort, when he returned from Palm Beach to Washington, Kennedy had to be lifted to the hatch of the plane by a crane, which showed just how much he hurt. Nevertheless, though one Republican congressman moaned, 'Now we've got an invalid for a President,' to the public at large, the Kennedy magic was still effective. When he got back to Washington and appeared in public, the youthful smile was back. So was the old spring in his step, once he had discarded the crutches.

But Berlin and the Khrushchev threats worried him deeply. Observers, like the Washington correspondent of the London *Times*, noted 'a new heaviness of features evident under the outdoor tan'. When dealing with other matters, many of them of crucial significance for his new administration, his mind would sometimes wander back to the Berlin conundrum. His repartee, once light and bantering, grew grimmer, and sometimes took on a morbid air. When a friend jokingly told him he had decided to build a swimming pool for his home rather than a nuclear fallout shelter, the President told him he had made a mistake.

Having established greater rapport with the Washington press corps than any previous occupant of the White House – he was, in fact, the last President to be protected by the press – Kennedy grew increasingly sensitive to press criticism. He would sometimes telephone newsmen to tell them off because of what their newspapers or broadcast organizations had said about him or the administration, at one time calling a correspondent during dinner with the opening line, 'I hear you bastards have done it to me again.' No doubt his aching back contributed to his irritability. But the pressure of events, as well as conflicting counsel from his advisers and from America's allies, didn't make things easier.

Despite Kennedy's vow to remain firm over Berlin, the first public move by the West after the Vienna summit was to give ground. Five days after the President's 'we-will-stand-fast' report to the nation, a meeting planned for Berlin of the upper house of the West German parliament was cancelled. It was to have been a symbolic gathering – it had been held regularly for years – to demonstrate a communion between the people of West Berlin and West Germany. But the Russians and East Germans condemned it as a dangerous provocation and Washington advised the West Germans to call it off.

Kennedy did not want to force the pace of events at this critical moment. He wanted to make certain that whatever was done would, as far as possible, be done under controlled conditions. He did not want to be distracted from the central issues by skirmishes over symbolic gestures. Though there was some grumbling about it in West Germany, the government in Bonn agreed that, under the circumstances, it was probably the wise thing to do. The Russians saw Kennedy's prudence in a different light: they saw it as confirmation of their belief that it wasn't a matter of a bad back for the President, more a case of no backbone.

As summer drew on, the temperature, political as well as climatic, was soaring in Washington. The American capital was becoming a cauldron of ideas on how to approach the situation. There were hardliners, softliners, and in-betweeners of various persuasions. There were specialists perturbed by the failure of others to grasp the finer points of the situation, and generalists who insisted the specialists were incapable of comprehending the bigger picture. There were some who, in the words of one old Washington hand, 'had all the answers and couldn't be told anything', and others who lost themselves in trying to tie together all available information so that specific recommendations could be made. There were people who said, 'Let's sit down and talk to the Russians about finding a way out of this mess.' There were others who insisted that when the Russians, as they had done, start giving America orders, there was nothing to talk about. And there were those who said, 'Yes, let's talk to them, but just to string them along.'

There was Kennedy's entourage of bright young advisers who had been through the Bay of Pigs debacle and were determined not to take another drubbing. There were some men in Congress who wanted to know why the United States had got into this mess to begin with when, as they believed, it did not touch on America's vital interests. And there were other congressmen who wanted to know who-the-hell the Russians thought they were.

There was the Berlin Mafia in Washington and at the United States Mission in Berlin; its members believed that any failure to confront the challenge to the freedom of the city would be disastrous for America and the rest of the non-Communist world. It seemed to them that every time the United States and the Soviet Union had negotiated over Germany since the war, the United States had been outfoxed and had ended up with 'less of the salami' than it had before. But there were others who held that the ideological village in which those honorary Berliners dwelled was not the global village, and that it was worth surrendering a little piece of 'the salami' to safeguard world peace.

Inevitably, one set of views was not always treated with respect or deference by those who espoused others. In addition, the White House contingent was convinced that the State Department was bogged down in bureaucratic hocus-pocus, and that it had no idea of how to cope with the developing crisis. State Department people, meanwhile, thought little of the Kennedy entourage. One State Department analyst said of them, 'They had such tremendous self-confidence, such élan, such assuredness and glamour – and then you'd discover they really didn't know the facts.'

Some Soviet affairs specialists in Washington, though believing they had no chance of getting a serious hearing in view of the crisis atmosphere following Kennedy's return from Vienna, were convinced the emergency was artificial. They tried as best they could to examine things through Soviet eyes and, sticking to the information provided by the various government intelligence services, believed that the Russians were nowhere near as strongly placed militarily as Khrushchev's bluster suggested they were. This, they maintained, had been confirmed by the failure of the Russians to follow through on previous threats.

Even if this view had made its way through the cumbersome machinery by which government departments and agencies reported to the White House, Kennedy would not have been prepared to take heart from such assurances in the atmosphere of nuclear posturing which prevailed. Besides, Llewellyn Thompson, America's man in Moscow, an astute and perceptive emissary, continued to pass word along that the Russians definitely were getting ready to deal with the Berlin situation within the next few months. The President had to prepare for all eventualities.

With war or peace thought to be at stake, weighing the options and deciding on a course of action was a worrying as well as a complicated process. Having to gain agreement on a course of action from America's chief allies made it even more difficult, especially when those allies were represented by such formidable individualists as British Prime Minister Harold Macmillan, French President Charles de Gaulle and West German Chancellor Konrad Adenauer.

Like Kennedy, all three men made appropriate noises about never abandoning West Berlin. But they were far from agreeing on how to respond to the Soviet challenge. It caused problems and prompted Kennedy to recall that Napoleon had once said that he won his battles because he fought them without allies.

De Gaulle's attitude was, ostensibly, the least complicated. He saw no reason at all to talk with the Russians about Berlin. There was, he said, simply nothing to talk about. The Allies were asking nothing of the Russians in Berlin, so any negotiations could only be based on the assumption that the West would concede something to them there – territory, rights, matters of principle, or all three. De Gaulle wasn't worried by Khrushchev's ultimatums. He had told the Soviet leader that if he signed the threatened separate peace treaty with East Germany, he would, in effect, only be signing the document with himself. It would be meaningless. The French President believed that when the Russians were prepared to talk seriously about the overall German problem, disarmament and other key international issues in which the West had something to gain, there would be time enough to talk with them about Berlin also. But the Russians had to know that if they interfered with western rights in the city, they risked war.

There was, however, more to de Gaulle's approach than merely keeping the Russians at bay. He also objected to negotiations over Berlin because they would inevitably be dominated by the Americans and the Russians, and would thus serve to perpetuate France's secondary status in international dealings. At the same time, with Britain linked in a 'special relationship' with the Americans and with West Germany not yet sitting at the top table, he saw the situation as offering France an opportunity to provide the distinctive, unsubmissive, 'European' voice in the Berlin dispute. All in all, de Gaulle was not greatly impressed with Kennedy or his policies. He thought of the American President as an attractive, reasonably clever young man, but with a great deal still to learn. Kennedy, on the other hand, greatly respected de Gaulle personally, but the Americans were cynical about the French: strong on advice, they were weak on action.

Despite the hard line in Paris, the French Berlin garrison could hardly be considered an impressive example of western defiance. The men who manned it were mostly on rest-and-recuperation after harrowing duty in the French colony of Algeria, where France had been unsuccessfully trying to suppress a bloody, guerrilla-sparked national liberation movement. With the bulk of its army tied down in Algeria and the rest of it braced for an attempted coup by generals infuriated by de Gaulle's intention to grant the country independence, France could not be counted on to carry its share of the military burden if the Berlin situation turned critical. In the city itself, the French interpretation of western unity of action was so narrow that if the American or British commandants proposed even a ceremonial military display the French commandant was required to clear it with his superiors in Paris before agreeing.

It was apparent that de Gaulle's dignified stand on principle could not be backed up with French deeds if deeds rather than lofty pronouncements became necessary. But Europe was centre stage for this episode and Kennedy knew he had to establish a strong measure of understanding among the Allies. His National Security Adviser, McGeorge Bundy, said, 'It would not have been to our advantage to be seen to be going it alone. We didn't want to get in a position where an ally would go to the sidelines because we were being unresponsive.'

To keep West Germany from going to the sidelines and just looking on was a particular concern at the White House and the State Department. A West Germany firmly linked to the western alliance was an indispensable element in America's vision of a strong, united western Europe, capable of containing Soviet influence on the continent. Any suggestion, however fictitious, that the United States government was toying with the possibility of making concessions in Berlin sent convulsive shudders through West Germany. Such concessions would have implied *de facto* recognition of the East German Communist state. They would have signalled American rejection of West German determination to reunify the divided country. The West Germans made sure that Washington, and every American with influential contacts in Washington, understood the depth of their feelings on that. The message got through, as testified by a letter to Deputy National Security Adviser Walt Rostow from William Griffith of the Massachusetts Institute of Technology Center of International Studies:

> Once the United States is no longer felt by the West German population to be completely committed to reunification, the West Germans will become unreliable allies for us . . . The stake here is what the Soviets have since 1945 tried to get: Germany. The Germans will be watching us to see if we display *any* sign of weakness, indecision or compromise. If we do, sooner or later, they will begin to look elsewhere.

If American interests were considered in isolation, there was no overriding reason why Washington, if able to extract a suitable *quid pro quo*, should not have agreed to the peace treaty the Russians were demanding for Germany, finally bringing the Second World War to a formal end – even if this did mean recognizing the East German regime – provided West Berlin's special status was absolutely guaranteed and the access routes were kept open (which was not what the Kremlin had in mind). After all, the United States extended diplomatic recognition to such other Communist countries as Czechoslovakia and Hungary, where Soviet forces were also stationed, which were also completely under Soviet control, and whose systems were equally in conflict with western values. No less a cold warrior than the late Secretary of State John Foster Dulles had once suggested that East German guards on the access routes might be acceptable as 'agents' of the Russians.

But East Germany had to be kept in pariah status and denied

western recognition. The West German government insisted upon it. It was the only way to keep alive the illusion, fundamental to West German policy at the time, that there would be no permanent division of Germany into East and West, that the country would be reunified in freedom and justice in the not-too-distant future, and that the Communist East German state was only a temporary aberration, soon to tumble onto the scrapheap of history. For the United States, Britain or France to have suggested otherwise, and to have recognized East Germany, might have busted the alliance wide open.

In effect, Adenauer claimed a veto over the western approach to the dispute. The United States government could, of course, not concede as much. An acceptable explanation had to be tortuously fabricated and was contained in a National Security Council memorandum:

> The fundamental reason why the United States, its allies and the uncommitted nations have refused to recognize the so-called 'German Democratic Republic' is that there is in actuality no such country. The area called the 'GDR' is in reality only one of the several occupation zones of Germany, the Soviet Zone, and it remains an inseparable part of Germany. According to the criteria of history, culture, language and tradition, according to the desire of the population and according to international agreements, Germany remains a single nation . . . Recognition of the 'GDR' by the United States in the face of the opposition of [West Germany] would jeopardize our entire post-war policy of integrating Germany with the West and utilizing its dynamism and military potential as an essential component of NATO.

That approach had to be ultimately futile, and not a few people in Washington were well aware of it. West Germany was bigger and economically stronger by far than East Germany, firmly in the western camp, and would soon have nuclear weapons based on its soil. It would inevitably dominate any reunified German nation. The threatening reappearance of such a nation in Central Europe would no longer have been tolerated by the Russians. It would have amounted to a setback of unacceptable proportions, foretelling a collapse of the Soviet East European empire and convincing Russians still mourning their war dead that their Motherland was once more under threat from Germany. Soviet paranoia, acute at the best of times, would have known no limits.

As a Catholic Rhinelander, West German Chancellor Konrad Adenauer personally didn't care all that much for Prussian,

Protestant Berlin, or for Berliners. Once, when John Foster Dulles, Secretary of State in the Eisenhower administration, in an effort to calm West German worries, had told Adenauer, 'If the Soviets push us too far, we'll go to nuclear war,' Adenauer's shocked response had been, '*Um Gottes willen, nicht über Berlin!*' ('For God's sake, not over Berlin!') Nor had he ever been much enamoured of that part of his country that was now East Germany. He was once quoted as saying that when he crossed the Elbe he felt like he was entering Asia. The Chancellor was, nevertheless, committed to stitching his war-splintered country together and removing all parts of it from Russia and Communist control. And that meant absolutely no concessions in Berlin.

As a shrewd statesman, the West German Chancellor made certain that the American commitment to reunification was not only firm, but publicly announced at every possible occasion. There were even times when the United States government was forced into pressuring the Olympic Committee to bar East German athletes from the Olympic Games so as not to give implied recognition to their Communist state. One administration figure in Washington recalled that, 'if you left a declaration of commitment to the reunification of Germany out of any speech, you could count on the West Germans to come around and ask if you changed your policy.' Another moaned at the time, 'How many times do you have to tell them you love them?'

As the crisis developed, they apparently weren't told often enough to get the West German government to clarify what turned out to be its confusing attitudes on Berlin. It adopted a hard line on the defence of western rights in the city, but recoiled at suggestions that the United States might use force to protect those rights. Having suffered greatly in the war, the West Germans feared their country might again become a battlefield. In addition, despite the absence of diplomatic relations, they had established lucrative trading relations with the East and were reluctant to see them jeopardized by an armed clash. To Washington, this quest after the best of both worlds was exasperating.

Britain's attitude on Berlin and Germany was no less complicated. To placate the West Germans, the Foreign Office offered ritual backing for German reunification, but the British would have been appalled if it had actually happened. They were already struggling, with limited success, to compete industrially with booming West Germany. The idea of having to match the economic might of a united Germany was too dreadful to entertain. Still recovering from the damage inflicted by the Germans in the war, the British were in the throes of their sixth serious economic crisis since the end of the war, while West Germany was on the threshhold of its 'economic miracle'. The man in the street in London or Liverpool needed no persuasion not to want to go to war again for any reason, certainly not to rescue 'bloody Germans'.

Nevertheless, Britain was deeply committed to the unity of the western alliance, including West Germany. British leaders were not to be outdone in declaring their determination not to be forced out of Berlin. Foreign Secretary Lord Home announced that the West was perfectly content with the status quo and could not see any need for a change. Member of Parliament Desmond Donnelly told the House of Commons that 'Britain's frontier is not at Dover but at the Brandenburg Gate.'

But the British had no intention of fighting to defend that frontier. They did not think it would ever become necessary. They firmly believed that negotiations could produce a mutually acceptable solution if undertaken with a full appreciation of the horrific alternatives. They did not at all like some of the ideas being batted about in Washington where, earlier in the year, Macmillan had sat in on a preliminary assessment of the situation by Dean Acheson. He had been horrified to hear the former Secretary of State revive General Clay's old proposal that, if necessary to break a Berlin blockade, tanks be sent storming down the autobahn through East Germany to West Berlin. He was apprehensive about what he called 'the absurd contingency planning of the Americans'. Not long before, he had told de Gaulle that 'he could not conceive of himself taking the responsibility for leading his country to appalling destruction simply for the sake of the future . . . of a German city'. The defence correspondent of the *Manchester Guardian* suggested that all West Berliners be evacuated to West Germany since their city was indefensible.

Under pressure from the United States, the British indicated they were prepared to agree to specific contingency plans to meet an increasingly likely Soviet squeeze on Berlin. But they wanted final decisions to be taken by the Allies in the light of circumstances prevailing when the crunch came. For American planners, that wasn't at all satisfactory. It meant that if the crunch ever did come, there would be delays, hemmings-and-hawings, and lengthy consultations, by which time the moment for effective action would have passed.

While the British thought there were too many trigger-happy people in Washington, the Americans thought that the British were sometimes remarkably naive in assessing the factors that might influence the Russians. This view seemed to be confirmed when, at the height of the refugee stampede, the London *Times* printed a letter to the editor suggesting that Khrushchev might have become so belligerent about West Berlin because he was not really aware of the flood of refugees who preferred not to live in East Germany. Perhaps, it was suggested, he might be discreetly informed so that he would better be able to appreciate its significance and revise his views accordingly.

The task of finding common ground for the Allies was an intricate one. American spokesmen gave assurances that the West would be united in facing the Berlin challenge. But one official conceded that it sounded like the classic alibi of a public relations executive whose client runs into embarrassing trouble: 'The situation is entirely normal – and we are doing everything we can to correct it.'

6

The Crisis Looms

ON THE MORNING of Monday 12 June 1961, personnel from the East German government's press office in East Berlin, supplied with rolls of West German ten pfenning coins, were dispatched across the sector border to make telephone calls; telephone communications between the two parts of the city had long before been severed by the Communists. They anchored themselves in street phone booths in West Berlin and passed along brief, precise messages to correspondents based there: 'Press conference. Chairman of the State Council of the German Democratic Republic Ulbricht. House of Ministries. Thursday. Eleven o'clock. You are invited.'

This was indeed to be a special occasion. Though never tongue-tied or hesitant, Ulbricht did not normally expose himself to the probings of people who might raise embarrassing questions. He saw no value in it. But now, exertions were being made by the East Germans to gain wide attention for what he would have to say. For the first time, the West Berlin press corps was being invited to East Berlin practically en masse. On the morning of 15 June, Vopos inspecting cars entering East Berlin had instructions not to be overly fastidious in checking western newsmen for forbidden newspapers they might happen to have in their possession on their way to Wilhelmstrasse and the press conference. Allowances were being made so as not to detract from the significance of the occasion.

An ornate banqueting hall, once used for special occasions by senior officers of Hermann Göring's Luftwaffe and now used largely for East German government receptions, was where Ulbricht was to meet the press. Facing a raised rostrum in the hall

1. Armed guards in a watchtower on the border between East Germany and West Berlin prior to the erection of the Wall, posted to prevent the escape of refugees to the West. The only route from East to West still open at the time was within the four-power city.

2. As the barbed wire barrier is strung dividing Berlin, East German soldiers, their backs to West Berlin, face a crowd of sullen East Berliners.

3. Members of an East Berlin 'Workers Battle Group' on duty at the barbed wire.

4. Hastily erected, the Wall, made of concrete blocks, at first collapsed in places under its own weight.

5. The Brandenburg Gate, once the symbol of Berlin and once astride Berlin's major Unter den Linden thoroughfare, sealed off from the East in 1961.

6. The same view in 1985, with the Brandenburg Gate still sealed off and inconspicuously patrolled by armed guards.

7. As the East Germans build the Wall with Soviet approval, British troops string wire around the Soviet War Memorial in West Berlin, ostensibly to protect it from enraged West Berliners.

8. East German soldiers armed with automatic weapons patrol a section of the sector border where concrete is replacing the original barbed wire barrier.

9. Separated from their relatives by the Wall, West Berlin parents hoist their children for grandparents in East Berlin to see.

10. A West Berlin bride and groom come to the Wall in the hope of being seen by relatives and other guests in East Berlin prevented by the Wall from attending their wedding.

11. West Berliners wave over the Wall toward East Berlin, hoping to be spotted by relatives there.

12. East Berliners fleeing West through buildings on the sector border.

13. The windows of an East Berlin border building are bricked up to prevent further escapes through them by refugees. Later this and all other buildings on the border were levelled to make a no-man's-land – easier to guard against East Berliners hoping to commit the crime of 'Fleeing the Republic'.

14. Vopos guard a hole in the Wall made by a heavy truck in which two young East Berliners crashed through to West Berlin.

were long tables dotted with little bottles of mineral water and flat orange soda. Well before the appointed time, more than three hundred correspondents, many from the East German and other Communist press but at least half from western media, were in place and speculating among themselves about the momentous announcement Ulbricht would make which had prompted him to grace them with his imminent presence. It was hot in the hall and the bottled mineral water was tepid.

Ulbricht, when he arrived, was flanked by other East German luminaries, including Gerhardt Eisler, in charge of the country's broadcasting operations, who some years before, after being convicted in America of spying for Russia, had jumped bail and had been spirited aboard a Polish ship out of the United States, where he had taken refuge during the Nazi years. But Ulbricht, the durable Communist leader of East Germany, was undoubtedly the star attraction that morning. A short, tight-lipped, grey man with rimless glasses and a squeaky voice, he looked like an aging office manager who had nurtured his neatly-trimmed goatee to lend his unprepossessing looks greater stature. It was not easy to imagine that this man had had the wit or good luck to survive the Stalin purges in Moscow, nor that he himself had been able to purge a fair number of colleagues who had dared to take exception to his rigid Stalinist policies.

After an introductory statement which contained no startling revelations, Ulbricht threw the floor open to questions, during which it was presumed those revelations would be forthcoming. It was hard to believe the press conference had been called for no specific purpose. Asked about a suggestion the day before by an influential American senator (Mike Mansfield of Montana) that all Berlin, rather than just the western sectors as the Communists proposed, be turned into a free city, Ulbricht replied that he had no idea who the good senator was. Asked about the future of West Berlin if he and the Russians had their way, he said its 'centres of espionage and subversion' would be put out of business. So would those involved in the 'slave trade', including, presumably, the refugee reception centre at Marienfelde. He said Tempelhof, still West Berlin's main airfield and likely to be used again for airlift purposes if it became necessary to break a land blockade, was a danger and nuisance in the centre of a big city and would probably close itself down. All access routes to Berlin through East Germany would come under the control of the East German authorities by the end of the year, after the peace treaty was signed with the Soviet Union.

It made a lively story for the assembled correspondents, but there was nothing earth-shakingly new in any of this. Though some of the questions put to him were pointed and designed to draw blood, Ulbricht fielded them without difficulty, sometimes simply by uttering what everyone there knew to be nonsense – like blaming West German restrictions rather than his own decrees for the inability of East Germans to travel legally to the West.

He took two or three questions at a time when he preferred to divert attention from a point a questioner wanted to clarify, thus shrouding the issue in a haze of verbiage. The East German leader had clearly learned a good deal about oratorical ducking and weaving in his long years of ideological shadow boxing in the Communist movement. Not one of the reporters in attendance saw any special significance in his gratuitous declaration that, 'No one intends to build a wall' in Berlin to stop the refugee exodus. He said it as if the very idea was absurd and, in fact, it did seem far-fetched.

As the proceedings dragged on and the hall grew hotter, some correspondents began to wonder why, after shunning the western press for so long, the East German leader had bothered to make himself available just then. Whatever he had said could just as easily have appeared in that morning's *Neues Deutschland* – indeed, much of it had featured in past issues of the newspaper. No one was given the opportunity to ask what it was all about. But Ulbricht's purpose later became apparent.

At that stage, despite his ultimatum to Kennedy, Nikita Khrushchev wasn't sure he wanted to risk a showdown by handing control of the western access routes to Berlin over to Ulbricht with the implied backing of Soviet forces in East Germany. Nor had he yet decided, as an alternative, to let the East Germans take action to stop the refugees. Worried that the Americans might respond forcefully or, more likely, that they might encourage and support a massive anti-Communist uprising among the disgruntled East German populace, Khrushchev was in no hurry to give Ulbricht, whom he neither liked nor trusted, what he wanted.

Now, to the great annoyance of the Russians, Ulbricht, fearing for the future of his regime, his personal position and the country's economy, was trying to force the pace and thus preclude another Khrushchevian climb-down. He trusted Khrushchev no more than Khrushchev trusted him. He recalled how the Soviet leader had dodged a Berlin showdown the previous year, after he had walked out of the Paris summit conference, with the words, 'We are realists. We shall never follow a reckless course.'

Ulbricht could not act against the wishes of the Kremlin, but he could influence events and attitudes. His presence at the press conference, and his words there implying that West Berlin would soon be his to do with as he pleased, were calculated to raise the level of tension already building up in the city, and they did. After his press conference performance was screened on East German television that night and splattered over the front pages of the East German press the following morning, the number of refugees checking in at the Marienfelde reception centre rose sharply, as the East German leader must have known it would. And two days later, Mayor Brandt, commemorating the anniversary of the 1953 East German uprising, responded to Ulbricht's rhetoric with rhetoric of his own. He vowed that the people of Berlin would never consent to write off the people of East Germany, 'who had the misfortune to find themselves living at the end of the war' in that part of the country.

A lot of people were getting very nervous. West German officials, fearful that Ulbricht's provocations might stampede the West into concessions to Russia to head-off an eruption of real trouble, tried to assure Washington that Khrushchev would never let East German hotheads drag him into an armed conflict. Fearing that hotheads in the American army might perform that task, Senator Mansfield called on President Kennedy to take steps to prevent such an occurrence:

> We should re-screen all ranking US military officers at home and abroad connected with possible Berlin operations, to make certain that the men who will give significant commands are persons with the highest sense of professional responsibility, completely disciplined, not given to politics or public relations, and fully cognizant of the significance of subordinating, without question, military action to the dimensions of the diplomatic decisions of the President and the Secretary of State.

At the request of the President, Chairman of the Joint Chiefs of Staff Lyman Lemnitzer prepared a report on levels of military supplies for the American garrison in Berlin, and on stockpiles of essential supplies for the civilian population of West Berlin. For the American troops, it showed eighteen days worth of ammunition and combat rations; for civilians, there were 440 days supply of solid fuels, fifty-six days supply of gasoline, 119 days supply of diesel oil, 180 days supply of dried milk, dehydrated potatoes and butter fat, and 182 days of medical supplies. Recalling the Berlin blockade, the President told Lemnitzer that improvements should be made 'immediately [for] the level reported for gasoline'. It was best to be ready. Kennedy aide and speech-writer Ted Sorenson came across a gloomy anecdote attributed to a Russian wise man and found it worth noting down in the presidential speech material file: Asked whether there would be peace or war, the sage replied, 'There will be no war – but it is doubtful that we shall survive the struggle for peace.'

Like people in the West, Russians, virtually all of whom had lost kin in the war, had no wish to find their country pushed into a conflict over Berlin. Talk of such a possibility aroused much anxiety among them. They were partially reassured on the day Ulbricht was trying to stir things up when, in a broadcast to the Soviet people, Khrushchev spoke admiringly of Kennedy. He repeated his warning that a peace treaty could no longer be put off and that the Soviet Union would meet force with force. But he assured his people that the American President was no nuclear lunatic. He said he had 'formed the impression that [Kennedy] appreciates the great responsibility that rests with the govern-ments of two such mighty states'. The Soviet Union, Khrushchev stressed, wanted a peaceful settlement in Germany.

People in America weren't so sure. With a few isolated exceptions, defiance rather than caution became the keynote in Congress and in the press: there were calls for an American military build-up to meet the Soviet threat; there were predic-tions that Soviet bullying, if successful, would not stop at Berlin; a line would have to be drawn somewhere, and Berlin was as good a place as any.

Having failed to elicit the desired response one way, Khrush-chev, beginning to flounder, tried another. On 21 June – the twentieth anniversary of the German invasion of Russia – to show he was serious about Berlin, he appeared in public in Moscow in the uniform of a Soviet lieutenant general, the rank he had attained as a political commissar attached to the Red Army during the war. Defining western refusal to give way as a threat to the entire Communist world, he declared, 'The might of the Soviet Union and the entire socialist camp has grown to such an extent that if the western powers mobilized all their forces in a senseless attempt to destroy the achievements of the peoples of the socialist countries, this time too, they [like the Nazis] would suffer complete failure.' In case that message wasn't getting through to Washington, he announced that Russia was prepared to resume testing nuclear weapons, suspended three years earlier, if provoked by the West.

The Soviet leader could no longer step back or procrastinate. The pressure on him to act was too great – and not only from the deteriorating situation in East Germany and the relentless Chinese assault on Soviet leadership of the Communist world. Several of his Kremlin colleagues – notably Foreign Minister Andrei Gromyko and Deputy Prime Minister Frol Kozlov – were pressing him to get on with the job if Soviet credibility was not to be damaged. Ulbricht had convinced the leaders of some of the other Communist countries of East Europe that if his regime went under, theirs were not likely to be far behind – Poland's western border was a mere sixty miles from Berlin – and they too brought their worries to the Kremlin; so did the Soviet military, which was fed up with tolerating the presence of western garrisons in the middle of East Germany where, they believed, those garrisons had no right to be. Marshal Vassili Chuikov pressed that point home:

> The historic truth is that during the assault on Berlin there was not a single American, British or French armed soldier around it, except for the prisoners of war, whom we freed. Therefore the claims of the United States, British and French ruling circles to some kind of special rights in Berlin are entirely unfounded. They did not take it. They came there to fulfill the conditions of surrender, and on the basis of the fulfillment of these conditions, the occupation of Berlin should long since have ended.

At the Vienna summit, Khrushchev had exploded angrily at Kennedy's concern about possible miscalculation leading to war. 'All I ever hear from your people and your news correspondents and your friends in Europe and every place else,' he said, 'is that damned word, miscalculation! You ought to take that word and bury it . . . and never use it again. I am sick of it!'

Sick of it or not, the Soviet leader had to face up to the very real possibility that he had miscalculated. Kremlinologist Robert Slusser has pointed out, 'An essential element in Soviet strategy was the calculation that it was an acceptable risk to raise the tension to a point where the West would yield to Soviet demands rather than accept the alternative of war.' A Soviet spokesman in Moscow could complain plaintively to western newsmen, 'We threaten you with a peace treaty while you threaten us with war.' In Washington, Soviet Ambassador Mikhail Menshikov could announce that he had reported back to Moscow that 'the American people will not fight for Berlin'. But Khrushchev's credibility depended on the West yielding – and that was not happening. Despite Kennedy's warning in Vienna, it looked very much as though he had misjudged and, in the process, had backed himself into a corner.

John Kennedy was in danger of doing the same. The magnitude of Khrushchev's conundrum did not filter through to Washington. The White House was under the impression that, though the Russian leader was being subjected to various pressures, he knew pretty much how he intended to deal with them. The fact that Khrushchev had been making the same threat to the Berlin access routes for almost three years without doing anything about them seemed irrelevant.

His aching back still acting up, Kennedy remained immersed in Berlin, brooding over the need to take action that might lead to war and the danger of doing so before all options had been fully explored. At his command, everything the Russians said or did with regard to Berlin was reported to him. He didn't want to miss a thing. He wanted to know everything and he wanted to know it now!

An analysis written later of administration practices during the Berlin crisis said, 'Washington bureaucrats will long remember John F. Kennedy as a President who stood them on their heads. Quick and impatient, he could not understand how Foggy Bottom and the Pentagon could take so long to answer his questions . . . [He tried] to force them to adapt the decision-making process to a world in which the President might have only minutes to make up his mind whether to blow up half the northern hemisphere.'

It made the State Department apprehensive as well as uncomfortable. Such presidential scrutiny could lend exaggerated importance to the blustery utterances emanating from Moscow. It could produce a distorted American response – and some would say later that it did.

But Kennedy was not overly impressed with the views of the State Department, which he called 'a bowl of jelly. It's got all those people over there who are constantly smiling.' Instead, he instructed the Department to tighten its procedures so that he would be better able to assess what was going on. He wanted communications with London, Paris and Bonn streamlined to complement Allied consultations in Washington, so that joint decisions could be more quickly reached. He wanted up-to-date assessments on nuances of mood in Moscow. He read all the cables from Berlin on what was happening there, and on what people thought was happening. He asked for reports on how, and at what point, the West could respond to any objectionable Soviet move with economic measures. He interrogated Treasury Department officials on how the crisis might affect the American domestic economy. He explored ways of seizing the propaganda advantage, so often forfeited by the United States through unimaginative planning. He ordered the Pentagon to report on how the armed forces should and could be beefed up to meet the crisis. He sought the views of foreign leaders who thought they were merely making ceremonial visits to the White House while passing through Washington.

Secretary of the Interior Stewart Udall, trying in vain to see the President about long-planned domestic campaigns to be initiated under the much-touted 'New Frontier' programme, said, 'He's imprisoned by Berlin. Ever since his Europe trip, Berlin has occupied him totally.' Others who had come with Kennedy to Washington after his election with visions of revitalizing America under the new administration found him equally out of reach.

According to Ted Sorenson, for the next weeks and months, the President 'saturated himself in the problem. He reviewed and revised the military contingency plans, the conventional force build-up, the diplomatic and propaganda initiatives, the budget changes and the plans for economic warfare . . . He talked to Allied leaders, to Gromyko, and to the Germans. He kept track of all the cables; he read transcripts of all the conferences.'

On 29 June, Dean Acheson, who had been asked to update his preliminary Berlin assessment, was summoned to the White House to present his report on Berlin to members of the National Security Council and key congressional figures. Incisive and unequivocal, Acheson's report and recommendations were sharply controversial. He maintained that Berlin was a problem only because the Russians wanted to make it a problem, and they wanted to do so for several reasons: they wanted to neutralize Berlin as a first step toward its take-over by East Germany; they wanted to weaken, if not break up, the western alliance; and they wanted to discredit the United States. Acheson said the Russians believed that if they could force the United States to back down over Berlin, American prestige and influence would be diminished everywhere, giving the Soviet Union greater opportunity to extend their areas of influence and control.

The former Secretary of State said that the Russians had to be shown that their assumptions about lack of American firmness and perseverance were dead wrong. The United States could threaten to take nuclear action to deter the Russians, but 'this I thought was not a real capability because it would not be believed . . . It would be perfectly obvious to the Russians we didn't mean it . . . A second step advocated . . . by some military people was a limited use of nuclear means – that is, to drop one bomb somewhere. I said this I thought was most unwise. If you drop one bomb, it wasn't a threat to drop that bomb – that was a drop – and once it happened, it either indicated that you were going to drop more, or you invited the other side to drop one back. This seemed to me to be irresponsible and not . . . adapted to the problem of Berlin.'

But Acheson urged the President to make his determination not to be booted out of Berlin clear to the Russians by declaring a national emergency and ordering a rapid build-up in American nuclear as well as conventional forces. United States forces in Germany should immediately be reinforced by two or three divisions, and military reserves in the United States should be increased by up to six divisions. Moscow would thus be sent a signal that if there was any backing down to do in this situation, it was up to the Russians to do it. The Russians would see that the American people were irrevocably committed to the freedom of West Berlin.

Acheson dusted off three 'essentials', drawn up as far back as 1958 to meet the threat then posed by Khrushchev, to define American vital interests in Berlin: there must be no threat to the maintenance of the western garrisons; there must be no disruption of western air and surface access; and there must be no interference with the freedom and viability of West Berlin.

If there was still an attempt to interfere with American surface access to Berlin, Acheson said, a 1948-style airlift should be launched. If, as was possible, that airlift proved inadequate this time because of greater supply needs in Berlin and improved disruption methods at the disposal of the Russians, two American armoured divisions should be sent up the autobahn from West Germany to force open the ground access routes. It would show the Kremlin that the United States was prepared to go all the way, to nuclear war if necessary, to protect its legal rights in Berlin.

Differences of views in Washington became more than academic. Kennedy now had to fix on an American response to Khrushchev's challenge and Acheson's hawkish recommendations served as a point of reference for the debate which gathered momentum in the weeks ahead. Some people participating in that debate came to be known as hardliners and others as softliners, a development which softliners complained about because it seemed to imply they were less firm than the hardliners in defending America's interests when that was their sole objective.

The hardline view was shared by, among others, Assistant Secretary of State Foy Kohler, the German desk at State, Assistant Secretary of Defence Paul Nitze and the Joint Chiefs of Staff at the Pentagon, Vice President Lyndon Johnson – whose influence in the White House, consistent with vice presidential tradition, was practically non-existent – and influential columnist Joseph Alsop, who said that unless there was a strong American military response, the United States was going to lose the cold war. All agreed that failing to take a demonstratively strong stance on Berlin would undermine the confidence of the Allies in America's protective umbrella, and that it would be a mistake to be seen to be overly anxious for negotiations.

With Moscow issuing demands, it was a potent argument. But, despite their fears of a wimpish image, the softliners who thought Acheson's recommendations both excessive and dangerous appeared to outgun those who lined up behind it. They included such formidable personalities as Ambassador Llewellyn Thompson, trusted Kennedy adviser on Soviet affairs Charles Bohlen, White House aide Arthur Schlesinger Jr, Senate Foreign Relations Committee Chairman William Fulbright, syndicated colum nist Walter Lippmann, and Henry Kissinger, who was at the time a Harvard professor called in as a White House consultant. Bohlen said, 'It seemed to us to be too extreme to put the country . . . into full mobilization for a situation like Berlin. This would have created dislocations, repercussions within the country and all over the world. It would have been regarded as proof of American hysteria.' Schlesinger called Acheson's proposals 'bleak choices'.

Thompson, summoned back from Moscow to participate in the debate, maintained that what Acheson suggested would be serious over-reaction. He said it was stretching things to believe that the Russians, in their Berlin probings, were bent on undermining the western alliance or doing damage to American prestige. Rather, he suggested, they were trying to consolidate their position in East Europe. Like the other softliners, he agreed that Moscow's Berlin demands should be resisted and that an American military build-up was advisable. But, like the others, he said that build-up should be far more modest than Acheson had proposed and should be accompanied by an American diplomatic offensive. The object would be to show that America's objectives were peaceful while the Soviet Union's actions were reckless. Kissinger called for a 'Kennedy Plan' for Central Europe to deal with an overall European settlement and not just Berlin. He said that, if handled properly, an offer to talk with the Russians would be seen as a sign of strength rather than weakness.

Compared with Acheson's detailed proposals, all of this was vague. Abram Chayes, the State Department's legal adviser who also took exception to the hard line, recalled, 'We didn't have the negotiating alternative very well worked out.' He was assigned the task of rectifying that omission. As Chayes set to work on plotting how to approach negotiations with the Russians on Berlin without damaging the West's position in the city or in Europe generally, Acheson told him, 'Abe, you'll see. You try but you will find that it just won't write.'

People at the Pentagon had, in the meantime, been doing some writing of their own, as was revealed in the 3 July issue of *Newsweek*, a month after the Vienna summit. What the magazine disclosed provoked considerable excitement in all the western capitals, and in Moscow as well. It reported that the Joint Chiefs of Staff had drawn up detailed proposals for steps to strengthen America's military capabilities. Included were the evacuation of a quarter of a million American military dependents in Europe; dispatch of forces to West Germany to reinforce the five divisions already there; deployment of forces in Europe into combat-ready positions; calling up four National Guard divisions and stepping-up the draft; and moving atomic weapons into 'ready' positions, resuming atomic weapons tests, or some other demonstration of United States readiness to use their nuclear capability.

Furious at the publicity it received and the anxiety it provoked at home and abroad, Kennedy immediately ordered the FBI to track down who leaked the report, which he had not yet officially received, much less approved. It turned out that *Newsweek*'s information was not altogether correct. But it was enough to impress Nikita Khrushchev, who immediately set out to prove publicly that he was as prepared to pick up the American gauntlet as the Americans appeared to be to throw it down. Barely had word reached Moscow before the Russians began offering their response.

Khrushchev sought out British Ambassador Sir Frank Roberts

at a reception and with characteristic vigour informed him that any western attempt to resist Soviet objectives in Berlin would prove futile. As waiters passed around them serving drinks, he told Sir Frank, 'Let me tell you, I can destroy your country with six hydrogen bombs.' A similar threat was directed at France, and West German Ambassador Hans Kroll was warned that his country could once again be reduced to rubble. In Washington, Soviet Ambassador Mikhail Menshikov advised presidential assistant Walt Rostow that America shouldn't count on its allies, and certainly not on West Germany. 'If the crisis intensified,' he told Rostow, 'the West Germans would leave West Germany as fast as the East Germans were leaving East Germany.'

This calculated bid to frighten the Allies and sow discord between them was the stick segment of a double-pronged Soviet campaign. A carrot was being brandished as well. On 5 July, presidential aide Arthur Schlesinger Jr, known by the Russians to be a softliner, received a visit from Georgi Kornienko, counsellor at the Soviet embassy in Washington. Kornienko said he was puzzled by the American attitude over Berlin. He pointed out that Khrushchev had said that the Soviet Union would guarantee the independence of West Berlin after the withdrawal of the western garrisons. He couldn't understand why the United States did not believe the Russians when they said they 'wish to keep things as they are in West Berlin', with only minor changes to the overall context of the situation. When Schlesinger said experience had taught the United States that Soviet guarantees were meaningless, Kornienko said, 'Why don't you propose your own guarantees? All we want to do is have a chance to discuss these things.'

It appeared to Schlesinger, Kissinger, and some others who favoured exploratory talks with Moscow, that this might be a genuine Soviet attempt to veer off the collision course to which the two countries were about to commit themselves. They saw it also as an opportunity for the United States to seize the initiative and test Soviet sincerity without losing ground in the process. Fearing that Kennedy was being provoked by Khrushchev's belligerence, Schlesinger urged the President not to overreact or to react prematurely. He advised him to hold hardline recommendations in reserve as a last-resort response to Russian transgressions in Berlin, to be invoked only if the other means failed to deter them:

If Khrushchev restrains himself [after a peace treaty with East Germany] from immediate physical violation of West Berlin and keeps saying that he will consider any guarantees for the continued integrity of West Berlin that we wish to propose, we will be very much on the political defensive. We will seem rigid and warlike, while he will seem filled with sweet reason.

Schlesinger touched a raw nerve when he reminded the President that the Bay of Pigs muddle had been caused by excessive concentration on operational matters and not enough on political implications. The President was warned that he might be in the process of being forced into the same position as he had been at the time of the Bay of Pigs – being asked by hardliners in Washington, in effect, 'Are you chicken or not?'

However, that seemed to be the question Moscow was asking when, a few days later, Khrushchev announced that a much-publicized programme for cutting more than a million men from the Soviet armed forces was being scrapped and that the Soviet military budget was being increased by one-third. Hardly had that news been digested when West German intelligence sources publicized reports that there were 67,500 Soviet and East German troops and 1,200 tanks in bases circling Berlin, within thirty miles of the city, 'the greatest concentration of modern forces in the world.' There was nothing new about those forces being there, but the atmosphere of crisis was noticeably thickening.

The time had come for the President to decide what to do. A nationwide public opinion survey indicated that the American public was prepared to back a hard-line response. An opinion poll commissioned by *US News and World Report* indicated that seventy-one percent of Americans were prepared to risk war to maintain Allied rights in Berlin; fifteen percent wanted to avoid war if possible, but wanted the government to remain firm; only fourteen percent said they were willing to yield rather than fight for the defence of Berlin.

Kennedy was afraid of letting the situation develop its own momentum. He continued to immerse himself in the implications and consequences of all possible moves. He even asked to be briefed on operational details. On 10 July, National Security Adviser McGeorge Bundy told Defence Secretary Robert McNamara that the President wanted to know, 'If we mobilize a million men, what would we do with them – how many would be combat troops, how many would be logistic support units, etc? Would we send the million to Europe, how long would it take to get them over, how many ships if by sea, how many would we plan to send by plane? How many days would it take to get all of them there? Where would they be positioned in Europe when they got there?' After the Bay of Pigs, there was very little the President was willing to take on trust.

When he was Secretary of State, John Foster Dulles had devised a straightforward, uncomplicated system for coping with the threat of Soviet aggression. The United States had a far greater nuclear armoury than Russia. If the Russians engaged in any aggressive activity contrary to the interests of the United States, it would risk massive nuclear retaliation. If it did not do so, it would have nothing to worry about.

It was an unrealistic, counter-productive, restrictive strategy, as Kennedy realized even before he took office. It was insanity to have a finger constantly poised over the nuclear button in a world where all sorts of disagreeable things happened, or could happen, all the time. It was sheer nonsense to say, as former Joint Chiefs of Staff Chairman Admiral Arthur Radford was reported to have told West German politician Franz Joseph Strauss, that if a single Communist soldier crossed the border into West Germany, the United States would unleash its nuclear weapons against the Communist bloc. Nor, as the Berlin crisis developed, did it seem at all credible to threaten a potentially suicidal nuclear war if the Russians or East Germans, to test Kennedy's resolve, blocked the autobahn with heavy trucks to stop an American convoy from getting through to Berlin.

Yet, as Robert McNamara, Kennedy's Secretary of Defence, had reported, the defence strategy which the administration had inherited required that any military challenge be almost immediately raised to the nuclear level. The United States did not have sufficient non-nuclear forces to cope on any other level. It was the big bang or nothing. More likely, it would be nothing – except the dispatch of diplomatic protests.

It meant that a conventional military build-up of some kind by the United States was inevitable if Kennedy's promise to stand by Berlin was to have any credibility. That presented an additional problem. America's European allies appreciated the logic of the situation, but were deeply suspicious of Washington's shift away from massive retaliation theology. They feared it would mean that Washington would develop a different perception of possible Soviet military adventures in Europe. Instead of threatening to unleash its nuclear response, it might see such Russian probes as purely European affairs in which the United States, as leader of the western alliance, would of course be involved, but which were to be confined to Europe, to be fought in Europe, and won or lost on European soil. The United States would commit troops, but would not itself be in danger of being devastated. No longer would America's commitment be total; and in time, though Russian expansionist objectives would be unchanged, American interest in European defence might fizzle out altogether.

Morale among the Allies was a factor Kennedy had to take into account as he prepared his response to Khrushchev. And that response had to be forthcoming soon because, though the debate in Washington and the nuclear concerns of the Allies were very much off-stage, very much on-stage were the refugees in Berlin. They were coming across into West Berlin in ever-increasing numbers. East Germany was being drained. It was increasingly evident that, whatever decision was finally made on trying to get negotiations going, and no matter how much time was left before Khrushchev's later-in-the-year deadline expired, something was going to happen very soon.

At times it seemed that Kennedy was more outraged by departmental dawdling within his administration than by anything the Russians might be up to. At one point during the crisis, he asked the State Department's Charles Bohlen, a trusted presidential adviser, 'Chip, what's wrong with that God-damned department of yours? I can never get a quick answer, no matter what question I put to them.'

He was infuriated when it took more than a month for him to receive a State Department draft of a reply to the formal Soviet ultimatum handed to him by Khrushchev in Vienna. That reply was supposed to inform the Russians officially, for the first time in the current crisis, where the United States stood on Berlin. Not only did Kennedy have to wait so long to see that draft but, when it did finally come, he found nothing in it to reflect the vigour, vigilance and imagination which he wanted his administration to display to Moscow. It stated the fundamental American position of firmness over Berlin, but Kennedy saw it as merely a dreary recital of old phrases and positions, devoid of spirit or freshness, limp, smothered in officialese. One Kennedy adviser called it 'a scissors and paste job' derived from previous documents. The President was described as 'totally disgusted with it.'

The President considered both the delay and the draft document to be confirmation of his belief that the State Department was a bureaucratic swamp. But State Department people saw the episode differently. According to Martin Hillenbrand, head of State's German desk at the time, a draft of a reply to the Soviet note had been sent over to the White House fairly promptly. After ten days, it was discovered that it had been lost there. When a new draft was sent over, it was locked up in the safe by a White House official who then went on two weeks leave. The entire, exhaustive, time-consuming process of consulting with the Allies over the document's contents was thus held up. State Department personnel who were involved were left with the impression that the people around the President found it more convenient to blame others for the delay than accept responsibility themselves.

As for the criticism of the style of the draft reply to the Soviet note, some people at State thought bitterly that if the President had wanted a public relations presentation rather than a diplomatic *aide-memoire* he should have gone to a Madison Avenue public relations firm instead. Some of the President's advisers felt that, in view of what they saw as the State Department's sluggish performance, that might not have been a bad idea.

A reply to the Soviet note was eventually patched together and sent off. However, the situation had gone past the stage of an exchange of diplomatic messages, and very likely would have done so no matter how soon the President had received a satisfactory draft of the message. The stage was now set for terminal public pronouncements and for action. Both were forthcoming from Kennedy on 25 July in his television report to the nation on what the United States intended to do in response to the Soviet challenge.

Few Presidents had ever worked harder to get the right words, establish the right mood and send the right signals. No President had ever believed more was at stake. Having buried himself so exhaustively in the crisis, Kennedy retired, as usual at weekends, to Hyannisport for the weekend of 22–23 July. There he studied the latest position papers, gathered his thoughts and painstakingly worked over the draft of the television speech. When he returned to Washington on Monday, the speech was chiseled into final shape by his aides for delivery that night.

The President's military adviser General Maxwell Taylor, McGeorge Bundy, Ted Sorenson, Edward R. Murrow, Dean Rusk and others in the President's entourage went over it word by word. Phrases were altered to add or soften emphasis. Ideas were clarified so there would be no misunderstanding, either in Moscow or Germany. 'With all changes and clearances completed and co-ordinated along the lines of the President's instructions,' Sorenson recalled, 'I took his reading copy for the 10.00 p.m. talk over [to him] around eight o'clock. I found the President sitting up in bed, a hot pad behind his back, scribbling out a personal note with which to close.' Then he looked over the speech and got ready to go on nationwide television to tell the American people, the Soviet Union and the world exactly where America stood:

> West Berlin has now become – as never before – the great testing place of Western courage and will . . . It is as secure . . . as the rest of us – for we cannot separate its safety from our own. I hear it said that West Berlin is militarily untenable. And so was Bastogne. And so, in fact, was Stalingrad. Any dangerous spot is tenable if . . . brave men will make it so. We do not want to fight – but we have fought before . . . We cannot and will not permit the Communists to drive us out of Berlin, either gradually or by force. For the fulfillment of our pledge to that city is essential to the morale and security of Western Germany, to the unity of western Europe, and to the faith of the entire world . . . We will at all times be ready to talk, if talk will help. But we must also be ready to resist with force, if force is used upon us . . . We seek peace, but we shall not surrender . . .

Nor did Kennedy intend for the United States to be impotent or unprepared if it was, in fact, to be put to the test. 'I must emphasize,' he said 'that the choice is not merely between resistance and retreat, between atomic holocaust and surrender . . . We intend to have a wider choice than humiliation or all-out nuclear action.' He announced that he was asking Congress for an additional three and a quarter billion dollars for defence, much of it to be spent on improved conventional weapons. There would be a fifteen-percent increase in the army's total strength, with the draft call sharply increased and certain reserve and National Guard units activated. Many ships and aircraft marked for mothballing were to be retained for active service. Civil defence programmes would be expanded and accelerated.

Kennedy had been careful to resist hardline urgings that he declare a national emergency or begin shipping troops to West Germany or West Berlin. He wanted to move one step at a time, in the hope that the next step in the escalation of the crisis would prove unnecessary. Khrushchev could turn off the heat in Germany just as easily as he had turned it on, leaving America looking foolish, or he could turn the heat on somewhere else in the world, making it necessary to move troops sent to Europe around like so much baggage.

Kennedy let the Russians know the United States wasn't looking for a fight and that he understood their concerns. He announced that America was prepared to sit down and talk about the situation, to resolve it with words rather than threats. Without specifying, he spoke of his 'readiness to remove any actual irritants in West Berlin', and recognized 'the Soviet Union's historical concerns about their security in central and eastern Europe'. He was, in effect, telling Khrushchev that it would be possible to discuss other matters of great concern to Moscow, like western recognition of disputed post-war borders in East Europe and assurances that no efforts would be made to undermine the stability of East Germany. Rejecting warnings that the Russians could not be trusted to negotiate in good faith, Kennedy was hoping he could reawaken momentum towards East–West talks, both to defuse the immediate crisis and to pave the way for more wide-reaching arrangements for peace and security in Europe.

But assurances from American spokesmen that the United States was willing to talk with the Russians were by then commonplace. Inevitably, to the surprise and regret of White House adviser Arthur Schlesinger Jr and other softliners, the 'let's talk' elements in the Kennedy speech were totally overshadowed by its defiance of Russian demands. Kennedy had meant to leave Khrushchev an 'out'. But it turned out to be an unmistakably tough speech. Boiled down to essentials, it said, 'We want peace, and you can have it if you want it. But you're trying to push us around and we're not going to let you do that.'

In the closing personal note which Kennedy had added to the speech, he told the American people:

> When I ran for the presidency of the United States, I knew that this country faced serious challenges. But I could not realize, nor could any man realize who does not bear the burdens of this office, how heavy and constant would be those burdens . . . In these days and weeks I ask for your help and your advice . . . In meeting my responsibilities in these coming months as President, I need your good will, and your support and, above all, your prayers.

Within minutes, telephone lines at the White House were jammed with callers promising all three. The following day, letters and telegrams of support began flooding in. Senators and congressmen of both parties praised the President. Former President Truman offered his congratulations, saying, 'The Russians are the greatest bluffers in the history of the world. When their bluff is called, they quit.'

Kennedy had touched a chord which warmed and excited the American imagination. There was a feeling that the United States could now recover from the Bay of Pigs humiliation. There was a belief that the freedom of West Berlin was an honourable cause, in the best tradition of American crusades. No doubt the effect of the President's words was strengthened by his stirring delivery, sustained throughout the length of the speech despite the sweltering heat of the Oval Office, where air conditioning had been turned off so as not to affect sound quality on television and radio.

Within days, army recruiting stations across the country reported a huge increase in enlistments. First reports from New York, Boston, Detroit, Chicago and other cities told of an increase of two to three times the number of volunteers coming forward to sign up. Newspapers across the country acclaimed the President, saying he had cleared away any doubts the Russians may have had about American determination. They pointed out, with many an historical reference, that the price of defending freedom is often steep.

This buoyancy was, however, not without outcroppings of concern and apprehension. Some newspapers urged that any remaining opportunities for negotiations should be carefully examined. Some people were concerned about what the increased defence spending would do to the budget deficit. Young men, parents, wives and girlfriends jammed the telephone lines of Selective Service offices to find out exactly who would be called to the colours in defence of West Berlin and when the call was likely to come.

The announcement that civil defence programmes were being expanded provoked widespread anxiety. How could it be otherwise when the President had given the dubious assurance that 'In the event of an attack, the lives of those families which are not hit in a nuclear blast and fire can still be saved – if they can be warned to take shelter and if that shelter is available. We owe that kind of insurance to our families – and to our country.' Much thought had gone into civil defence, as shown in a National Security Council memorandum drawn up shortly before the President's speech:

> The suggested programme . . . provided for fifty-four million shelter spaces in existing buildings at the end of four years. To

achieve even five or six million of these by 1 January 1962 would require a large effort . . . It is in order to remind ourselves that while five million shelter spaces are nothing, the lives that they might save in the event of general war represents not the difference between zero and five million casualties, but more like the difference between forty million and thirty-five million.

After the Kennedy speech, people beseiged local civil defence offices to inquire about measures to protect themselves in case of nuclear war. There was an overnight boom in the sale of prefabricated shelters. Houses up for sale which came equipped with nuclear fallout shelters were gobbled up at prices well above their market value. Stories appeared in newspapers and magazines of how to stock the family nuclear shelter properly with food and other essentials. A California scientist made a name for himself by announcing that his preference in supplies was for beer and encyclopaedias. The Department of Agriculture drew up a food storage scheme which involved commandeering grain surpluses for emergency stockpiles to feed nuclear survivors.

Defence Secretary Robert McNamara was quoted as saying that he doubted the value of any effort to evacuate Washington in case of a nuclear threat because the warning time would be too brief to make a successful evacuation possible. Thinking along the same lines, Washington's Civil Defence Director George R. Rodericks announced plans to survey public and commercial buildings in the nation's capital to pinpoint suitable space for fallout shelters. New York's Mayor Robert Wagner commissioned a civil defence 'nuclear survey' of his city. Plans were made by the authorities of other major municipalities to do the same. Air-raid sirens were regularly tested in various places, with announcements made on radio beforehand so that people would not be alarmed. It was joked that the tricky Russians would choose the appointed time for the test alert to launch a real attack.

One point of great significance in the Kennedy speech which was carefully noted in the Kremlin was virtually overlooked in the press. The President referred several times to America's commitment not to Berlin, but to *West* Berlin. To members of the Berlin Mafia, this amounted to telling the Russians that, contrary to four-power agreements, they could do anything they pleased in the city so long as they left West Berlin alone.

James O'Donnell, who had worked as a newsman in Berlin during the Berlin blockade and after, and who, in 1961, was speech-writer for Under Secretary of State George Ball in

Washington, was shown a near-final draft of the presidential speech by Ted Sorenson on 25 July, prior to its delivery. Kennedy, whom O'Donnell had known for many years, apparently had told Sorenson to let O'Donnell see it to show him that, contrary to rumours circulating among some insiders, the President was not of the SLOB (Soft Line On Berlin) persuasion. However, as a charter member of the Berlin Mafia, O'Donnell immediately spotted the distinction being made between Berlin and West Berlin.

He told Sorenson, 'Ted, if you want to make that speech perfect, take the word West out from in front of Berlin.' He pointed out that it was practically an invitation for the Russians to tighten their control over East Berlin, effectively ending the city's four-power status. Sorenson flatly dismissed O'Donnell's objection. He told him that the Russians had exercised control over their sector of the city for many years, no matter what the four-power agreements said. Besides, he said, 'this speech has been churned through the mills of six branches of government. We have had copies back and forth for ten days. This is the final version. This is the policy line. This is it.'

Karl Mautner, who had been stationed at the American Mission in Berlin some years before and who was now at INR (Intelligence and Research) at the State Department, was among those badly shaken by the Kennedy reference only to West Berlin. 'There was,' Mautner said, 'an "Oh my God!" feeling. We knew immediately what it meant. But the White House didn't know. Even if we felt our commitment was only to West Berlin, we shouldn't have said so openly. We were undercutting our own position.'

National Security Adviser McGeorge Bundy, who was intimately involved in drawing up the final version of the speech, says he cannot recall anyone objecting prior to the speech by saying that the specific reference to *West* Berlin might be construed as Kennedy announcing he didn't care what happened to *East* Berlin. But, says Bundy, even if someone had said it then, his impression is that the President would have replied, 'It's West Berlin I want to talk about.'

It was true that all of Berlin came under the four-power agreements. But, as Sorenson had told O'Donnell, the fact was that the Russians and the East German Communists had long been doing whatever they wished – interfering with cross-city traffic, and arresting and imprisoning people, some of whom disappeared forever, without what westerners would consider reasonable cause or due process. The only reaction from the western powers to these violations of four-power agreements was to file routine protests with the Soviet Commandant in East Berlin.

The theory of joint control was there. In practice, the western powers had less influence over what transpired in East Berlin that the Soviets had in West Berlin. While East Berlin was openly designated by the Russians the capital of Communist East Germany, no one dared arouse Soviet fury by suggesting that West Berlin would, in the foreseeable future, be the capital of West Germany (which was improbable anyway because of the distance between the two). While troops and military vehicles of the East German army were, in violation of agreements, to be seen in East Berlin by permission of the Russians, it would have been unthinkable to station West German troops in West Berlin.

These restraints were self-imposed by the western powers. Joint four-power jurisdiction over the entire city had long before lapsed. To think otherwise was dismissed by Prime Minister Macmillan as indulging in 'excessive legalism'. By making reference in his speech to the freedom of only West Berlin, the President and his advisers, to the extent that they weighed up the matter at all, believed they were being realistic, though their approach revealed a readiness to give up bargaining points without extracting something in return. That was something of which the Russians could never be accused. However, aside from the Russians, only a comparative handful of Kremlin-watchers seemed to recognize that.

The Kennedy speech was generally as well received in London and Paris as it had been across the United States, though Macmillan regretted that Kennedy had made so much of a point of civil defence and would have liked him to rattle American sabres less noisily. De Gaulle approved of the tone of the speech, though his spokesmen made it clear that, if the matter was to come up again, France still saw no reason why the West should enter into negotiations over Berlin. The West Germans, who seemed to expect to be betrayed, once more displayed their nervousness about American reliability. They were pleased with the President's declared readiness to back up American policy with armed force, but worried that Washington appeared prepared to extend some form of recognition to East Germany if only the Russians could be persuaded to calm down. They wanted none of that.

For John McCloy, Kennedy's special assistant for arms control, the timing of the President's speech was trouble. McCloy was in Russia for disarmament talks, with instructions 'to explore the widest possible area of agreement'. At the moment when Kennedy was upping the ante over Berlin, he was very much involved in that exploration process as Khrushchev's guest at the Black Sea resort of Sochi. Until word of the Kennedy speech came through, the Soviet leader had been the perfect host – courteous, gracious, friendly, exposing his visitor to none of his customary threats and warnings. But as soon as he learned what the President had said, Khrushchev's mood and attitude darkened.

Questions of arms control and disarmament were abruptly dropped by the wayside. In their place, McCloy was subjected to a blistering tirade. He was told that Kennedy's military build-up and his obstinacy over Berlin were virtually equivalent to a declaration of war on the Soviet Union. If the Americans wanted war, Khrushchev roared, they could have it, and if there was a nuclear war over Berlin, John F. Kennedy would be the last President of the United States. He said there was still time for the Americans to realize how perilous the situation was, that he still hoped that Kennedy would come to his senses, but that the existing Berlin situation would have to be changed.

The stage was set for the showdown. Both Kennedy and Khrushchev had now delivered public presentations of their respective positions and each had pronounced the other's unacceptable. Not even the softest of the softliners in Washington could assume any longer that the Russians would wait much longer before doing whatever they intended to do about Berlin. Not even the hardest of the hardliners in Moscow could still insist with total conviction that when snarl came to push and push came to shove, the Americans would prove faint-hearted.

Though scheduled to participate in other disarmament talks in Europe, McCloy was summoned back to Washington immediately for a personal report to the President on his meeting with Khrushchev. Kennedy wanted as accurate an account as possible of what had transpired at Sochi. Upon his return, McCloy told the press he had been 'entertained very hospitably' by the Soviet leader in a 'very pleasant' atmosphere. The President was spared such flim-flam. McCloy told him that Khrushchev was in no mood for negotiations of any kind; he seemed determined to have his way, no matter what the cost. He demanded that the West give way because he did not intend to.

Time had become a factor for Khrushchev. The Twenty-Second Congress of the Communist Party of the Soviet Union, scheduled for October, was already in preparation. He had hoped to get the Berlin mess satisfactorily sorted out before then so that he would be able to devote his energies exclusively to what he considered the main task at hand – shoring up his position as Soviet leader by neutralizing remaining rivals within the Soviet hierarchy, notably Deputy Prime Minister Frol Kozlov and party theoretician Mikhail Suslov, who had never been happy with his de-Stalinization campaign and generally objected to the style and substance of his leadership. And always nipping at his heels was Ulbricht who, with the discreet backing of those rivals, continued to press for urgent action on Berlin, offering almost desperate assurances that Kennedy was bluffing:

> We simply do not believe and cannot believe that it is the desire, the ambition of the United States to appear before the whole world as an aggressor . . . We would be pleased if certain people would refrain in the future from answering our peace offers time after time with foolish sabre-rattling.

The press in the East kept headlining statements from East German government officials, party functionaries, trade union spokesmen and ordinary citizens that the long-delayed peace treaty was essential for peace and stability in Europe and that, courtesy of the Soviet Union, one would soon be forthcoming – no matter how many sabres the Americans chose to rattle. It issued assurances that the days were numbered for 'the espionage activities', 'the slave trade', 'the kidnapping', and other nefarious practices made possible in Berlin by violation of what should long before have been East German sovereignty over the access routes.

The earlier exchange of fulminations by the superpowers had already accelerated the refugee flow, as had abortive efforts to require East German workers to make good production losses resulting from the exodus. Now, many East Germans who had been thinking of maybe going West some time in the future, as well as many who had never before given it much thought, decided it was time to leave, and to leave in a hurry. *Torschlusspanik* (panic to escape before the door slammed shut) set in across the German Democratic Republic and rapidly became contagious.

Longer and longer lines formed up at the Marienfelde Refugee Reception Centre in West Berlin. More than a thousand persons from all over East Germany were passing through East Berlin en route to West Berlin each day, getting out before it was too late. Barely a subway or an elevated train crossed over from the Soviet to the western sectors without its share of passengers seeking directions to Marienfelde, and heading there in droves, as if it were a shrine. On the weekend after the Kennedy television speech, 3,859 refugees registered at the reception centre. It was turning into such a torrent that the American Mission reported back to Washington on the possibility that, unless something intervened, as many as four million East Germans would flood into and through West Berlin before the end of the year.

Publicly, the Kremlin tried to ignore the stampede. No word of it was mentioned in the Communist press anywhere, or by Communist officials. Questioned by western newsmen, Soviet diplomats in East Berlin insisted it was vastly exaggerated by the newspapers and claimed that most East Germans who went West came back after they had had a taste of how corrupt life was under capitalism. But those diplomats knew what was happening, and so did Khrushchev, as he revealed later:

> The drain of workers was creating a simply disastrous situation in the GDR . . . If things had continued like this much longer, I don't know what would have happened. I spent a great deal of time trying to think of a way out. How could we introduce incentives in the GDR to counteract the force behind the exodus of East German youth to West Germany . . . ? How could we create conditions in the GDR which would enable the state to regulate the steady attrition of its working force?

Khrushchev would soon have an answer to those questions. With his approval, the desired 'incentives' would soon be introduced and the elusive 'conditions' would soon be created.

As their workers flooded out, the East German regime struggled to retain some vestige of credibility. Its much-trumpeted planning programmes which were to herald future prosperity for the people were in tatters. House construction, machine building, the chemical industry and just about every other major component of its detailed economic plan were way behind schedule. In an effort to retain some sense of reality, factories were sharply reducing planned production levels. In some cases, they were closing down altogether. Unable to pretend otherwise, Deputy Prime Minister Willy Stoph had to concede it was proving difficult adequately to supply the population with bread, butter and meat.

The Communist press carried on as if it existed in another

world. It carried photos of happy workers toiling for peace and socialism. It told of tens of thousands of people who had volunteered their free Sundays to work on farms because bringing in the harvest would bring a peace treaty nearer. At a time when refugees transplanted to West Germany were sending back glowing news of the jobs they had found almost immediatly upon arrival, it warned that men lured to the West by West Berlin 'slave traders' were drummed into the West German army and trained to be cannon fodder for the Americans, while young women tricked into abandoning their homeland were forced to become prostitutes.

Accusations were made that 'blood money' was dangled in front of people by West Germany to lure them across the border. West German Minister for All German Affairs Ernst Lemmer, himself a former refugee, denied that his government was doing anything of the kind. Lemmer said that, on the contrary, he feared the exodus of East Germans would leave a vacuum which would be filled by migrants from East European countries, thus diluting the German character of the region and diminishing hopes for ultimate reunification of the country. Totally unfounded rumours circulated in Berlin that plans were afoot to import Chinese labour to flesh out the East German workforce in the factories and on the land. That anyone could believe such a story was an indication of how thoroughly that workforce was being depleted.

In trying to cope with the refugee problem, the East German authorities felt they had no alternative but to compound the labour shortages the refugees created. The security forces and bureaucracy required to cope with the growing crisis were both substantially expanded and given priority in taking on additional personnel. But, as if fleeing a plague, the procession of absconders continued to grow.

7

Bracing for the Showdown

SHORTLY AFTER he became Secretary of State, Dean Rusk learned by accident that a planned American military operation related to delicate diplomatic manoeuvrings in south-east Asia had been cancelled. That he hadn't been consulted before the cancellation offended and appalled him. But he was downright astounded by the fact that, though he might have had to engage in discussions or make public statements related to those delicate manoeuvrings, he hadn't even been notified afterwards. It had not been a deliberate attempt to keep the Secretary of State in the dark. The frightening fact was that the State Department had no machinery operational at all hours of the day to keep him, or anyone else in the department, automatically informed of things they had to know.

It was different at the Pentagon. A war-room nerve centre had been set up there years before, ready to deal with emergencies and keep top brass in the picture around the clock. But despite incessant international diplomatic brawls and occasional bouts of much worse, ever since the United States had emerged from the Second World War as a superpower, the State Department, the limb of the American government with responsibility for matters of consequence outside the country, had no central twenty-four-hour-a-day facility to co-ordinate responses to crises, or even to keep posted on them as they developed.

Each of the many divisions within the department dealt independently, on a nine-to-five basis, with any problem that arose in its area of expertise and responsibility. The Office of German Affairs dealt with Germany; The Office of East European Affairs dealt with East Europe. The Office of West

116

European Affairs dealt with West Europe. Communication between the various divisions was usually cumbersome and time-consuming, and was often obstructed by departmental rivalries or personality clashes.

If something happened out of office hours, it was left to a communications clerk, who was rarely fine-tuned on international affairs, to determine whether it was serious enough to contact a divisional duty officer at home, or wherever he might be. If, when contacted, that duty officer thought the development serious enough to drag him away from a dinner party or out of his bed, he would drive to Foggy Bottom, size up the situation and decide whether to contact someone senior enough in the department to make a decision on further action – not something that was encouraged in the middle of the night or at weekends. The dangers built into such a system were glaring.

Shocked by his own experience with it, Rusk set about changing things. He ordered that an Operations Centre be established in the State Department. It was to be a watch bureau and a crisis centre, keeping abreast of developments and co-ordinating intelligence within State so that the department would be equipped to respond to emergencies at any time of the day or night, and so that he and his senior subordinates would never again have to rely on luck to learn of developments in world trouble spots.

This Operations Centre, nicknamed the 'Rumpus Room', was set up on the seventh floor of the State Department building, not far from Rusk's office. Among other things, it was to house and service special 'task forces' whenever one was organized for the purpose of gathering all pertinent facts bearing on a specific problem in foreign affairs and producing recommendations for action.

The centre was, however, not equipped to co-ordinate the State Department's resources with those of other government departments and agencies. Analysts at State and the Pentagon and the CIA often looked at world problems as if the others did not exist. There were occasional interdepartmental consultations on international problems. But those had never been systematic and had always been plagued by intense rivalries, notably (as is still the case) between State and the Pentagon. Nevertheless, it was obvious that Berlin planning by the various government departments and agencies had to be co-ordinated. After Kennedy got back from his rough-and-tumble with Khrushchev at the Vienna summit, he issued instructions that a Berlin Task Force be established for that purpose.

At first, a State Department telegraphic watch centre for Berlin was set up. Copies of all cables coming into the department related to Berlin – from Moscow, Bonn, London, Paris and Berlin itself – were funnelled into that centre for scrutiny, so that developments in any of those places would not be assessed in isolation. But as the crisis developed, the actual Berlin Task Force took shape. Its assignment was to acquire information, draw up recommendations, get authority from whatever level of government had to approve them, and issue instructions for them to be carried out.

Set up in a bank of offices opposite the Operations Centre, it was basically a joint State Department–Pentagon effort, with Assistant Secretary of State Foy Kohler and Assistant Secretary of Defence Paul Nitze its joint guiding spirits at first. Kohler soon took sole charge, it being recognized that the State Department was best equipped to co-ordinate the Task Force's operations. Personnel, mostly from State's Office of German Affairs but also Colonel Wilbur ('Bur') Showalter from the Pentagon, were detached from other duties and moved full time onto the Task Force. Gradually, people from other State Department sections – including Intelligence and Research, the Legal Department, and the United Nations desk – and from the Pentagon began participating in informal Task Force meetings, as did personnel from the CIA, the United States Information Agency, the Treasury Department and, later, the White House.

Informal sessions of the Task Force were open to anyone in an official capacity who was instructed or wished to participate in the assessment of what was going on with regard to Berlin and how to deal with it. At times, there were as many as sixty people from nine different departments in attendance. There was some confusion as to who was a Task Force staff member. At the conclusion of one of those early mass sections, Martin Hillenbrand, Director of the Office of German Affairs, who was chairing it, called on 'everyone from the Task Force' to stay on for a staff meeting. 'At last,' someone said, 'we'll find out who's on it and who's not.' According to Task Force member John Ausland, 'Those who thought they were on it stayed behind.' While various others made important contributions to its workings, the basic Task Force staff consisted of Kohler in charge, Hillenbrand his deputy, Frank Cash, Ausland, Arthur ('Pete') Day, David Klein and Jerry Holloway, all from the State Department, and Showalter from the Pentagon. Klein remained on the Task Force when he was recruited onto the White House staff later during the crisis.

In its early stages, Kohler, who retained responsibility for the workings of the Task Force even after Hillenbrand took charge of its day-to-day operations, thought of the open sessions as a place where anyone who thought he had something to contribute could sound off. According to Karl Mautner, a participant sharply critical of the failure of the American government to take a stronger line with the Russians, complainers were made to feel free to continue their verbal sniping. But, said Mautner, 'It was made clear we were not to expect to be loved for it.'

The Berlin Task Force didn't find its stride until after the Kennedy television address of 25 July. Even then, it took a while till operational procedures became routine and questions of interdepartmental rivalries, which might have hampered its operations, were resolved. Ausland recalls that the first exchange that he (State) and Showalter (Pentagon) had at the Task Force was an agreement to be above board with each other. Neither of them saw anything remarkable in the fact that such an agreement should be thought necessary between officials of the same government.

One of the Task Force's jobs was to make arrangements for Washington meetings of the 'quadripartite group' – the ambassadors of Britain, France and West Germany and Foy Kohler – to co-ordinate Allied responses in the crisis. The arrangement proved not altogether satisfactory. The French ambassador, Herve Alphand, who never forgave Kennedy for his condemnation of French policy in Algeria when he had been a senator, was very much on his dignity at all times. He seemed perpetually ready to take offence. The West German ambassador, Wilhelm Grewe, was not at all taken with the bright young problem-solvers who ran the American administration. He was an intensely humourless man, much given to administering longish lectures which were thought to insult the intelligence of those exposed to them. In due course, Bonn was discreetly advised that Grewe was perhaps not the best man to represent West Germany in the United States and he was replaced.

There was no difficulty for the Americans with the British ambassador, David Ormsby-Gore, a close personal friend of Kennedy. But in view of the personality problems with Alphand and Grewe, the Task Force took to arranging for lower-level diplomats of the four Allied powers to take over the job of consultations. Things went more smoothly after that, though fundamental differences with the French remained unresolved and American and West German attitudes never quite converged.

Well aware of differences within western ranks, the Russians had embarked on a systematic campaign to engineer a deeper division among the Allies. In Washington and in European capitals, Soviet diplomats joined in a co-ordinated chorus of complaints about the slowness of the West in responding to Khrushchev's proposal that West Berlin be turned into a 'free city', as if Kennedy's rejection of it had been no response at all. Russian envoys on the black-tie-and-cocktail circuit in London, Paris, Rome, Geneva and other cities parroted the same line: it was not too late; if the West acted quickly and made serious counter-proposals, it would be in a better position to extract guarantees from Moscow for West Berlin's independence after the East Germans assumed control of the access routes, than if it waited until the Russians acted unilaterally. The British, with their battered economy, seemed to the Russians particularly susceptible to the argument that a few changes to remedy the 'abnormal' situation in Berlin and bring the world back from the brink of war were worth considering.

At the Moscow end of the new Soviet manoeuvre, the Russians reverted to a double-pronged, hard-soft assault on the position Kennedy had spelled out. The Soviet foreign ministry declared that when the Russians spoke of turning West Berlin into a free city, they didn't really mean anything as specific as that. It just meant that the Soviet Union was ready 'to settle, jointly with interested parties,' what West Berlin's status would be after the overdue peace treaty was signed. To persuade people that Kennedy was making far too much of the Berlin imbroglio, Khrushchev protested that 'We do not intend to change West Berlin's social and political system.'

At the same time, the Soviet leader used every opportunity to try to terrify western nations by brandishing his missiles. Visiting Italian premier Amantori Fanfani was told by the Soviet leader in Moscow that his country, like others in the western alliance, would be devastated by Soviet nuclear weapons if the Berlin dispute led to armed conflict: 'Not only the orange groves of Italy but also the people who created them and who have exalted Italy's culture and arts, people in whose good intentions we believe, may perish.' To the Greek ambassador, he said, 'I will not issue orders that bombs be dropped specifically on the Acropolis. But we will not hesitate to strike a blow at the military bases of the North Atlantic bloc which are located in Greece.'

Khrushchev was making history. Never before had nuclear weapons been brandished in a bid to conquer territory.

In early August, as forebodings spread through the West like a nasty rash, Allied military liaison teams, based at Potsdam in East Germany and accredited to the commander of Soviet troops there, stepped up their patrols. They were looking for intimations of Russian moves against the access routes. Those liaison teams had been stationed in East Germany since the end of the war, just as Soviet military teams had been stationed in West Germany. Though originally designed purely as liaison units to maintain official contact between Soviet and western occupation forces, and though they had primarily fulfilled that function during the brief post-war East–West honeymoon fling, they had soon also become deeply engaged in active spying operations, seeing what the other side's military forces were up to. That was openly recognized and reciprocally tolerated as such.

American, British and French military personnel, in uniform and in military vehicles, scouted around East Germany, staying clear of restricted areas when under tight security, but keeping an eye on military matters – troop reinforcements, troop deploy- ment, the introduction of new equipment – as best they could. (Soviet liaison missions in West Germany did the same.) They were often on the road for days on end, but were rarely without a tail of Communist security personnel, generally believed to be KGB. Colonel Ernest von Pawel, the chief of the American Liaison Mission in East Germany at the time, had previously been US army attaché in Warsaw and recognized one of his 'shadows' as someone who had tailed him in Poland. Once, when von Pawel was out on a reconnaissance mission in East Germany, they parked across the autobahn from each other and the man waved amicably at him.

There were occasions on both sides when liaison officers were chased off or detained for being where they were not supposed to be in their search for military information. But there were no incidents anything near as serious as the one in 1985 when United States Army Major Arthur Nicholson was shot dead by a Soviet sentry as he photographed Russian equipment.

As the Berlin situation grew more inflamed, the Allied liaison teams reported considerable Soviet military activity on the autobahns and roads outside the city. That bit of news was not overly revealing. The Russians had tens of thousands of troops in these areas. Engaged in training exercises, they were continually moved about to familiarize them with the increasingly sophisti- cated weapons with which they were equipped.

At one point, British military intelligence in Berlin received an alarming report about Soviet military movements in East Germany. The report said there were so many Soviet armoured vehicles on the autobahn not far from the city that it could only mean a move against West Berlin. A Chipmunk reconnaissance aircraft was dispatched from the British airfield in the West Berlin suburb of Gatow to investigate. It reported back alarmingly that the information was correct – there were so many Soviet armoured vehicles that the autobahn was practically jammed. A British liaison team vehicle was sent to take a look and discovered that the emphasis of the Chipmunk report had been wrong. The road wasn't *practically* jammed, it was *completely* jammed. Two Soviet divisions on training missions had met face to face and couldn't disentangle themselves.

The liaison missions in East Germany, like western military intelligence organizations based in Berlin itself, did not concern themselves with the activities of civilians in the East – the Communist authorities, the refugees, or anyone else. They were interested exclusively in the Soviet military presence in the area – particularly unusual deployments of troops, the arrival of additional forces, the introduction of new weapons, the construction of additional barracks – anything that might indicate that the military balance in Germany was being altered.

There was a lot of ground to cover. Soviet forces were deployed in great strength near Berlin. The Russians occupied former German barracks at Oranienburg, Bernau, Potsdam and Koepenick, all within ten miles of the city. Planes coming in to land at Gatow made their approach over the Soviet barracks at Dallgow, where a division of Soviet troops was based. There was a Soviet military headquarters at Zossen, twenty miles from Berlin. Jueterbog, forty miles from the centre of the city, was the headquarters of one of the five Soviet armies in East Germany, with something like two divisions of troops based there.* Any of those units, which were always on the move anyway, could have been deployed against the access routes.

Unlike the Allied liaison missions, the commandants in Berlin had more than only military responsibilities. They were in direct supreme command of the city. They were obliged also to take

---

*Though most western officials appreciated the seriousness of the situation, the lack of understanding of some dignitaries who passed through Berlin was baffling. When, with the aid of a map and a pointer, an official at the American Mission explained the geographical complications and outlined the Soviet military deployment, a visiting congressman asked him in amazement, 'Do you mean we're surrounded?'

into account the well-being of the populace in their sectors and the maintenance of public order as well. As disenchantment with the Communist regime intensified throughout East Germany, the western commandants were faced with the possibility of uprisings in the East, more specifically in East Berlin, from which trouble might spill over into the western sectors.

In Washington, the State Department reported that 'the Soviets were sitting on top of a volcano.' There was no doubt that drastic efforts would be made by the Communists to control the refugee flood if it continued, that this would magnify discontent in the East, and that a subsequent uprising was a real possibility. It was further believed that if a revolt did break out in the Soviet Zone the Russians would deploy whatever military strength was necessary to crush it; therefore, the United States should make no effort to encourage an uprising. That did not rule out gaining as much propaganda mileage as possible out of an anti-Communist insurrection if one occurred.

In addition to worrying that their sectors might be affected by civil disturbances in East Berlin, the western commandants had another concern – the possibility that the Communists, as they had before, might send strong-arm squads into West Berlin to stir up trouble, perhaps using that as a pretext for calling on Soviet forces to restore law and order. To prepare for such a contingency, the western garrisons in Berlin took to practising riot control. Teams of American soldiers, in civilian clothes and armed with sticks, played at being rioters sent in by the Communists, while other troops, in uniform, were deployed to contain and control them. Officers carefully monitored this training but the men, enormously enjoying these simulated scrimmages, had trouble taking them seriously.

East German security forces, meanwhile, were playing a different game. They were attempting more vigorously than ever before to stem the refugee tide. To justify their efforts, they claimed that West Germany was suffering from a polio epidemic from which East Germans had to be shielded. Vopos and transport police scoured all trains from the East German hinterland to East Berlin and from East Berlin into West Berlin. Just about every second passenger was interrogated and had his papers examined. A dozen or so people would be ordered off each train for questioning as a matter of course, so that word would spread of the dangerous gauntlet that had to be run to reach the West. People carrying luggage or packages were automatically searched. Those who were thought possibly to be en route to the West were ordered home and their local police were informed. Those believed definitely to be on their way out were arrested and charged with attempted *republikflucht*. Police patrols combed the forests and fields around East Berlin to winkle out people who had got off trains before reaching East Berlin to evade detection, and were trying to make their way westward on foot. Communist vigilante squads, from Worker Brigades and the Free German Youth, roamed districts east of the sector borders in search of refugees to turn over to the police. Vopo strength along the borders was increased, and more and more people were questioned and harassed when crossing into West Berlin.

Fear of arrest and loathing of the authorities grew in intensity. Worry about the future was widespread. A man who fled with his five children said he had been stopped by a Vopo who, while examining his papers, had whispered that he also would be going across if he had children. Throughout East Germany and East Berlin, people resorted to complicated subterfuges to make good their get-away.

A doctor, believing himself watched by his local Vopos, began elaborately decorating his new house, calming suspicions and relaxing the scrutiny directed at him, before slipping away one night and making for the West. Families split up and went in different directions, to meet again at Marienfelde with as much relief as if they had escaped from a labour camp.

There was a series of widely-publicized show trials in which would-be refugees and those who helped refugees were sentenced to as much as fifteen years in jail for promoting West German war preparations. The logic was simple. If people emigrated to West Germany to work there, and if West Germany was, as the Communists maintained, bent on war, then those people were, *ipso facto*, accessories. East German Supreme Court Judge Horst Hetzar fled west, charging that, 'The administration of law has sunk to such a level [in the East] that one is ashamed to be a lawyer.'

The crackdown on *grenzgängers*, whom the authorities could more easily control, was also intensified. They were ordered to give up their jobs in West Berlin and register for work in the Soviet Sector. Neighbourhood party activists went to their homes after they had returned from work in the evening to harangue them. Letters to newspapers asked why East Germany should put up with 'free-loaders' who creamed off the benefits of socialism without contributing to its construction. People were barred from buying refrigerators, washing machines and other major manufactured goods in the East unless they could prove they worked there (which was no great punishment because such items were not readily available even to those who could afford them).

When these tactics produced few results, a more effective approach was attempted. The cross-border commuters were ordered by the Communist authorities to pay their rents and utility charges in west marks, which continued to be worth five times the equivalent in east marks. Their children were banned from the state schools. In a joint protest to Soviet Berlin commandant Colonel A. I. Solovyev about the harassment of the commuters, the western commandants insisted that 'the principle of freedom of movement is basic to the agreements regarding Berlin which are binding on the four powers responsible for this city'. It had no effect whatsoever.

Some *grenzgängers* bowed to the pressure and gave up their jobs in West Berlin. Others chose to give up their homes in East Berlin and finally move west altogether. Weary of being harassed and harangued, a garage mechanic, a wizard with motors (at least he was with my car), was one of those who reluctantly gave up his East Berlin residence to settle in the West. He said he was paid too well for his skills in West Berlin to settle for what an East Berlin garage would be able to offer. Besides, in the East he would be spending all his time trying to scrounge up hard-to-find spare parts rather than tinkering with the insides of cars.

As the haemorrhage of refugees continued unstaunched, Ulbricht's pleas to the Kremlin to let him finally do something effective to stop the exodus took on a desperate tinge. East German newspapers, which Ulbricht knew were monitored by the Soviet commandant's office, were permitted to tuck away on the bottom of inside pages normally-censored reports of worrying developments in the Soviet Zone.

The Karl Marx Stadt *Volkstimme* ('Voice of the People') disclosed that slogans circulating in a local factory dared to call for the reunification of Germany. The *Leipziger Volkszeitung* quoted a worker as demanding unrestricted travel to West Germany. Another newspaper reported that workers were brazenly walking out on lectures given by SED officials. The Russians might scold the East German Communist leadership for permitting such impermissible slippage in revolutionary discipline. Nevertheless, the point, if it still needed making, was made. Command of the situation had to be retrieved before reactionary subversion could contaminate the entire country. The long-simmering pot of trouble was about to boil over.

A countdown to the crunch was also underway on the western side. There were pre-dawn practice alerts in West Berlin, with Allied tanks and troop-carriers rumbling through town and machine-gun positions set up at street corners. In Washington on 1 August, Congress voted 403 to 2 to grant President Kennedy's request for funds to boost America's conventional military strength. The two opposing voters were congressmen who believed the United States should, as before, rely on nuclear weapons to deter the Russians from threatening America's vital interests. On that same day, a curfew was imposed on American forces in Europe. Unless on leave or on an overnight pass, officers and men had to be back in their quarters by midnight – 1.00 a.m. on Sundays. No more than fifteen percent of personnel were to be off base or off duty at any one time.

Five days later, the biggest manoeuvres by United States forces since the Second World War were launched at Fort Bragg, North Carolina. Forty thousand troops took part, including units of the Strategic Army Corps and the National Guard. Manoeuvres include a massed jump by 5,000 paratroopers. Publicity was provided, in the unlikely event that the Soviet Union failed to notice.

By then, the foreign ministers of the United States, Britain, France and West Germany had met in Paris for an urgent review of the situation. They sought once again to firm up a common approach to the Berlin problem. However, agreement remained stubbornly elusive. The Americans and, even more so, the British continued to press for talks with the Russians, if only to avoid miscalculation by either side. Secretary of State Rusk believed that if the West pushed for negotiations, it would be able to chart the direction those negotiations would take. The West Germans, in the middle of an election campaign and fundamentally wary of negotiations anyway, feared that agreeing to talks could be interpreted as paving the way for western concessions to the Russians on the future of Germany. The French insisted that talks, if they took place at all, should be delayed until after the projected western military build-up. What it all meant was that no accord was reached, except that western rights in Berlin would not be surrendered.

Presidential aide Walt Rostow had already advised Kennedy that as the situation developed, America might have to go at least part of the way alone:

I argued that the somewhat hesitant mood of our Allies, while understandable, did not justify a weakening of the American position. I recalled that Washington, not London or Bonn, had its finger on the atomic trigger. It was one matter to face the possibility of atomic war if your political leaders have their finger on the trigger; it is a quite different matter if someone else's leaders are in that position . . . The Allies might stay together to the end . . . but . . . we ought to be prepared in our minds for the possibility of a relatively lonely stage; and, recalling *High Noon*, we ought to accept it without throwing our sheriff's badge in the dust when the crisis subsided.

In view of the unrelenting Soviet diplomatic campaign to get the West out of Berlin, it was deemed necessary to make continually certain that everybody concerned understood the whys and wherefores of the situation – that it was right rather than might that justified the Allied presence in the city. Once more, Secretary of State Dean Rusk publicly explained the American position: 'We are in West Berlin under the same arrangements which led Allied forces to withdraw from Thuringia and Saxony, large parts of which are now Eastern Germany with a population of some eight million persons.' The implication was clear. If the Russians wanted the West out of Berlin, they should announce their readiness to withdraw from parts of East Germany in which almost half the population of that country lived. And the Russians weren't about to do that.

On 2 August, rumours circulated in Berlin that Ulbricht had left the city, perhaps for Moscow for consultations in the Kremlin. His presence in the Soviet capital, for an important meeting of the leaders of the Warsaw Pact countries, was confirmed the following day. Having been less successful in penetrating the Warsaw Pact than the KGB had been in penetrating NATO, western intelligence services had no way of knowing that Khrushchev was about to reveal what he had decided to do about Berlin.

All sorts of plans had been drawn up in Washington for responding to a Soviet move against the western presence in the city. As the crisis built up, there were two file drawers full of them which, when later reduced to a single document for quick reference purposes, still amounted to over one hundred pages. Soviet or East European vessels en route to Cuba could be turned back in a counter-blockade. The Soviet fleet in the Mediterranean might be harassed. Soviet shipping might be halted at random, as randomly as American convoys were stopped on the autobahn into Berlin. A unit to oversee such action had been set up, under the code-name SEA SPRAY, at United States Naval Headquarters at Norfolk, Virginia. In a study of the possibilities for the Pentagon, the Rand Corporation think tank had advised that the West should not feel constrained to confine its reaction to Berlin or Germany. It was said that Soviet leaders could be made 'aware of the fact that their broader and more important political interests will suffer if they carry out their threats on any local front where the Soviet Union happens to have superiority'.

However, there was a drawback to that approach. The Russians might well be prepared to accept a reverse somewhere else if it meant they could claim West Berlin, believing that a blockade of Cuba or any other western retaliation would prove pointless and be phased out in due course. Primary emphasis was, therefore, placed on plans for direct military responses to keep the lifelines to West Berlin open and functioning. These would be under the direction of LIVE OAK, the code-name for an Allied military headquarters set up (and still in existence) outside Paris under the direction of General Lauris Norstad, the Supreme Allied Commander in Europe. Among LIVE OAK contingency plans was General Clay's old proposal to send an armoured column from West Germany through East Germany to West Berlin to brush aside any Communist obstruction of the ground access routes.

According to that plan, the armoured column was to start its trek across East Germany at Helmstedt, on the border of that part of West Germany where British NATO forces were based. Accordingly, British troops were to be the vanguard of the column. A Russian-speaking British officer, Captain Michael Burkham, was to be in the lead vehicle. If stopped, he was to say, in effect, 'We come in peace. Please, clear the road.' No instructions were available (they would be later; they still are – and remain classified) on what to do if the Russians, or the East Germans, did not let the column through.

Burkham was stationed at British military headquarters in West Germany at Rheindahlem. One evening early in August, as he and his wife were getting ready at their Düsseldorf home not far away to go to a party thrown by a fellow officer, there was a knock on the door. When Burkham opened it, he found himself face-to-face with a stern-countenanced military police corporal. 'This is it,' he thought, and prepared to tell his wife to take the children, hop into the car and head West because he was about to set off in the other direction. As it turned out, the MP had only come to report that the officer throwing the party 'sends his compliments but his child has come down with the chicken pox and the party is off.'

As things appeared to be approaching a climax, and LIVE OAK and SEA SPRAY reviewed and updated their operational procedures, individuals began looking to their personal contingency plans. If their dependents were with them, Allied military personnel in West Germany stored jerrycans of gas in the trunks of their cars in case a sudden emergency made it advisable for their dependents, like Burkham's, to scamper to safety without having to join the long lines that certainly would form immediately at gas stations. In West Berlin, where my daughter was born in mid-July, my wife and I decided to get a separate passport for her at the American Mission rather than, as was customary, having the baby put on her mother's passport. It was impossible to forecast what sort of evacuation procedures would have to be followed if the access routes came under threat.

Real-estate values were plummeting in West Berlin, and so had rents in gentrified districts as many propertied West Berliners of a nervous disposition emigrated to West Germany for safety's sake, putting their homes on the market. They included the architect who had built the ranch house not far from the West Berlin border with East Germany in which my family and I lived. He had meant to live in the house himself, and take pleasure from its delightful, apple-tree-studded garden, but had felt the danger of a Communist take-over was too great. He had transferred his residence and practice to Düsseldorf several months before. Among those who were joining him in resettling in West Germany were many who had earlier fled to West Berlin from the East, and who now decided it was time once and for all to put themselves well out of reach of the Communists.

A lot of West Berliners who would eventually stay put debated whether to join them. It wasn't only the incessant threats and warnings from Moscow and East Berlin; nor was it only the sight of the refugees now jamming Marienfelde in headline-making numbers; nor the stepped-up refugee airlift out of Templehof. The effect of these images of flight and escape was compounded by the boom of Soviet jet fighters mischievously breaking the sound barrier over West Berlin, as if claiming possession of the sky. The chatter of machine-gun fire coming from the direction of the training grounds of the western garrisons did little to convince people that there was nothing to worry about.

There was no panic, no end-of-the-world frenzy, no pervasive gloom, certainly not enough to keep people from their poppyseed strudel and whipped cream on the patio of Kempinski's or the Kranzler on the Ku'damm – if they were lucky enough to get a seat out in the open – nor to keep the movie houses from filling up. There was, however, a deeply implanted uneasiness, only lightly masked by Berlin's big city sophistication.

People going about their everyday affairs quipped about being the West's expendable frontline troops. Their *galgenhumor*, their flippancy on the precipice, was contagious. When a garbage truck rumbled past our home in the dark, early hours of the morning, waking us, my wife and I joked about it being a Russian tank casing the neighbourhood. We figured we would learn what had happened during the night by whether we would find the Communist *Neues Deutschland* on our doorstep in the morning, rather than the West Berlin newspapers that were normally delivered to our home.

People joked, but the atmosphere was thick with expectation. It was also so thick with rumour that it was often difficult to distinguish between what was fake and what was not. As the only city in the world where western and Soviet influences co-existed, Berlin was a magnet for all sorts of eccentric personalities, situations and ideas, as countless spy novels and movies have testified. Rarely was it believed that the truth behind any development had been fully disclosed. There was always more to come. The 'real story', in its myriad variations, would invariably follow, only to be subsequently updated, revised, and sometimes stood on its head.

Rumours were a dime a dozen and, though without substantiation, sometimes blown up into major revelations. The head of the East German intelligence service had fled to West Berlin; no he hadn't – it was one of his junior subordinates and it had happened two years earlier; yes, that's the way it was, except that he was proved to be a KGB plant. The dependents of American military personnel in Berlin were about to be evacuated to West Germany to get out of harm's way; yes, they would be evacuated, but only if they wanted to be; no, such an evacuation had been contemplated, but it was decided it would be taken by the Russians as a sign that the Americans weren't as firm over Berlin as they said they were.

Rumours which started in Berlin were often built upon elsewhere, and magnified out of proportion. After feeding a broadcast report on the refugee situation to New York one afternoon, I mentioned to the editor on duty there that I had heard an interesting rumour which I wanted to try to substantiate. I told him I had heard that the Russians would demand that since, as they insisted, East Berlin was the capital of East Germany, West Berlin, rather than all of Berlin, be made a four-power city. According to that rumour, Moscow would propose that a Soviet garrison should move in to take up residence alongside the American, British and French garrisons in the western sectors of the city.

Returning the next morning by car through the Brandenburg Gate from a fruitless attempt to get a spokesman at the Russian Embassy to comment on the rumour, I was flagged down by Carl Hartman of the Associated Press, who flashed in front of my windshield an early edition of *Der Abend*, a West Berlin afternoon newspaper. Not only did it headline my rumour on the front page, but it quoted me by name as the source, or rather my 'absolutely reliable sources' in the East. Several weeks later, Soviet Deputy Premier Anastas Mikoyan did, in fact, suggest that West Berlin should come under four-power jurisdiction, a theme which soon was to become an official Soviet proposal.

The creeping malaise in West Berlin was due less to a lack of trust in the Allied 'protectors' than to a sense of powerlessness about the anticipated Communist move to choke off the refugee flow. No one believed the Allies would simply pull out overnight, leaving them to Ulbricht's questionable mercies. But the feeling of impotence about the refugees was infectious – there was gut despair that the bigger battle for Berlin might eventually be lost no matter what John F. Kennedy promised. It was a deeply troubling suspicion for those in West Berlin who considered the Ulbricht regime to be a despicable tyranny – and there were few who did not.

No one, neither in West Berlin nor elsewhere, doubted that Ulbricht had the wherewithal ultimately to deal with his refugee problem. The *New York Times* pointed out, 'There has never been any East–West agreement that would prevent the Communists from closing the border between East Germany and East Berlin. Why they have not done so in the past is something of a mystery.' Senator William Fulbright, chairman of the Senate Foreign Relations Committee, said, 'I don't understand why the East Germans don't close the border because I think they have a right to close it.' In fact, they did not have that right in Berlin. Fulbright said later that, in view of the perils inherent in the situation, he was not overly concerned with legalisms fashioned

many years before in different circumstances. He was interested
primarily in preventing the dispute from turning into an avoidable
armed clash. Whatever his reasons, it was thought by many, and
particularly by the ever-suspicious West Germans, that the
senator was expressing a view which Kennedy shared but dared
not voice for fear of alienating Adenauer.

Kennedy at that stage was, however, giving little thought to
whether the Communists did or did not have a legal right to close
the border. But without knowing it, Fulbright had been very close
to voicing the President's attitude, as Kennedy made clear in a
passing remark to Walt Rostow early in August:

> Khrushchev is losing East Germany. He cannot let that happen. If
> East Germany goes, so will Poland and all of Eastern Europe. He
> will have to do something to stop the flow of refugees – perhaps a
> wall. And we won't be able to prevent it. I can hold the Alliance
> together to defend West Berlin but I cannot act to keep East Berlin
> open.

When asking Washington about contingency plans, Allan Lightner, the minister at the American Berlin Mission, was informed
that decisions would depend on 'the situation at the time.'
Lightner was left with the impression he was being told if the
Communists 'left West Berlin alone, we would have nothing to
worry about,' and he was not to 'rock the boat.'

The western powers were thus reconciled to Communist action
to deal with the refugees on their own side of the border. Nor did
all westerners find that prospect altogether disagreeable. Though
sympathizing with the refugees, many saw the East German
exodus as a potentially perilous phenomenon. They feared that,
unless halted, it would generate instability and uncertainty in all
of East Europe. Confusion would follow in the Kremlin, where a
powerful bloc of back-seat luminaries had been pressing their
belief that Soviet détente with the West was an illusion. It was
feared by pundits in Washington, London and elsewhere in the
West who vastly overestimated Soviet military capabilities that, if
the views of the Moscow hawks prevailed in the Kremlin, peace
and security in West Europe could be endangered.

De Gaulle, who thought in more grandiose terms, was troubled
by another possibility. He feared that the mass German migration
westward would create a vacuum which would draw hordes of
Slavs into parts of Central Europe which had been German since
the sixteenth century, altering the ethnic balance of the area.

However, it did not occur to East German leaders that anyone in the West could exhibit such qualms, and if it had, they would have suspected it was a calculated deception. They were convinced – and drew proof from West German promises of ultimate German reunification – that an insidious plot was afoot to destroy Communist rule and the East German state, and that it could very well succeed unless they were vigilant and took drastic steps to foil it. Erich Honecker, a member of the SED Central Committee and the man in operational control of preparations to seal off West Berlin, maintained that 'West German monopolies' were planning a step-by-step take-over of the East German economy. The West, he claimed, had engaged in a campaign of slander to promote the refugee outflow and had sent saboteurs into East Berlin to commit arson and create panic among East Germans. Honecker later said, 'It became more and more obvious what a danger [the open border] represented to peace.'

The belief that the West was bent on destroying the first ever German workers' state was genuine and widespread in Communist ranks. It couldn't be otherwise among people who believed Communism was inevitable, and that civilization was reaching the stage where it was due to come about. It followed logically that only conspiracies and plots were holding it back. Many East German Communists, particularly the older ones, had become cynical puppets of the Soviet Union. The belief in justice which had originally motivated their political involvement had long before been shattered by the tyrannical injustices they had been obliged to excuse and explain away. (Wolfgang Leonhard has described how docilely they had accepted the arrest by the NKVD in Moscow of German Communists who had sought refuge from the Nazis, including, in his case, his mother.)

But not all East German Communists accepted that the panicky police state then existing in East Germany had the makings of a true people's democracy. Many of them believed – and some were imprisoned for presuming to say so – that the day was still to come when they would be able to feel pride in their Socialist Fatherland, and not merely try to explain away its shortcomings. But except for a few who would go West, either physically or spiritually, even those Communists who were pained by the injustices committed in the name of Communism subscribed to the Robespierre's revolutionary rationalization, 'You must break eggs to make an omelette.' They believed with a virtually religious passion that any system but Communism was wrong and that capitalism was, by definition, criminal and wicked. They hoped to construct a brave new world whose inhabitants, untrammeled by what they deemed to be the trivializing pseudo-rewards of capitalism, would be able to develop their full potential. If that involved disagreeable tactics, that was regrettable.

It was estimated that if free elections had taken place in East Germany, the Communists, in power for more than fifteen years, would have gained only between ten and twenty percent of the vote, even after the refugees had gone. But that ten to twenty percent were prepared to fall into line no matter how many eggs their leaders chose to break in their desperate effort to serve up the Communist omelette.

On Friday 11 August, as John Kennedy looked forward to going off to his cottage in the Kennedy compound at Hyannisport for what had become his regular weekend rest and rehabilitation retreat, as Dean Rusk mulled over how next to go about trying to pin down a concerted Allied policy on dealing with the Russians over Berlin, and as Nikita Khrushchev sustained his terror campaign with a warning that 'hundreds of millions' would die if there was war over the status of the city, the East German *Volkskammer* was summoned into special session in East Berlin to hear from Walter Ulbricht what had transpired at the Warsaw Pact meeting in Moscow the previous week. It received only a sketchy report. Details were not yet to be revealed. There was too great a danger of a leak. But *Volkskammer* members were told that a moment of crucial decision had arrived and the long-promised effective action against the refugees was about to be taken. They then went through the motions of giving Ulbricht and his Council of Ministers full authority to do whatever was thought necessary to protect the security and interests of the German Democratic Republic.

Khrushchev's decision on what to do about Berlin had been reached a little more than two weeks earlier, when Kennedy's 'stand firm' position had been outlined on television. Although he had reacted in fury at the time, and had made repeated doomsday threats since, he had realized that it was he, not Kennedy, who would have to back off. He would have to postpone dealing with the access routes. Plans to lever the Allies out of their malignant enclave behind Soviet lines would have to be shelved for the moment.

It wasn't only tough talk from the West which influenced his decision. Reports from Soviet intelligence agents had an important bearing as well. The Russians were well served by strategically-placed spies in Washington and at NATO. Among them was Lieutenant-Colonel W. H. Whalen, a United States Army intelligence officer assigned to the Joint Chiefs of Staff and a KGB agent of long standing who was unmasked and arrested several years later, and George Paques, a Frenchman on the NATO staff who was arrested as a Soviet spy later in the year.* Through them and other Soviet operatives, Khrushchev had learned a great deal about American nuclear contingency plans, some of which, though frightening, were more ambitious than practicable. He had learned enough to accept that Kennedy was not bluffing. He had no reason any longer to doubt that, instead of yielding in the face of Soviet war warnings as he believed he would, the American President seemed actually ready to use his far superior nuclear weaponry to have his way in Berlin.

Ending the Allied presence in West Berlin was high on the Soviet agenda, but it was not as overridingly important to the Russians as Kennedy insisted remaining in Berlin was to the Americans. Khrushchev's main priority was leading his country along the road to Communism. Despite his impulsive nature, he realized he couldn't very well do that by exposing it to nuclear destruction for a prize it could manage very well without, and which would still be there for the taking at a more auspicious moment in the future.

But there was still the refugees. The Kremlin had considered them a serious but subordinate problem which could wait until the territorial jurisdiction issue was resolved before the year was out. It would then more or less resolve itself. That problem now had to be upgraded and dealt with because, with no overall, satisfactory solution to the Berlin hassle in sight, the population drain-away posed a serious threat to the future of the East German state. And that *was* a vital Soviet interest.

Nobody in the Soviet hierarchy – neither Khrushchev nor any of his colleagues – liked the idea of letting Ulbricht build a barrier between East Berlin and West Berlin to choke off the exodus. Aside from being a public admission of Communist failure in open competition between two systems operating side-by-side, it was a blatant violation of a written agreement to which the Soviet

---

*Secretary of State Rusk told the author that, knowing Soviet spies were planted at NATO, he later used the certainty of intelligence leaks there to pass messages he did not want misunderstood to the Soviet government. The Russians were so security conscious that he believed that route would guarantee those messages more urgent attention in Moscow than if they were delivered by the American ambassador.

Union was a party. Like all nations, the Soviet Union was not averse to playing fast-and-loose with treaties which were loosely defined, but the agreements on four-power Berlin were clear and unambiguous. Freedom of movement throughout the entire city was guaranteed. It could be argued that a Vopo crackdown was a police exercise within the purview of the civil authorities. But to build a permanent barrier would be a blatant treaty violation which would invite reprisal and which the Russians were reluctant to commit unless it was unavoidable.

There was an alternative. With the border between East Germany and West Germany sealed, and with that part of East Germany which bordered directly on West Berlin having also long before been made escape-proof, only the sector border in the middle of the four-power city remained open. If people in East Germany were prevented from getting to East Berlin, they would not be able to get close enough to West Berlin to make good their escape. Traffic between the two parts of the city would then be much reduced, enabling the Vopos to do a more thorough job of turning back East Berlin residents wanting to head West. The refugee problem would thus be solved. What was more, sealing East Germany off from East Berlin would be undertaken exclusively within what the Allies still regarded as the Soviet Zone, where it would be nobody else's business.

However, the plan had several obvious drawbacks. It would require a tremendous, permanent police operation on all trains and roads to Berlin. Past experience with a system of spot checks on travellers indicated it didn't work very well. And a good many East German citizens would be denied right of access to what the Communists insisted, despite western objections, was their own capital city. The operation would be cumbersome, difficult to maintain, expensive and probably futile in the long run.

To his regret, Khrushchev realized that if the refugees were to be stopped, and East Germany saved from collapse, West Berlin would have to be fenced off, no matter how badly such a move would reflect on the qualities of the Communist system. It was the only way to save the good people of the German Democratic Republic from being exposed to siren calls from the capitalist world, to which they had proved so susceptible. The leaders of the Warsaw Pact countries had been called together at the Moscow meeting to be informed of Khrushchev's decision and to agree to it. Like the United States, the Russians wanted to make sure all their allies were in accord with their policies. Khrushchev had an easier time persuading them.

The final communiqué of the Warsaw Pact conclave said nothing about the Berlin decision. It did, however, again express 'the inflexible determination of all its participants to achieve a peace settlement with Germany before the end of the year'. Expecting major developments, decisions, pronouncements, western analysts monitored all public statements and speeches emanating from the meeting for new developments. They found none. Waiting anxiously for a replay of Russia's Berlin blockade, the West was successfully diverted from suspecting what the Russians were really up to. Intelligence and Research at the State Department innocently reported, 'Purpose of Moscow 3–5 August meeting was to impress the West with bloc determination to conclude a separate treaty with the East German regime if necessary and to enhance the bloc's bargaining position in negotiations.'

Having decided on a plan of action, the Russians stepped up their stick-and-carrot propaganda campaign to confuse the West into operational paralysis. Two days after the Moscow Warsaw Pact gathering, Khrushchev publicly urged, 'Let us sit down honestly at a round conference table. Let us not fan up war psychosis.' At the same time he warned that if the United States unleashed a war, its people would taste the horrors of thermo-nuclear conflict and would face devastation of a kind they had not experienced since their Civil War.

His olive branch was designed to sustain hope in the White House that Moscow would back off before crossing the line Kennedy had drawn. It would thus discourage the President from authorizing precipitous action which might disrupt Soviet plans. The simultaneous nuclear threats were meant to convince Kennedy – as they did – that he might nevertheless finally be forced to order the launching of America's nuclear missiles, with calamitous consequences for Americans as well as Russians. He would thus be set up to be stunned into a stupour of relief when he realized that the Russians did not intend to push him that far.

The success of the Soviet campaign in artificially generating an atmosphere of morbid apprehension was demonstrated by the uncharacteristically emotional reaction of veteran diplomat George Kennan, otherwise one of the most perceptive and creative modern American foreign policy thinkers. As the crisis mushroomed, Kennan told Arthur Schlesinger, 'I do not propose to let the future of mankind be settled, or ended, by a group of men operating on the basis of limited perspectives and short-run calculations. I figure that the only thing I have left in life is to do everything I can to stop the war.'

It was hard not to worry when Khrushchev boasted that the
Soviet Union had developed the capacity to develop a one-
hundred-megaton, deliverable nuclear warhead, and warned that
Soviet missiles 'are not for slicing sausages.' On 9 August, the day
he made that statement, 1,926 East German refugees fled West.
Also on that day, Soviet intelligence officer and British spy
Colonel Oleg Penkovsky learned in Moscow of plans to divide
Berlin four days later. He was, however, in no position to pass
word along to his British contact before the event.

On 10 August, it was announced that Soviet war hero Marshal
Ivan Stepanovich Koniev, former supreme military commander
of the Warsaw Pact, had been appointed commander of Soviet
troops in East Germany. It was a position for which he normally
would have been considered too senior. His appointment was
another step in the escalation of Soviet threatening gestures.
Koniev had a wartime reputation for capturing enemy-held cities
by severing approach roads. He had once said, 'A city is like the
branch of a tree – cut the roads leading to it and the city will fall.'
It was an ominous thought in view of the vulnerability of the
Berlin access routes.

Koniev's arrival coincided with a flood of rumours that the East
German *Volkskammer*, scheduled to meet the following morning, would soon – possibly within a matter of days – announce
measures to restrict travel from East Germany to East Berlin –
the plan Khrushchev had rejected. On that day, twenty-four
hours after East Berlin *grenzgängers* were ordered to give up
their West Berlin jobs and report to labour offices in the East to
be assigned jobs within the Soviet Sector, 1,709 refugees showed
up at Marienfelde. Personnel at the refugee reception centre,
already bulging at the rafters, were bracing themselves for a
record weekend.

8

Something Funny at the Border

A s THE ONLY western correspondent resident in East Berlin, Reuters correspondent Adam Kellett-Long had an advantage over his colleagues based across the sector border in West Berlin. Hungry for diplomatic recognition by the West to remove any doubts about its legitimacy, the East German regime was gratified by the decision of the reputable British Reuters agency to man an office in East Berlin, rather than having the city covered only from West Berlin. It was a measure of recognition, even if it was not yet backed by the British government. Kellett-Long was, therefore, sometimes allowed access to Communist sources which other western newsmen were denied. After the special *Volkskammer* session, he managed to buttonhole a senior figure in the government to ask what was going on. The man declined to be specific, which was no more than expected, but he mysteriously advised, 'If I were you and I had plans to spend this weekend away from Berlin, I wouldn't.'

Though pleased to receive what appeared to be an extremely unusual tip-off at a time of great suspense in the city, Kellett-Long found himself in a quandary. Speculation that the Berlin tinder box was about to ignite had been rampant on a daily basis for the better part of a month. Western newsmen in the city were under pressure from their home offices to stay on top of the story. Some of the major American broadcast networks had beefed up their Berlin coverage, ferrying in senior correspondents from less tempestuous posts in Bonn, London and elsewhere to lend appropriate gravity to the story on their news programmes. Espying pay dirt, freelance journalists flowed in from everywhere.

News agency reporters – especially those at the fiercely competing United Press International, Associated Press and Reuters – were in a particularly tricky position, being regularly pressed to explain why they had missed (sometimes dubious) stories a rival agency had circulated to its subscribers. Mindful of Reuters' reputation for caution and reliability, Kellett-Long – twenty-six years old and on his first overseas assignment – had tried to stay well clear of far-fetched stories based on speculation and rumour, except when reporting the more credible ones and labelling them as such. He had, in fact, been expending much effort and time on checking out stories which proved to have no basis in fact. His wife, Mary, noted in her diary, 'Adam is getting tired of having to keep on throwing down these stories. Of course one day [one of those stories] will be true and then I hope he gets it first.'

Now it looked very much like Kellett-Long *would* be getting it first. Exclusive, genuine tip-offs from senior Communist officials on breaking stories of critical importance were few and far between. However, regardless how eminent its source (whom he was bound by the rules of the game not to identify), advice not to go away for the weekend could have meant many things – still tighter police controls, new systems for checking on East German train passengers making for East Berlin, stiffer penalties for apprehended refugees – or nothing at all.

Nevertheless, bright and early on Saturday morning, Kellett-Long sat down at the teleprinter in the East Berlin apartment which served as both his office and his home and tapped out a morning lead to London that was to cause him much anguish over the next sixteen hours. 'Berlin,' it began, 'is holding its breath . . .' Reviewing developments over the past few days, his story strongly suggested that the implementation of drastic measures to halt the flow of refugees to the West was imminent.

In the meantime, East Germans who had waited for the weekend to take leave of the German Democratic Republic were descending in great numbers on East Berlin en route to West Berlin and sanctuary. Efforts by Vopos, scouring inter-city and suburban trains, to spot refugees among people from the East German hinterlands who had chosen a Saturday in August for innocent visits to the big city were swamped by the volume of passenger traffic. The same was true for their attempts on the sector border, and on the Berlin subway and elevated trains.

Many were turned back. Many were arrested. But by noon it was apparent that the record for the influx of refugees at

Marienfelde on a single day would be broken. The lines of new arrivals from the East were growing longer and longer, and were creating problems. Mayor Willy Brandt's director of staff at the town hall, Heinrich Albertz, telephoned George Muller, deputy political adviser at the American Mission, to say food supplies on hand at the centre were just about exhausted – could the United States Army spare extra field rations? Muller got onto the army quartermaster and arranged for them to be delivered. Meanwhile, processing procedures were accelerated and still more planes were chartered to ferry refugees to West Germany.

While that was happening, Ulbricht's Council of Ministers, now formally empowered to 'implement all measures necessary to safeguard peace,' met in East Berlin to put a halt to the flood of refugees. Without dissent or question, it formally authorized action by East German security forces to place 'under proper control the still open border between Socialist and capitalist Europe.'

At 4.00 p.m. that Saturday, Ulbricht, as chairman of the East German National Defence Council, signed the order formally instructing Erich Honecker to proceed with his task of sealing the border between East and West Berlin. At 11.00 p.m., Honecker's command staff, by now gathered at East Berlin's central police headquarters, set in motion the operation for which they had been preparing under a blanket of secrecy for weeks. Among those also present were Minister of Defence General Heinz Hoffmann and Minister of State Security Erich Mielke, who were playing key roles in the operation. Without knowing why exactly, security forces under their command had already been put on the alert. It was time to give them their orders.

By nightfall, Kellett-Long was worried. His editors in London had been asking what he had to back up his morning lead suggesting that the Berlin climax was around the corner, and he had nothing of substance to offer them. He drove to the Ostbahnhof, East Berlin's main railway station, to get a copy of the early edition of *Neues Deutschland*. He hoped it would carry something that might substantiate his forecast. The Communists often broke major stories in the official press rather than through government press offices. But not this time. (At that moment, in fact, other staffers having been sent home, a hand-picked, politically-reliable skeleton staff at *Neues Deutschland* was preparing a special second edition of the newspaper that would tell the story for which Kellett-Long was waiting.) The only unusual thing he saw at the station was a surprisingly large number of black-uniformed railway police coming off trains arriving from out of town. That was curious – but hardly an earth-shattering development in view of the heavy policing to which East Berlin was being subjected.

Feeling like an amateurish blunderer, Kellett-Long drove back to his office to try to figure some way out of the hole he thought he had dug for himself. He sat down at his typewriter and began working on the night lead he was due to file to sum up the day's East Berlin developments. It began, 'Contrary to expectations . . .' And there he stopped. It was so limp and transparent. His wife Mary had gone to bed but, though also tired, he decided that before winding up his story and transmitting it he would wait until the East German news agency, ADN, had closed down its wire service for the night – at around 1.00 a.m. Though headline-grabbing events were unlikely so late at night, ADN was often used by the East German regime for special announcements.

At midnight exactly, twenty-five miles from the centre of Berlin, the piercing hoot of a siren sounding through the barracks of the militarized East German border police (*Grenzpolizei*, known as Grepos) shattered the slumber of Grepo Sergeant Rudi Thurow. Thurow thought it was just another practice drill, of which there had been an increasing number of late. But he quickly donned his uniform and, to a chorus of curses, went through the barracks prying from their beds men who, despite the siren, were trying to cling to sleep.

At about the same time in West Berlin, George Muller received another phone call from Heinrich Albertz, not about additional rations for the refugees this time. 'Something funny is going on,' Albertz told him. 'There are more *S Bahn* trains going East than are coming West.' That was strange, Muller thought, because it was believed that if the East Germans were planning to cause trouble in West Berlin, the movement would be the other way, with Communist militia men posing as workers streaming west by train and on foot, perhaps to try to seize a West Berlin government building and foment unrest.

There was a contingency plan for that involving the West Berlin police and, if necessary, Allied troops. But that clearly wasn't what was happening. What was taking place instead was a clamp-down on train services between the two parts of the city. As would soon become evident, the *S Bahn*, one of the most heavily-trafficked refugee arteries – used also by tens of thousands of Berliners who travelled back and forth between East and West every day – was being severed. This was confirmed when late-night West Berlin travellers and carousers leaving East Berlin by *S bahn* began trudging wearily and grumpily on foot up to the sector border. Their trains had been stopped at the last station in the East. They had been shooed off and made to walk the rest of the way. But although, as Albertz had told Muller, it was 'funny', there was as yet no indication that it was any worse than that; perhaps it was only another of the games the Communist authorities in East Berlin played now and again to show their dwindling population who was in charge.

At 12.20 a.m., Sergeant Rudi Thurow, having pried his men out of bed and got them to form up in combat dress on the parade ground outside, was summoned to the office in the barracks of his company commander, Oberleutnant Witz. When all of the company's officers and NCOs were assembled, Witz announced that this was not just another dry run. The leaders of the German Democratic Republic, he said, had finally been forced to take vigorous steps to block attempts to undermine the Socialist Fatherland. The flesh merchants in West Berlin who preyed on the citizens of the GDR would be put in their place. The activities of the *grenzgängers* who benefited from living in East Berlin while serving the West would no longer be tolerated. The espionage and terror centres in the western sectors were about to be dealt a crippling blow. Some upstanding and loyal East Germans might be hurt by what was about to happen and that was unfortunate. But the interests of the people's republic had to come first.

'Is it war?' Sergeant Thurow wondered, as Oberleutnant Witz lectured on. There was a sense of foreboding when the company commander, who had himself been briefed only a half-hour before, picked up a brown envelope marked 'Top Secret', tore it open, took out a document and started reading from it. 'In accordance with the declaration of the member states of the Warsaw Pact . . .' he began. It was a long declaration, replete with condemnations of West Germany, and it stressed the need to take action to preserve peace. All of that had been heard often before. This time, however, it was announced that, 'To block the hostile activities of the revenge-seeking and militaristic forces in West Germany and West Berlin, controls appropriate for all sovereign states will be established on the borders of the German Democratic Republic, including along the borders of the western sectors of Berlin.' There it was! That was how the refugees would be stopped. Contrary to four-power agreements on free movement throughout the city, Berlin was to be split in two.

Silence followed. Then somebody mumbled, 'Will the West stand for this?' Through RIAS and other western broadcast media readily picked up in the East, the proclaimed determination of President Kennedy and other western leaders not to be pushed around over Berlin was widely known. But Oberleutnant Witz had been briefed to deal with the concerns of his men. He told them no military response from the West would be forthcoming because the Soviet forces in the area, which greatly outnumbered the Allied Berlin garrisons, had been alerted, as the West well knew. Soviet tanks were already taking up positions around Berlin; the men had heard them rumbling by their barracks as they had shaken off the last remnants of sleep and poured themselves into their uniforms less than an hour before.

The deputy head of the American Military Liaison Mission in Potsdam, Lieutenant Colonel David Morgan, had also heard the tanks. When he got in a Mission car to drive out to see what was happening, he got no further than two hundred yards, just short of the highway, before being stopped by a Vopo and kept there until the tanks had passed, heading for positions around Berlin.

Just before 1.00 a.m., Kellett-Long, still with nothing new of substance to report and despairing of surviving the weekend with his credibility intact, prepared to face the grim necessity of winding up his night lead and dispatching it to London. As he set to it, his telephone rang. A man, speaking German and declining to identify himself, said, 'I strongly advise you not to go to bed tonight.'* Another mysterious tip-off! First not to go away for the weekend, now not to go to sleep. A few minutes later, at 1.11 a.m., the ADN teleprinter in the Reuters office began to chatter. After announcing that an important statement had been issued by the member nations of the Warsaw Pact (the statement drawn up at the Warsaw Pact meeting in Moscow the week before), it began churning out the turgid officialese in which government pronouncements, whether important or trivial, were invariably couched: 'The governments of the member nations of the Warsaw Pact have striven for many years to reach a peace settlement with Germany.' The statement went on to describe the

---

*Kellett-Long thought he recognized the voice as that of someone he knew at ADN. He later thanked the man, who responded with a blank look.

dangers that were inherent in the prevailing situation and the great patience which the Soviet Union and its Warsaw Pact allies had displayed, patience which now was at an end:

> The present traffic situation on the borders of West Berlin is being used by ruling circles of [West Germany] and intelligence agencies of NATO countries to undermine the economy of the German Democratic Republic. Through deceit, bribery, and blackmail, West German government bodies and military interests induce certain unstable elements in the German Democratic Republic to leave for West Germany. These deceived people are compelled to serve with the *Bundeswehr* [West German army], and are recruited for the intelligence agencies of different countries to be sent back to the GDR as spies and saboteurs . . . In the face of the aggressive aspirations of the reactionary forces of West Germany and its NATO allies, the Warsaw Pact member states must take necessary steps to guarantee their security and, primarily, the security of the GDR . . . The governments of the Warsaw Pact member states [propose to the parliament, government and working people at the GDR that] . . . reliable safeguards and effective control be established around the whole territory of West Berlin.

West Berlin, and its dangerous influences, was to be quarantined. The Warsaw Pact declaration was careful to reassure the Allies that the access routes, upon which the Russians had so skilfully focused the West's attention, would not be touched: 'It goes without saying that these measures must not affect existing provisions for traffic and control on communications routes between West Berlin and West Germany.' The Russians were, in effect, telling Kennedy, 'You told us not to step over the line you drew and we have not done so. There is to be no interference with the access routes, no encroachment on West Berlin. You have nothing to worry about.' Moscow had shook a threatening finger in one direction and then, when everyone was looking that way, had moved off in another direction. For all its contingency plans, the West had been braced for something that was not happening.

By the time ADN had begun dispatching the text of the Warsaw Pact communiqué, the East German border-bolting operation was already well in hand. Units of the East German army and police were already on their way to the sector boundaries. Rolls of barbed wire, concrete posts, wooden horses, picks, shovels and other construction tools which had earlier been loaded onto trucks for unspecified 'construction projects' were also en route to transform one the largest cities in Europe.

At the Reuters East Berlin office, having phoned London as soon as the Warsaw Pact communiqué had come over his ADN teleprinter and having learned that the communiqué was simultaneously being released in Moscow (a more important dateline), Kellett-Long went down into the streets to see what was happening. His immediate impression was that nothing at all was different. His street, Schoenhauser Allee, was dark, silent and deserted, as it always was late at night. He got into his car and drove toward the East–West crossing point at the Brandenburg Gate. Just short of the gate, he was stopped by a Vopo brandishing a red-beamed flashlight. The Vopo told him he would not be allowed to proceed further. '*Die Grenze ist geschlossen*,' he said ('The border is closed'), and motioned him away. When he turned around and drove off to see what was going on elsewhere, his car was again stopped by a Vopo at Karl Marx Platz. This time it was because a column of trucks was passing in the direction of the border. What exactly was taking place wasn't yet clear. But troops and military vehicles were in motion and the border area was being cordoned off. Vindicated at last, Kellett-Long, the first westerner to know that West Berlin was being closed off from the East, hurried back to his office to report to London. He tapped out a 'snap' – 'The East–West Berlin border was closed early today . . .' before filing a longer story on what he had seen.

It was the beginning of a very long night for him, and for many others in Berlin. West Berlin taxi-drivers, sensitive as always to the winds of change, had begun radioing their dispatchers an hour before not to accept any requests that involved trips into the Soviet Sector. Reports began flooding in to West Berlin police headquarters from police positions and police patrols telling of troop-carriers and armoured cars arriving at various places along the eastern side of the border. On Bernauer Strasse, where the borderline between the Soviet and French Sectors ran down the middle of the road, a line of trucks had rolled up on the eastern side of the street and were just sitting there, headlights blazing. Reports of truck convoys came in from other locations as well. Soon, streets bordering sector crossings began resounding to the clatter and clank of bales of barbed wire and concrete posts being unloaded from the trucks, and to the shouts of police and army officers as they deployed the men pouring out of armoured troop-carriers and other vehicles.

When it became unmistakable, by 2.00 a.m., that a major operation was in progress, West Berlin police headquarters

roused Deputy Mayor Franz Amrehn and word was passed along
also to western duty officers. Awakened at home, officials of the
American Mission in Berlin were reluctant to jump to conclusions
or send out alarm signals. They recalled that when the Communists had closed the sector border during the Evangelical Church
Congress in Berlin the previous month, it had been only a
temporary operation. Officers of the Mission knew they were
regarded in Washington as overly excitable, with a tendency to
transform Berlin trivialities into cosmic catastrophes.

In this case, not only was it the weekend and night-time, when
officials in Washington weren't likely to appreciate being disturbed, but there were no reports of any problems within West
Berlin. So far, everything seemed to be happening in the Soviet
Sector. It had earlier been rumoured that new identity cards
might soon be issued by the Communists to all East Germans as
part of the clamp-down on refugees and *grenzgängers* – a massive
operation which, if it was happening, would account for the
hubbub on the border. If that was all it was, the western powers
would issue the usual formal protest about the East German
military presence in Berlin, officially forbidden in the four-power
city. There was no reason to get people out of bed for something
like that.

After checking with the British military police, Bernard
Ledwidge, political adviser at the British Mission, decided
somebody should be awakened in London, if only the resident
clerk at the Foreign Office whose duties included being roused
when needed. Ledwidge put a call through to the Foreign Office.
He said there was tumult on the border but that as yet he hadn't
much more to report. Patrols were out scouting the terrain and he
would report more when he knew more.

The operation was only just beginning. Ringing all of West
Berlin's 103-mile perimeter with an impenetrable barrier was an
immense project. It would take time to complete. Men had to be
deployed. Materials had to be transported and unloaded. Not all
parts of the border could be dealt with at once. The first to get
concentrated treatment was Potsdamer Platz, normally the
busiest East–West crossing point in the world; it was usually
almost deserted in the early morning hours, but not now. As
hastily-reinforced West Berlin police and a gaggle of angry West
Berliner night owls looked on, East German soldiers and Vopos
went about their business of bisecting the square. With rifle-
toting guards in front of them facing west, men with pneumatic
drills jackhammered out cobblestones and trolley tracks, blasting

holes into the ground for posts on which barbed wire could be strung. Some positioned the bales of wire for stringing, while other guards, cradling sub-machine-guns in their arms, faced into the Soviet Sector from the border to make certain that, though night owls had not been much in evidence in that part of the city for a long time, no one from east of the borderline attempted to interfere with this massive and bizarre construction project.

By 3.30 a.m., obstructions were being installed on all the major streets which had previously been crossing points. Vehicles with East Berlin licence plates and East German pedestrians attempting to traverse them to the West were being turned back, while West Berliners trying to return home from the Soviet Sector were required to show identity papers before being let through. People living near the border were soon awakened by the clamour in the streets. In tenements nearby, windows were dotted with the faces and shapes of pyjamaed people peering anxiously down at the proceedings below. Those on the eastern side who ventured into the street to get a closer look were quickly shooed back indoors by Vopos.

Many East Berliners living further in from the border were also aware that this was no ordinary night. They had been awakened by the sound of trucks and military vehicles rumbling down their normally silent, night-time streets and, as dawn approached, by the wail of sirens as police cars escorted tanks and more convoys of trucks and armoured vehicles to the borderline.

Some of those East Berliners went down to see what was happening. They drifted in the direction of the convoys and toward the din on the border. But when they got there, they were kept well back. Others, having expected the crackdown on the refugees to come at any moment, instinctively realized what was up. If they did not, they had only to switch on their radios and listen to RIAS which, by 4.00 a.m., was providing the first sketchy reports of the barbed-wire barriers. Having already planned to flee West, several East Berliners grabbed what they could and hurried through nearby crossing points or border wasteland patches before guards had taken up positions there and before the barbed wire that would lock them in was properly strung. But most East Berliners, like most West Berliners, would not know till they awoke in the morning what had transpired during the night. For them and others living under Communist rule in East Germany, going West at will was becoming a thing of the past.

From just after 2.00 a.m., senior officials of the Allied Missions in West Berlin had been almost continually on the telephone trying to sort out an accurate account of what was going on and taking calls from others seeking the same information. With the barrage of reports of activity on the sector border pouring in, it was evident that whatever was happening had serious political dimensions. Minister Allan Lightner of the American Mission realized that what was needed was a first-hand report of what was going on. Richard Smyser, one of the junior officers in the Mission's eastern affairs section, was roused from deep sleep and told, 'There seems to be something going on in East Berlin. Go over there and take a look.'

Smyser dressed quickly and, with Frank Trinka, another junior officer at the Mission, climbed into Smyser's bluish-grey Mercedes convertible, putting the top down so they could see better. They drove to Potsdamer Platz, where the building of the barbed-wire barrier had already been going on for the better part of two hours but where wire was still being clatteringly unrolled to be strung from the concrete posts. When Smyser drove up to the barrier to go through into the Soviet Sector, Vopos stepped forward to order him to turn around. Motioning to the official United States licence plate at the front of his car, Smyser told them, 'We are officials of the American forces. You have no right to stop us.' The Vopos huddled together for a moment, exchanged some words and then rolled back some of the barbed wire to let them through. They had instructions not to interfere with the movement of Allied officials – not yet. Nothing was to be done to complicate the immediate task at hand.

Off stage, the commander of Soviet forces in East Germany kept close watch on the proceedings. Marshal Koniev was prepared to move in and take direct charge of operations if things threatened to get out of control. This was, however, designed to be an exclusively East German affair. Its main objective was to stop the refugees. But it was also meant to demonstrate that, though the Allies could proclaim from here to eternity that Berlin was a four-power city, they had no say or influence whatsoever in East Berlin. The western powers had been insisting that it remained the Soviet Sector and nothing more, but exclusive sovereignty over East Berlin was herewith being both proclaimed and demonstrated, with Moscow's blessings, by the East German regime, the same regime which the three western powers and West Germany insisted did not legally exist.

Though put on full alert and threateningly deployed around the city, Soviet forces were keeping clear of Berlin itself, as was reported by the licensed spies of the Allied Liaison Missions. They had been busily scouting the area without serious interference from the Russians. The preliminary report of American liaison officers was concise:

> Soviet 19th Motorized Rifle Division, combined with 10th Guards Tank Division and possibly the 6th Motorized Rifle Division moved out early this morning and moved into position around Berlin. Elements of the 1st East German Army Motorized Rifle Division moved out from Potsdam and are presently unlocated. Soviet units deployed and moved off the autobahn, deploying units into small outposts and roadblocks composed of three or four tanks, an armoured personnel-carrier and several troops. These outposts were established about three or four kilometres apart, and appear completely to ring Berlin.

The Soviet commander positioned his forces conspicuously. The Americans were to be discouraged from thinking they might be able to do something about the East German army units which had moved into East Berlin to play a major role in the seal-off operation. Though they had been on display in East Berlin before – at parades and ceremonial occasions – the Allies had the right, on paper, to march into East Berlin and arrest the East German troops for being where they were forbidden. The prospect of anything like that happening was remote, but the Russian forces ringing the city were telling the Allies that the East German army units would not stand alone if there was trouble. Nor was that all. Soviet rocket forces in East Europe had also been put on the alert. The Allies were to be under no illusions about the strength of the Soviet commitment.

Neither the Russians nor the East German leaders knew how the men on the front line, those assigned to build and guard the sector barrier, would stand up to the job. No doubt they would obey orders, form up as instructed, drill holes in the pavement, plant the concrete posts, unroll the barbed wire and string it up. But they had never been tested under pressure. How would they react if, as was possible, American tanks roared up to the border, or if American troops moved in on foot to tear apart their handiwork?

Though they had been pressing the Russians for permission to slam the border shut, the East German leaders knew that things could go disastrously wrong. If there was trouble, would the men break ranks? Would they panic? And what would happen then?

Indeed, while many of the East German police and soldiers on duty at the borderline wore expressions of defiant determination, others seemed glum and nervous, as if wishing they were somewhere else.

In previous weeks, several Vopos and some East German soldiers had themselves become refugees seeking sanctuary at Marienfelde. Many who did not go West were equally disenchanted with the Communist regime. Vopo officers had reported that some of their men had been less than enthusiastic in carrying out the pre-Wall crackdown on *grenzgängers*. Some had been observed on duty treating border-crossers with nothing like the severity they deserved. Several had been warned that they had to bring greater enthusiasm and diligence to the job of dealing with enemies of the Socialist Fatherland or they would have to answer for their shortcomings.

It was easy enough for the officials organizing the operation to exude confidence when assuring the Russians and Ulbricht that everything would work out as planned. But officers on the spot who knew the men and who were responsible for the details of the border closure weren't so sure. They wondered how those men among the Vopos and Grepos whose relatives had already fled as refugees would stand up to physically preventing others from doing the same. They wondered how those who happened to be Berliners would react to standing guard while their city was broken in two. Berliners tended to be less submissive to authority than most other Germans. Berlin was where the 1953 anti-Communist uprising began and where it had been carried to its greatest extremes before being bloodily crushed. How would the men react in the days to come when they had to turn back not only *grenzgängers*, not only would-be refugees committing the crime of 'Fleeing the Republic', but also harmless, ordinary East Berliners merely wishing to visit brothers or cousins in the West, or go to a movie there, or simply cross over to buy a Coca Cola from a West Berlin border stand? Members of the security forces had all been required to attend regular indoctrination sessions. But the fact that some of them had still chosen to go West left troubling suspicions that others might also be smitten with doubts about which side they were on.

Officials at the Allied missions in Berlin had a problem of a different dimension. Something peculiar was going on in the middle of the city and they couldn't tell for sure what it was. In addition to trying to piece together a picture of what was happening, they were fielding countless phone calls from others wanting to do the same. George Muller of the American Mission recalled: 'The phone kept ringing. The United States establishment in Berlin was huge and practically everybody had something to report or questions to ask. You could hardly sit back and collect your wits.'

No effort was made at that stage to file a report to Washington. It was realized the Mission could never beat the news agencies in getting information across to the United States. It took from four to six hours to transmit an official telegram through channels from Berlin to the State Department. Besides, official reports were expected to be more analytical than 'what-when-where' wire service flashes. 'We decided,' Muller said, 'to hold up our reporting till we knew exactly what this was about.'

Around 6.00 a.m., Richard Smyser and Frank Trinka returned from their reconnaissance expedition in East Berlin and told a story of considerable activity there. There was a lot of movement of armoured personnel-carriers, trucks and other police and military vehicles in various parts of East Berlin close to the sector border. Judging from what the two men had seen crossing into and out of the East, they were part of a very major population-control exercise, the extent of which was still unclear.

Victims of this exercise had been seen in sharp relief by Smyser and Trinka when they had parked near the Friedrichstrasse train station a mile from the American Sector and entered the station hall. With its tired brown walls, the hall – dimly lit and cavernous – seemed like the inside of a huge bunker. There was a crowd there, people of all ages, including small children. They carried packages and suitcases. Some sat on them. Their faces were masked by anguish and worry. Some were weeping. These were would-be refugees, their escape route abruptly choked off. Smyser thought the expressions some wore conveyed a feeling of 'Oh, my God, if we'd only gone twenty-four hours earlier.' For them, there was no doubt that the border closure was final, that the escape hatch was closed for good.

Some people in the station hall, uncomprehending, tried to get past the guards and onto the platform where westbound trains normally arrived. They were held back, though some of the Vopos seemed not overly happy with the task they had to perform. A few Vopos distributed printed leaflets containing a proclamation explaining, among other things, that citizens of the German Democratic Republic wishing to visit West Berlin would henceforth require special passes, which, it was said, could be obtained at their local police stations. But except for a handful of

East German intelligence officers sent West to size up the situation there, no such special passes were available.

It was just after dawn of a bright summer's morning when Smyser and Trinka approached the Brandenburg Gate to drive through to West Berlin again. The gate had not been sealed, but it was heavily policed and their car was waved to a halt by a Vopo on the East Berlin side. Though informed that they were officers of the American forces, he kept them from driving on and went into the guard house nearby to consult a superior before letting them pass. It was later reported that a senior East German government official had been posted in that guard house to make certain no unnecessary difficulties arose at the gate. Everybody was being very careful.

When they gave their report at the American Mission, Smyser and Trinka were pointedly asked whether they had seen any Russians in East Berlin. They reported that they had not. Regardless of who was sponsoring the border closure, the nuts and bolts of it were being provided by the 'non-existent' East German regime rather than the Russians, making it a twin challenge to the West.

Among East Berliners who had jobs in West Berlin were restaurant employees, cleaning women, hotel porters and others who worked on Sundays and who normally got to work early in the morning. Around 6.00 a.m., many of them, in the dark about the night's developments, started off for work as usual. They didn't get very far. They found that the gates to the entrances of all twelve East Berlin stations on crosstown subway lines had been padlocked hours before. Turned away by police, they couldn't at first grasp what was happening and just stood there, bewildered. Some appealed to the Vopos to let them through, not realizing that even if the gates were unlocked and they were let through, they still wouldn't be able to get to West Berlin.

Though the subway system was still operating, trains shuttling under East Berlin from one part of West Berlin to another were not permitted to stop in the Soviet Sector. The only exception was at the Friedrichstrasse station Smyser and Trinka had visited, where people from the West could still enter East Berlin if permitted to pass through the tight security cordon there. What was more, Vopos had been posted in the subway stations to keep would-be refugees who managed to slip into the train tunnels from finding their way to freedom on foot. Cross-border commuters who normally went west by elevated *S Bahn* also quickly discovered that their way was blocked.

Early morning *grenzgängers* were soon joined in their despair by other East Berliners who were setting out to visit relatives and friends in West Berlin for the day. Some grew explosively angry when told that was no longer possible. Grepo Sergeant Rudi Thurow heard one man defiantly denounce the government for keeping him from seeing his own mother. Others were equally outspoken. One of Thurow's men, Private Gottfried Herrman, confessed to the sergeant that he was ashamed of himself for what he was required to do. It wasn't long before Herrman vaulted the barbed wire to the West and made his way to Marienfelde. Fed up, Thurow was to follow him soon afterward.

As the morning drew on, another factor was appearing in the equation. Despite the early hour, clusters of angry West Berliners had been gathering at places along the sector borders to look on and hurl catcalls at the Vopos as the barbed-wire barrier was being laid. West Berlin police were getting worried that hotheads among them might try to assault the Vopos. But it wasn't only the Communists who were the object of their derision. Voices were raised in mockery of their supposed protectors, the Americans. Though the Communists were already sending men to relieve those who had been on duty since midnight, the Americans had not even bothered to send a company of troops to the border in response to this gruesome provocation. The city they had made such moving promises to defend was being ripped apart, and there was no sign of them. Few of those watching it happen were in any mood to examine the fine points of American policy, which had long before acquiesced to undisputed Communist rule in East Berlin.

Whatever his own gut reaction to the situation, the American commandant did not feel free to use his own judgment. As tension had built up over the previous weeks, Major General Albert Watson Jr had been strongly advised not to be provoked into impetuous action. Watson was careful to observe that admonition. He was in an unenviable position. A tough but even-tempered soldier-soldier (rather than a diplomat-soldier, of which the United States Army has many more today than it did then), he had been American commandant in Berlin only three months. But that had been more than enough time for him to realize that he was expected to be little more than a messenger boy.

Though the situation might change from day to day and events worthy of immediate response might occur, he was required to tread very carefully in making decisions. He was directly responsible to American Ambassador Walter Dowling in Bonn, an experienced foreign-service officer who was officially chief of the Berlin Mission, as well as to General Bruce Clarke in Heidelberg, the U.S. Army Commander in Europe, both of whom, in view of the delicacy of the situation, relentlessly peered over his shoulder and made sure he knew it. He was also responsible, through Clarke, to General Lauris Norstad at NATO headquarters in Paris. There were times when Watson's instructions, usually but not always identical, came through both military and diplomatic channels. There were times when both channels were silent. That morning was one of those times, and yet a decision had to be made – to do something or to do nothing.

There were no reports of Russian military activity in Berlin or of East German provocations in the city, so there was no reason in those early hours to disturb people at army headquarters in Heidelberg, and the political side of his Mission had already begun filing dispatches to Bonn. Later in the morning, he would alert his garrison and send a helicopter over the border area for a look at developments. But to send troops to the sector border just to watch the East Germans get on with whatever they had in mind might have been deemed a pointless and humiliating over-reaction which he would be called upon to explain by Dowling and Clarke, who were both still fast asleep far away in their respective beds. As the crisis developed, General Watson was, as one officer put it, 'in a hell of a box'.

9

'Why Didn't We Know?'

S URPRISE, WHEN IT happens to a government, is likely to be a complicated, diffuse, bureaucratic thing. It includes neglect of responsibility, but also responsibility so poorly defined or so ambiguously delegated that action gets lost. It includes gaps in intelligence that, like a string of pearls too precious to wear, is too sensitive to give to those who need it. It includes the alarm that fails to work, but also the alarm that has gone off so often it has been disconnected. It includes the unalert watchman, but also the one who knows he'll be chewed out by his superiors if he gets high authority out of bed. It includes the contingencies that occur to no one, but also those that everyone assumes somebody else is taking care of. It includes straight-forward procrastination, but also decisions protracted by internal disagreement. It includes, in addition, the inability of individual human beings to rise to the occasion until they are sure it is the occasion – which is usually too late. . . . Finally . . . surprise may include some measure of genuine novelty introduced by the enemy, and possibly some sheer bad luck.

Thomas C. Schelling

There was a six-hour time difference between Berlin and Washington. Early morning in central Europe was late night of the previous day on the east coast of the United States. If Honecker had deliberately timed his operation for when American leaders would be least prepared to respond quickly, he had chosen shrewdly. There weren't many people in the American capital – or in any of the places they had gone to get away from the oppressive heat of the city – sharply attuned on a Saturday night to the latest developments far away from home.

156

Washington was to remain very much in the dark about the story unfolding in Berlin for many hours after the bales of barbed wire were first pushed off the trucks on the sector border. A lot of disjointed reporting came in at first – bits and pieces of news being passed along by the wire services: East German troops and police had taken up positions on the sector dividing line; they were tearing up pavement; they were stringing barbed wire. But news agency reporters in Berlin were not reading too much into what they were at first able to see happening. For one thing, they were too busy covering the story as it developed in the dark of night. For another, like everyone else there, they didn't know exactly what the Communists had in mind. Pedestrian, vehicular and train traffic between the Soviet and western sectors was being interrupted. The Communists, as always, were making extravagant declarations. It was a good enough story without speculative forecasts about how long the East Germans were prepared to go on with the prodigious effort and expense of manning a barbed-wire, city-centre frontier with troops and police.

Having fielded their share of unfounded rumours and exaggerations at various times during the previous few weeks, the main bureaus of the news agencies were being cautious. Though he needed no such instruction, Joe Fleming, United Press International bureau chief and newshawk in Berlin, was soon to be advised by New York to be careful not to make it seem that the Third World War was about to break out.

In Washington just after midnight (6.00 a.m. Berlin time), John Ausland, Berlin Task Force duty officer for the weekend, was telephoned at home by the State Department's Operations Centre and told that things were happening along the Berlin sector border, though it wasn't yet exactly clear what. There had, as yet, been no report from the Berlin Mission; just wire service squibs. Ausland, who had gone to bed early, left word that he was to be called back when more specific information was available, and went back to sleep. It was almost four hours later before he was awakened again with a more comprehensive report. He got out of bed, dressed and alerted Berlin Task Force member Frank Cash by telephone before driving to the State Department. Cash said he'd join him there after taking his wife to the airport later that morning.

President Kennedy was still fast asleep at his Hyannisport retreat, and would be for several more hours. Edward Tomkins, head of the Western Department of the British Foreign Office, who normally spent his weekends at his Buckinghamshire home an hour and a half from London, was alerted by the Foreign Office resident clerk shortly after breakfast and drove immediately to his office in Whitehall. But the news was still patchy when he got there. 'No one knew what was happening,' Tomkins said. Whatever it was, the western commandants in Berlin could not delay a response of some kind, if only for the sake of appearances. They, and the Soviet commandant, were supposed to be in charge of the city. Now they were being shown that they were not in charge.

Armed East German forces – not even Russian – were presuming to draw a line through the city, and were deciding who may or may not pass through that line. A decree by East German Interior Minister Karl Maron, who had no legal status or authority in the eyes of the western commandants, announced that Berlin border-crossing points were to be reduced from eighty-eight to thirteen, all to be controlled by East German security forces. There would be no new restrictions on foreigners crossing the border, but they would have to show their passports. West Berliners 'with peaceful intentions' would be permitted to enter, but would be required to show their personal identity cards when doing so. 'Agents of West German militarism' would be banned from East Berlin. East Berliners were being forbidden to enter West Berlin. If any of this was allowed to stand, even the pretence of four-power status for the city would be consigned to the history books, and the face of Berlin would be totally transformed.

At 10.00 a.m., the western commandants and their political advisers gathered at the Kommandatura to confer on developments. Some of those attending had not slept at all, or had slept very little during the night, and their faces were scarred with fatigue. The role of Kommandatura chairman rotated among the commandants and the job had fallen to Watson for August. It was his job to outline the facts to his colleagues, as far as they were known. At that point, five things were known: 1) the Communists were setting up a barrier which, if completed, would effectively seal East Berlin off from West Berlin; 2) in permitting the East Germans to do this, and to issue various decrees, the Russians were violating four-power agreements; 3) there had so far been no encroachment by the Communists on West Berlin; 4) the western powers were committed to defend their rights in West Berlin and might soon be obliged to live up to that commitment; 5) there was no sign as yet of Russian military forces being directly involved, though at least two Soviet divisions had been deployed around the city.

Questions were asked for which no answers were available.

Would the access route lifelines to West Berlin across East Germany be blocked? Would the Russians continue to stay clear of the operation? Would the East Germans continue to confine their activity to East Berlin, or was it a prelude to some sort of move against West Berlin, about which reports might come in at any moment? It was, for example, learned that not only troops and Vopos were manning the border and laying barbed wire, but also East German border police (Grepos like Sergant Thurow), transport police (Trapos), and even East Berlin firemen. In addition to fresh troops and Vopos to relieve the men who had been on duty through the night, units of the Worker Battle Brigades,* the paramilitary Communist militia, armed with automatic weapons, had just taken up positions at some places along the border. The East Germans were deploying every man they had.

The atmosphere at the Kommandatura meeting was grim. The sense of impotence that had overtaken West Berliners in anticipation of a Communist clamp-down on the refugees was now shared by the western commandants. There was a reflexive recollection of the blockade thirteen years earlier. Anxious questions were asked about the level of essential supplies in the city. Would they last until a new airlift could be organized if the ground access routes were again severed? Nor did it escape the imagination of some in attendance that their deliberations might serve no purpose whatsoever, that they might be witnessing the opening act of a major East–West clash in which the comparatively puny western garrisons in Berlin would quickly be overrun.

But such speculation was pointless and distracting. The commandants had to weigh up the circumstances prevailing then and there. And further developments could be expected momentarily. No one suggested doing anything about the barbed wire. Nor was there talk of other possible counter-measures. The possibility that action might be taken to wrest the initiative away from the Communists was not raised. All three commandants, and their political advisers, awaited instructions from their respective governments. They knew there was nothing else they could do. Their meeting was dominated by forebodings about what might lie ahead.

*The previous Thursday, when Adam Kellett-Long had gone to the Diplomatic Services Bureau in East Berlin to check on the supply of fuel for his office-apartment, he had seen a full field pack in the corner of the office. The man there, a member of a workers' brigade, had said there was going to be some sort of exercise over the weekend.

Realizing that at least a gesture should be made while they waited for their masters to decide what was to be done, Watson suggested that the commandants dispatch a message of protest to their Soviet counterpart in East Berlin. Though reluctant to go along until instructions came from London, the British commandant, Major General Rohan Delacombe, was persuaded to agree. But Major General Jean Lacomme, the French commandant, regretted that not only did he require authorization from Paris to send a note of any kind, but that Paris would insist on reviewing the contents of the note before approval would be given. The way things happened in the French capital during the vacation month of August, that could take days.

However, the French general agreed there was no reason why a public protest, rather than a formal message to the Russians, could not be made and the aides of the three commandants were instructed to draft a suitable statement. It was to condemn not only the violation of four-power agreements, but the abuse of human rights as well. It would not remove the barbed wire, but it would at least show both West Berliners and the Communists that the western commandants were deeply concerned by developments.

Before the commandants adjourned their meeting, Willy Brandt was invited to join them to give his view of what was happening to his city. Running against Adenauer in the following month's elections for West German Chancellor, Brandt had arrived back in Berlin from a campaign tour of West Germany only that morning. When the border-sealing operation had begun, he had been asleep on a train heading from one campaign rally to another. At around 5.00 a.m., a railway official had knocked on the door of his compartment to tell him what was happening. He and his entourage had left the train at Hanover, its next major stop, made quickly for the nearby airport and taken the first flight back to Berlin. Arriving at Tempelhof, Brandt had gone directly to Potsdamer Platz, where he had been devastated by the sight of the barbed wire and the armed East German troops and police posted like guards at a prison camp. The full dimensions of the operation weren't yet evident. Trucks were unloading more barbed wire, more concrete posts, additional loads of rubble to firm up and extend the job begun during the night.

Brandt was at first profoundly saddened rather than angered by what he saw and by what he heard from West Berlin police about what was going on. The Communist barrier ran down the middle of streets, dividing neighbourhoods and separating neighbours. It was cutting through churchyards, cemeteries and wooded areas, it ran along canals, zigzagging through the city, faithfully following the contours of the Soviet Sector. Trolley tracks had been torn up, paving stones had been gouged out, trenches had been dug, trees had been cut down to block off streets. Machine-gun nests had been set up at the Brandenburg Gate – where Brandt had gone next – the guns pointing down the Street of the 17th of June (named to commemorate the East German uprising of 1953) towards West Berliners who had gathered in fury and disgust on their side of that monumental architectural symbol of Berlin. 'It was hard,' Brandt recalled, 'to remain calm and composed.'

But when he got to the Kommandatura to confer with the western commandants, he seemed stunned and flabbergasted. Under the circumstances, it was not surprising. Brandt was a moody man, a man of deep if generally undemonstrative emotions. Sometimes at meetings, as debate swirled around him, he would say nothing, his long, dark face seemingly clouded in thought. At other times, he could be articulate and emotionally engaged. Now he was subdued and sombre, the layers of distress that had engulfed him only gradually lifting. It was, remarkably, his first visit to the Kommandatura and he was surprised to see hanging there, alongside pictures of the western commandants, a picture of General Alexander Kotikov, the last Soviet Berlin commandant to participate in the activities of the Kommandatura before the Russians had walked out thirteen years before. It had not been removed, and a place for the Russians was still reserved at the main Kommandatura conference table, as symbols of continued Allied insistence that Berlin was a four-power city.

Once he rose from the doldrums, Brandt's main concern that morning was that both East and West Berliners might be so enraged by the barbed wire drawn across their city that they would erupt uncontrollably in violent protests. By 10.00 a.m., 150 angry West Berliners had gathered at Potsdamer Platz to jeer at the work crews tearing up the pavement and feeding out the wire, and at the armed guards in front of them. By 10.30, the crowd there had swollen to 500 and was expanding all the time. By 11.00, 2,000 indignant protesters had congregated west of the Brandenberg Gate.

Brandt feared that the Russians would not hesitate to send in their tanks if there was an explosion of popular wrath on the other side of the border. Blood would be shed. People would be killed. But something had to be done. At the very least, western patrols should be sent to the border to show West Berliners that whatever was happening in the East they were not endangered. When informed that the commandants intended to issue a protest to the Soviet commandant, Brandt replied softly, 'If all the commandants do is issue protests, people in the East will laugh themselves sick from Pankow* all the way to Vladivostok.' 'Scanning the troubled faces of my American friends,' he wrote later, 'I could imagine what had happened. They had alerted the Pentagon, the State Department and the White House, only to be told that ungovernable reactions must be avoided at all costs.' In fact that had not yet happened.

By mid-morning on Sunday, the barbed-wire barrier, six feet high in some places, was firmly installed along long stretches of the sector border. Where it wasn't, a beginning had been made. The air was still filled with the chatter of pneumatic drills battering holes into the ground for concrete posts. Bulldozers were ramming mounds of rubble into position along some parts of the border. All over there were armed men – soldiers, Vopos, Grepos, Trapos, Worker Battle Brigadesmen.

On the eastern side of the wire, but kept back, small knots of East Berliners, stunned more than frightened, bewildered rather than angry, gazed on at the proceedings. The full significance of what they were seeing had yet to sink in. They had trouble grasping the fact that streets they had casually crossed day in day out for years – as readily as people in New York, London or Paris cross a street – were not only out of bounds, but barred to them by uniformed men who were prepared to shoot them.

On the West Berlin side, all available police were on duty to control ever larger, ever angrier crowds. Many people who lived well away from the border and only now showed up had learned of developments only when called by anxious relatives elsewhere in West Berlin or in West Germany, who had heard radio news reports. Some people in the city had been telephoned by West Berliners out of town or out of the country on business or vacation, who feared for the safety of their families or who, in the confusion of the moment, worried that they might not be permitted to return home. Some West Berliners had learned what was happening from fellow parishioners at early morning church services. Many who went to join the protesters at Potsdamer

*East Berlin suburb in which there was a district reserved for residences of senior East German Communist officials.

Platz and elsewhere along the wire called out pleadingly or bitterly to the East German police and troops, asking them whether they weren't ashamed of themselves and if they had the nerve to still call themselves Germans.

For a summer's Sunday morning when momentous things were taking place nearby, Karl-Marx-Allee, East Berlin's showcase boulevard, was strangely quiet. There were no clusters of anxious or curious residents milling about or locked in public discourse on the developments of the night. There was no to-ing and fro-ing of people seeking the latest news. The street was virtually deserted. It was as if people living along it, most of them equipped with the untarnished political credentials required to have been allotted accommodation in the new buildings there, had received advance word of a tornado and, not having access to the old, Kansas-style cellar sanctuaries, had shut themselves in their new, showcase apartments till things blew over.

Nearer the border, however, gatherings of East Berliners continued to expand, swollen by those who realized to their bitterness, grief or amazement – or all three – that they had been cut off from parents or offspring, brothers and sisters, friends and jobs just a few minutes away. One East Berliner who had been organizing his permanent shift to West Berlin little by little, and had rented an apartment there to which he had been furtively carting his portable possessions one by one, had slept in his West Berlin home-to-be that night to find in the morning that he was separated from his wife, now apparently stuck behind the barbed wire.

Others, though shaken by developments, were not deterred by the newly-installed barrier. A middle-aged East Berlin couple, having only learned of the night's developments at 9.00 that morning, went down to see for themselves. Spotting a stretch of wire barrier that was still incomplete and, for the moment, unguarded, the man said to his wife, '*Hop oder top*' ('Now or never') and across they went to find their way to Marienfelde.

Others did the same, some after carefully reconnoitering the border barrier for weak spots, some on impulse when overcome by the implications of what they saw. A Vopo, the first of several to come through in the following days, came across just before noon. A Volkswagen came crashing through, the first of a number of vehicles to make the attempt – some successfully, some not. Some East Berliners jumped into the Teltow Canal which marked part of the East–West boundary and swam to the far side, where waiting West Berliners helped them out of the water. Among them was a young couple with their three-year-old son strapped to his father's back. The border guards weren't yet shooting at escapers, but each believed he was risking his life. As the hours passed, as more and more barbed wire was strung, it became increasingly difficult to get through. But during the first few days of Berlin's new era, an East German or East Berliner determined enough, daring enough, knowledgeable enough and capable of making a thorough tour of the border could have found a way through to the West, and not necessarily by swimming a canal. Between dawn and dusk of the first day, 800 refugees checked in at Marienfelde.

However, most people, and especially those from the East German hinterlands, had no idea that it was still possible to get out. The easiest routes, the ones which had earlier been most commonly used for crossing the border, were now sealed. At midday, Alexanderplatz, at the heart of East Berlin, began taking on a surrealistic aspect no less nightmarish than the scene Richard Smyser had witnessed in the Friedrichstrasse railway station the night before. People shuffled back and forth through the square, some clutching small suitcases, some with small cardboard cartons tied with string, going nowhere, sometimes stopping to look off into the distance, as if expecting a reprieve or a saviour. One man, apparently recognizing that I was not one of their number, approached and started to say something to me, but stopped short and turned quickly away, perhaps suspecting me of being a police spy.

Some people were trudging around the perimeters of the square as if actually going somewhere. Some just squatted forlornly on their cases or cartons. Like the frustrated travellers at the Friedrichstrasse station, they had learned too late of the border closing – or hadn't believed what they had heard – and had left home for East Berlin in order to cross into West Berlin. Now they had to come to terms with the fact that Marienfelde was as much beyond their reach as Mars. They had no place to go but the homes they had forsaken, perhaps to face the consequences if their attempt to 'Flee the Republic' had come to the attention of the local police.

The East German authorities were, in the meantime, relieved that the operation was proceeding as planned, with no sign of either Allied interference or serious repercussions in the streets of East Berlin. But there was a long way still to go before the operation could be deemed a success. The West was certain to make some kind of protest, whatever form that might take. Remaining gaps in the border were still to be closed. There was more barbed wire to string, more embankments of rubble to bulldoze up where such barriers would prove more suitable.

As Sunday wore on, more and more police and troops and Communist militiamen were bussed to the border area, many from outside Berlin, to take part in the operation. No hitches were reported. But it remained to be seen what the workers of East Berlin, people like those who had rioted against the government eight years earlier, would do when they gathered at their jobs the next morning and could co-ordinate their reaction. An East German army officer who later fled to the West said that, though the deployment of Soviet and East German army divisions around Berlin was meant to discourage Allied countermeasures, they were primarily positioned to deal with the greater danger of popular uprisings, if any occurred.

East German radio was now broadcasting regular reports, not about barbed wire being drawn across the middle of Berlin, but about unspecified 'measures' being implemented to protect the Socialist Fatherland by blocking off the 'slave traders', 'kidnappers', and 'currency swindlers'. A single city, a single people was being monumentally split in two, but radio broadcasts in the East sought to belittle the significance of that aspect of the event by announcing repeatedly that the controls being introduced were of the kind 'customary along the border of any sovereign state'.

Such announcements, and vivid accounts by RIAS and *Sender Freies Berlin* of the border proceedings, attracted still more people to the eastern as well as the western approaches to the border. Some East Berliners complained heatedly when stopped by Vopos from getting within a block of the barbed wire as it was being strung and reinforced. In one case, a Vopo beat up a man who insisted the authorities had no right to divide Berlin in that way. Another Vopo, sickened by the sight of such brutality, found a gap in the barbed wire soon afterwards, and went West.

But, for the most part, unless physically provoked, the East Berlin police refrained from assaulting protesters, or even arguing with them. They had been instructed to be firm but unprovocative. East German leaders remained haunted by visions of a violent reaction from the people they were fencing in. They had been told by the Russians that no such reaction would be tolerated, that Russian forces would move in to deal with riots if necessary, before they could spread, even if it meant that this elaborate display of East German sovereignty in East Berlin would be sacrificed by their intervention.

Where the situation did threaten to explode into violence, Vopo reinforcements, held in reserve in strategic locations in the city, were rushed in to disperse the crowds – gently if possible, roughly if not. When a group of youths refused to back off when ordered, shouted condemnation of the East German regime and demanded their usual access to West Berlin, tear gas grenades and smoke bombs were thrown to scatter them. In some places, the police waded in with nightsticks. But, though their presence was an intimidating factor, T-34 and T-54 tanks of the *Volksarmee*, held in reserve on sidestreets near potential trouble spots, were not needed to maintain order. East Berliners vividly recalled how ruthlessly the 1953 uprising had been quashed and how the West had merely looked on as it happened.

Expecting the security forces to come under popular pressure, operation co-ordinators instructed officers of the Communist youth organization to organize morale-boosting exercises. By early afternoon, the guards at the border and the troops and police held in reserve were receiving cheering visits from pink-cheeked, flower-bearing, blue-shirted boys and girls of the Free German Youth, who thanked them and praised the work they were doing on behalf of the peace-loving citizens of the German workers' and farmers' state.

In West Berlin, Mayor Brandt was emerging from the numbing shock of what he had seen at the border and the implications of what was happening. Now furious, he called a special session of the West Berlin Chamber of Deputies to condemn the Communist action. He told the deputies, 'The concrete posts which now split our city have been driven into . . . the living organism of Berlin.' Brandt said the people of Berlin expected the western powers, from whom nothing had yet been heard, to take 'energetic steps' in response.

But there was more anguish and desperation than substance to what he was saying. The energetic steps of which he spoke would have been mere gestures – sending Allied patrols to the sector border as he had urged the commandants to do and vigorous Allied protests to the Russians and the Warsaw Pact countries. He later noted bitterly, 'Twenty hours elapsed before the military patrols I had requested appeared on the city's internal border . . . Seventy-two hours elapsed before a protest – couched in terms that were little more than routine – was lodged in Moscow.'

But neither Brandt nor the western commandants had any

suggestions to offer for action that would produce any significant change in the situation. The barbed wire, the armed East German troops and police, would still be there. Crowds of West Berlin demonstrators, continuing to grow in front of the wire, did, however, offer a few suggestions. 'Hang Ulbricht!' they shouted, 'Open the border!' 'Ivan go home!' They sang the West German national anthem, and then sang it again, and they shouted slogans: 'There is only one Germany! There is only one Berlin!'

At one point, a group of West Berlin youths tore open a gap in the barbed wire and called out to East Berliners who had managed to get close and were watching from the other side to hurry through, but the youths were quickly driven back by Vopos who advanced on them, some with fixed bayonets, others with their truncheons drawn. At another place along the border, a Vopo was beaten up before others could come to his rescue and before West Berlin police could push back his assaulters.

When a crowd of enraged demonstrators surged toward the Brandenburg Gate and appeared to be threatening to march into East Berlin, East German water-cannon vehicles moved into position, unleashed high pressure jets on the would-be invaders and drove them back. When the vehicles and the Vopos at the gate were then bombarded with stones, steel-helmeted East German troops clutching their rifles moved forward and West Berlin police were able to coax the demonstrators back down the street and out of trouble.

The West Berlin police were particularly worried about the two Soviet soldiers ceremonially guarding the Soviet War Memorial in the British Sector, a few hundred yards into West Berlin from the Brandenburg Gate. Those soldiers would have been quickly overwhelmed if rushed by the mob, and the demonstrators jeering at them were growing increasingly abusive. The mere sight of Russian uniforms on West Berlin territory, and of the monument's two Second World War Russian tanks – said to be the first to have entered Berlin when the Russians overran the city in 1945 – infuriated the demonstrators. Police reinforcements were hurriedly rushed in to block any move against the monument.

In Washington, Berlin Task Force duty officer John Ausland had reached the State Department at around 5.00 a.m. (11.00 a.m. Berlin time). Reviewing the available reports from Berlin, he realized that the Task Force was about to earn its keep. There was work to be done. Acting Task Force director Martin Hillenbrand was away on vacation and incommunicado on an island off Virginia. Task Force members Pete Day and David Klein were also away. Their vacations had been arranged when it had been believed that the Berlin crunch was not likely to come until the autumn.

Ausland contacted Colonel Showalter who hurried right over. When he got there, he put a call through to United States military headquarters in Europe, outside Paris, but the duty officer there knew only what was being reported about the Berlin situation by the wire services. This was ten hours after the East German operation had begun! It was later learned that senior United States diplomats in Bonn had been completely in the dark until later that day, when they had returned from an embassy-sponsored Little League baseball game and turned on the radio. The duty officer at the American Embassy in the West German capital had seen dispatches from the Berlin Mission arriving at the message centre, had marked them 'noted', and had not bothered to contact anyone or extract further details from Berlin. He was subsequently punished for this incomprehensible over-sight by being relieved of the onorous task of ever again having to serve as night or weekend duty officer!

At 6.00 a.m. in Washington, things looked serious enough for a senior State Department official to be alerted. Ausland tried to reach Foy Kohler by telephone, but got no answer. He felt that he didn't yet have enough solid information to rouse Secretary of State Rusk at that time of day. But a White House duty officer who had been monitoring the news agency reports telephoned the Task Force office to find out if Ausland could provide an update on the situation. He said, 'We need something for Salinger' (the presidential press officer), in case the President wanted to issue a statement when he woke up in Hyannisport and was alerted to developments. Ausland drafted some points the President might consider. They included the fact that, as far as reports indicated, what the Communists were doing was confined to East Berlin. The Warsaw Pact declaration had given assurances that the access routes would not be affected. Much as what was happening might be deplored, it was not something about which, according to declared policy, the United States was prepared to take military action.

Shortly after 7.00 a.m., having delivered his wife to the airport, Frank Cash arrived at State. Ausland had been trying without success to find the file with a contingency plan for dealing with the latest Berlin developments. When Frank Cash arrived, he was able to locate the file. There turned out to be nothing in it at all relevant to the situation that had arisen. All the planning in

Washington had been directed toward coping with other contingencies – a Communist move against the access routes and an East
German uprising in the event of a refugee clamp-down. Despite
weeks of gradually escalating tension, despite streamlined procedures for consultations between government departments and
between the Allies, the Berlin Task Force hadn't yet got around
to contemplating more far-fetched possibilities – like the lowering
of the Iron Curtain in the middle of Berlin. There was no plan for
doing something about it and no plan for doing nothing. Later,
Kennedy would complain to a Task Force officer, 'Why, with all
those plans, do you never have one for what happens?'

At the time, official communications between Washington and the
American Mission in Berlin took forever. Officers were required
to use only secure telephone lines. The process for doing so was
absurdly complicated, involving specialized equipment that was
not readily accessible. So no direct voice contact had been made.
With reporters in Berlin still out covering their story, press
accounts of what was going on were still sketchy and inconclusive.
Embarrassingly, the most detailed early morning report on
developments in Berlin reached the State Department through an
unofficial channel – Lothar Loewe, a West Berlin correspondent
based in Washington. A diligent and personable reporter, Loewe
had established close personal contacts with some State Department officials. When he heard a radio report of trouble on the
sector borders, he checked with the State Department crisis centre
but was told they didn't know all that much. He then did what State
Department officials were not authorized to do. He telephoned
West Berlin on an ordinary commercial line and reached Albert
Hemsing, the press officer at the American Mission, who gave him
a run-down on the situation as far as he knew it. Loewe also
telephoned journalist colleagues in Berlin and got a detailed report
from them as well. He then went to the State Department to pass
on his information to people at the Task Force.

'Where did you get your facts?' they asked suspiciously.

'It was simple,' he replied. 'I called Al Hemsing. Why didn't
you?'

'We have to go through channels,' they explained limply.

As more information became available, Ausland again tried to
get through to Foy Kohler on the telephone and finally was able
to reach him. Though he had also heard radio news reports of the
Berlin developments, unlike those who were working up a head
of emotional steam, Kohler was not overly alarmed. Apprised of

what the Task Force was up to, which was not much more than trying to gather information, Kohler said that Cash and Ausland appeared to have the situation well in hand and that he, therefore, would not be coming in.

After conferring subsequently with Rusk on the telephone, Kohler did, however, get in, just before 10.00 a.m. Rusk also arrived then to take charge. Kohler was first brought up to date on developments by Cash and Ausland and then went to Rusk's office to discuss the situation. It was decided that it was time finally to contact Kennedy, who presumably had not yet been alerted since there had been no calls for information from Hyannisport, and no further contact with the White House duty officer since 6.00 a.m. Before calling the President, Rusk wanted to confer with the American Mission in Berlin. Not to waste time, he had Kohler disregard the rule on security in such matters and had him put through a call on an open line. There wasn't much that would be said that could be of use to the Communists, who were presumed to be tapping the telephone line as it ran through East Germany.

Allan Lightner in Berlin took the call from Kohler and filled him in on the latest developments at the border and on the proceedings at the commandants meeting. He reported that the commandants had decided to issue an open protest to the Soviets. After conferring with Rusk, Kohler said no. Though the Americans in Berlin had worked hard to persuade their reluctant British and French counterparts to agree to issuing the protest, they were ordered to make no statement whatsoever. The situation was deemed too serious to be left to the diplomats and generals in the field. Whatever official comment was to be made would come, in due course, from Washington. Having long been irritated by insinuations from their American colleagues in Berlin that they were too weak-kneed to face up to the Russians, personnel at the British Mission were not overly distressed at seeing them stamped on from above.

Barred from issuing a protest on the spot, officials at the American mission waited with great anticipation for the protest to come from Washington. As they waited, a sense of frustration set in, nourished by the conviction that Washington could not grasp what was at stake. Howard Trivers, political officer at the Berlin Mission at the time, complained, 'It was exceedingly difficult to make the Kennedy administration see beyond its abstract preconceptions and come to understand the actual situation in West Berlin.' His deputy, George Muller, said, 'Washington, the President, the administration didn't know or didn't want to know that there were many residual threads that wove all Berlin together.' Richard Smyser said that Washington 'didn't understand that what was happening in East Berlin would affect the vitality of West Berlin.'

The White House, on the other hand, remained convinced that personnel at the Mission were afflicted by a disorienting disease known as 'Berlinitis', the prime symptom of which was an unshakable belief that Berlin was the centre of the universe and that each incident there, no matter how commonplace in the greater scheme of things, was earthshaking. Even the American Embassy in Bonn, to which the Mission was responsible in the chain of command, didn't completely trust the judgment of Mission officers, who were believed to be supersensitive to every move the Russians made. Martin Hillenbrand, who had himself earlier been an official at the Berlin Mission, later observed, 'We always noted that when we sent people to Berlin, they became Berliners by adoption and adopted the psychological atmosphere of Berlin. They did not have the view that Washington had in a nuclear age.'

Members of the Berlin Mafia in Washington shared the disquiet of the Berlin Mission. But those in the higher councils of state, notably Rusk, displayed no sense of urgency about responding to what the reports he received said the Communists were up to. Upon taking office in January, John Kennedy had named the low-keyed Rusk to be his Secretary of State because he really wanted to do the job himself. He and the bright young advisers he had brought with him to the White House were confident that they knew pretty well how to deal with international questions in such a way as to protect America's basic interests while keeping the world at peace. Unlike Dean Acheson and John Foster Dulles, his forceful, policy-pushing predecessors at the State Department, Rusk had been made to understand that his job was merely to run the State Department bureaucracy efficiently and carry out White House instructions on policy.

As the Berlin crisis developed, Kennedy regularly consulted Rusk, who had wide experience in international affairs and whose judgment he valued. But hungry for fresh ideas which might point the way out of the crisis, he sometimes also conferred with lower-level experts at State, telephoning them out of the blue without Rusk even knowing about it or being told the conclusions drawn from such exchanges. Whatever his feelings about Kennedy's *modus operandi*, Rusk, a mild-mannered, unassuming professional with a keen understanding of both how to administer foreign policy and keep his advice to himself when it wasn't wanted, had been content to work according to the Kennedy ground rules.

But thus hamstrung, the Secretary of State could only wait for instructions from the President at Hyannisport on the course to follow as the Berlin signals began flashing that Sunday morning. With those signals indicating that western interests were not under threat, Kennedy had been shielded by his solicitous aides from unnecessary bother when he awoke that morning. As much as possible, the President's weekends away from Washington were meant to be brief escapes from presidential pressures. Kennedy had gone off with his family to 10.00 a.m. mass at the Church of St Francis Xavier in Hyannisport. (It was already 4.00 in the afternoon in divided Berlin.) He then returned to his Hyannisport home to change his clothes for a relaxing cruise on Nantucket Sound aboard *The Marlin*, his father's yacht.

At about the time *The Marlin* was setting off from shore, details of the trouble in Berlin were finally being relayed from Washington to the presidential message centre set up by the Signal Corps in the basement of Hyannisport's Yachtsman Hotel. When it was received, a messenger was dispatched to deliver it to the President's military aide, Brigadier General Chester Clifton, who was acting as presidential on-shore duty officer while the President was at sea.

Clifton opened the sealed envelope in which the report came, read the contents and contacted the secret service agent aboard *The Marlin* by walkie-talkie. The President, the agent was told, had to return to shore at once. A message had been received from Washington which required his immediate attention. Kennedy was informed, and he ordered *The Marlin* to turn back to shore. (It seems remarkable that the President had not been alerted earlier. It remains possible that he had been informed, but that the seriousness of the situation had not been fully appreciated – not something the White House would have wanted publicized.)

The news from Berlin infuriated Kennedy – but not because of the action the Communists were taking. That struck him as ugly and despicable, but they had been expected to do something about the refugees. What angered him was the realization that all the effort he had personally ordered to be put into forecasting what the Communists would do, and into preparing an appropriate response, had been in vain. To McGeorge Bundy he would complain on the phone later in the day, 'Why didn't we know?'

But first he telephoned Dean Rusk in Washington for a more comprehensive picture of the situation than the comparatively brief telex message could provide. He wanted to know if there were any signs that the access routes were being blocked and whether West Berlin was in any way affected. He was relieved to hear that the answer to both was no. Rusk said there was no sign of panic in West Berlin but, like Brandt and the Russians, he felt there remained a danger of an uprising by people in the East which might spill over into the West, and which could lead to Soviet military intercession with unpredictable consequences.

However, he said that from all reports the situation could not be considered critical – certainly not yet. There was no need for the President to rush back to Washington. 'Time was not of the essence,' Rusk said later. 'We had previously discussed the refugee problem and were sure the Russians and East Germans would have to plug that hole. But they were not moving against West Berlin.' As Kennedy had made clear, the United States was prepared to go to war to keep the access routes open or defend the freedom of West Berlin. What might or might not occur in East Berlin, no matter how heavy-handed and deplorable, had never been thought of as a possible *casus belli*. The point of greatest significance for the President at that moment was that a Communist internal security operation, which is what this seemed to be, in no way heightened the threat of nuclear confrontation with which the President had been living since his encounter with Khrushchev in Vienna.

Some administration figures made no effort to disguise their absence of concern and their relief that it was nothing worse. When told by Ausland that morning, 'People are going to ask what we're going to do about this,' Assistant Secretary of State Kohler had replied, 'Let's not worry about it. That refugee flow was getting out of hand.' According to McGeorge Bundy, Kennedy himself did not feel a sense of relief, more a 'sense of irritation, accompanied by an awareness that this was not the issue on which we had decided we would have had to take a forceful stand.'

It was, nevertheless, an illegal act, unilaterally violating four-power agreements. Even if no forceful response was contemplated, the United States, as primary 'protecting power' in West Berlin, was obliged to issue a public condemnation. Rusk read Kennedy a prepared statement observing that the East German authorities, in a confession of failure of the Communist system, had denied their own people access to West Berlin. Satisfied that the statement did nothing to complicate or aggravate a situation that was still in the making, the President gave his approval and it was duly released to the press:

. . . Available information indicates that measures taken thus far are aimed at residents of East Berlin and East Germany and not at the Allied position in West Berlin or access thereto. However limitation on travel within Berlin is a violation of the four-power status of Berlin and a flagrant violation of the right of free circulation throughout the city . . . These violations of existing agreements will be the subject of vigorous protest through appropriate channels.

It was thought by Kennedy and Rusk that this statement soberly and responsibly dealt with the situation, at least until the dust settled. The United States registered its unqualified disapproval of the Communist action but, in planning to protest 'through appropriate channels', it was signalling Moscow that, in the volatile situation which prevailed, no hasty, scatterbrained overreaction was being contemplated.

The statement was also calculated to avoid encouraging an East German uprising. At the time of the 1956 Hungarian rebellion against the Russians, the United States had, with some justification, been accused of encouraging the rebels with praise for their hunger for freedom while never intending to come to the aid of Hungarians who dared to take to the streets against Russian tanks. Nothing was to be said this time that might be taken as promoting civil disturbances in East Berlin.

Besides, no one yet imagined that splitting the city would turn out to be the high-water mark of Soviet action. The Russians were still expected to trigger the real confrontation with their threatened move against the access routes. It was thought that civil disturbances in East Berlin could goad them into moving in that direction sooner than they had intended, and before America's military build-up in Europe had got into full stride. All chances of negotiating an end to the Berlin squabble from strength would be undermined.

Kennedy and Rusk agreed that British Foreign Secretary Lord Home was right to have warned that panic pronouncements could prove self-fulfilling. No crisis atmosphere was to be nurtured. The President advised Rusk not to cancel his plans to go to a baseball game that afternoon. He himself was going sailing again. Everything was to appear perfectly calm and controlled.

Ironically, as the Communists moved ahead with settling their Berlin problem their own way, people in Washington were reading in their Sunday newspapers reports which had been written earlier about Kennedy planning a major 'peace offensive' to rally support around the world by dramatizing the Soviet threat to peace in Berlin and its foot-dragging on arms control. It was reported that the President might make an appearance at the United Nations General Assembly in September to kick off that campaign. Whatever preparations had been going on at the White House for that appearance would have to be modified in the light of the campaign the Communists had already kicked off in the streets of Berlin.

Dean Rusk's public statement may have reassured the Russians that the Americans were not going to overreact, but it stunned West Berliners. Was that all their protectors were going to do? There were armed Communist troops on the sector border. East German machine-guns were trained west. The city was being cut in two. Ulbricht was making fools of the Americans. And all the United States was going to do was 'protest through appropriate channels'!

General Watson was keeping a close watch on developments. But his primary concern at that moment was the military situation – in particular, the deployment of Soviet forces around Berlin. Soviet troops stationed at Teltow, just south of Berlin, were actually closer to his headquarters than the troubled sector border. With things in flux and Soviet intentions uncertain, among the questions to which Watson had to give priority consideration was whether his garrison, his command post, the entire American establishment in Berlin, would be overrun if the situation escalated. Compared to that, barbed wire being strung on the Soviet side of the sector border didn't seem to amount to much.

In Britain, Prime Minister Macmillan was on a hunting holiday in the north of England and didn't intend to break it off. Though officers of the American Berlin Mission agonized over the unruffled response from Kennedy and Rusk, Macmillan believed the situation, while not yet dangerous, could turn so, 'partly because the Americans have got very excited.' He was convinced the best approach was to stress the importance of negotiations. The possibility of western counter-measures did not seem credible to the British leader, nor to the London *Times*, where an editorial writer was pounding out his comment on the situation for Monday morning's edition: 'All that the West can do at the moment is to protest against this further infringement of the Berlin agreements and the freedom of East Germans.' With Foreign Secretary Lord Home vacationing in Scotland, the task of co-ordinating the British reaction was left to the Prime Minister's secretary, Philip de Zulueta. 'I suppose,' Macmillan wrote in his private journal, 'the newspapers will criticize us for being on holiday during the Berlin crisis, but actually this is nonsense.'

Had there been any criticism of de Gaulle's absence from Paris at the time, he would not even have deigned to recognize it. The French President was at his country home at Colombey-les-Deux-Eglises, maintaining a haughty seclusion. All senior officials and just about everybody else at the French foreign ministry were also away on their annual vacations – the Quai D'Orsay, like much of the rest of Paris, was pretty much closed down for August. In Bonn, Chancellor Adenauer, who had returned from his summer holiday that morning, issued a strong condemnation of the border closure but, like the Americans, had little to suggest.

In Washington that Sunday afternoon, with Rusk having gone to his baseball game and Kohler having gone home, Berlin Task Force members decided there wasn't much they could still do that day. They fixed a time for a meeting for the morning, and went home also. Returning from vacation and expecting to see people at work, Pete Day hurried over to State, but finding no one else in the Task Force suite, he went home too.

Around 3.00 p.m., James O'Donnell received a telephone call at his Washington apartment from journalist Marguerite Higgins, who was an old friend and, like O'Donnell, a charter member of the Berlin Mafia. Higgins was calling on another matter, but she pointed out that her neighbour – in Chatham, Massachusetts – was General Clay whom they had both known when they were covering the Berlin blockade. She said she was going to talk to Clay about the Berlin situation and asked O'Donnell what Washington was doing about it. O'Donnell, who had called in at the State Department earlier and talked with colleagues there, told her what he knew.

Not long afterwards, after Higgins had called on him, Clay also telephoned O'Donnell for an update. O'Donnell told him the State Department line was basically to lie low and do nothing because there was nothing the United States could do in East Berlin. Clay, who retained a feeling of special responsibility for Berlin, was greatly disturbed by this attitude. He said that he might volunteer to go back to Berlin on behalf of the American government to try to salvage the situation.

O'Donnell suggested that if he really meant it, he should get in touch with Attorney General Robert Kennedy, the President's brother, who had greater access to the President than anyone else in Washington. Clay replied that, though he had great respect for

John Kennedy, he couldn't abide his brother. O'Donnell said that Marguerite Higgins was nevertheless a good friend of the Attorney General, which made him the best available channel for Clay to get a message through quickly to the White House. Clay discussed the matter with Higgins and she called Robert Kennedy, who passed word on to the President. But there it stood for the moment, although O'Donnell passed word along to German correspondent Lothar Loewe, who had proved so useful an informant that morning, that Clay would be volunteering to go to Berlin. He also told German journalist Peter Boenisch, who telephoned him from Berlin that night. He hoped the news would make West Berliners feel that they weren't being abandoned by the Americans. But Loewe was too convinced at the time that the White House crowd 'was a bunch of amateurs' who couldn't grasp the situation. And while Boenisch passed word along to Willy Brandt's adviser and friend Egon Bahr, it did not go further than him. The story, which was premature anyway, was therefore stillborn.

As 13 August drew to a close, with the barbed-wire barrier already virtually complete and work to fill remaining gaps continuing under floodlights, the East German Communists and the Russians had good reason to be satisfied. Little by little, protesters on both sides of the border were detaching themselves from the clusters of demonstrators and trudging home. But the operation was still in its early stages. There was much more to come. Would the Americans, who had promised to remain firm in defence of their rights in Berlin, react on Monday with the same restraint they had displayed on Sunday? Still to be seen and dealt with would be the reaction of East Berlin workers when they gathered at their factories and construction sites in the morning, exchanged views and shared feelings.

In the meantime, a lot of East Berliners had to quickly rethink their personal situations. The *grenzängers* were now out of work. Dropping in with a colleague at the Adlon Hotel in the East that night to refresh himself at the bar after a long, hard day's work, Reuters man Kellett-Long was greeted by the doorman, which was interesting because there hadn't been a doorman there since the war. It became even more interesting when Kellett-Long recognized the doorman as the man who, until the previous day, had been doorman at the Hotel Am Zoo on the Ku'damm in West Berlin. He was still wearing the same cap, but with the name of the West Berlin hotel torn from above the brim. Here was one commuter who had wasted no time relocating.

10

Postmortem

AFTER THE FACT, it seemed astounding that the Allies did not know, or even suspect, that the Communists would plant a virtually impenetrable divide down the middle of Berlin to stop the refugees. How could they have failed to learn about so huge a project, requiring such extensive and elaborate preparation? Once Ulbricht had been given permission to proceed at the Moscow Warsaw Pact meeting during the first days of August, Honecker had installed himself and his staff at police headquarters in East Berlin from which he was in 'constant contact' with the commanding officers and staffs of the armed forces, district committees of the SED, central government departments, and the municipal councils of the major cities.

Few of the officials with whom Honecker dealt were told what exactly his intentions were when he gave orders and made requests. Members of the Central Committee of the SED did not have to explain themselves. But it must have been apparent to many that he was engaged in. a major undertaking, involving a large-scale security operation, and not a few must have had a pretty good suspicion of what was about to take place. Berlin was a city of spies, divided loyalties and rumours. People were passing back and forth all the time. It was a situation in which confidentiality might reasonably have been considered impossible to maintain. Yet the Allies were caught totally by surprise.

Balancing too long on the edge of a crisis in which another party is prime mover generates a kind of mental torpor. The options are reviewed and analysed over and over again until they seem to have only a paper reality, remote from here and now. After a while, dramatic factors – threats of nuclear conflagration, troops geared up for armed clashes in the middle of a metropolis – lose their capacity to generate new ideas. The unrelenting sameness of a tense and protracted situation is stupefying.

So it was with Berlin as the climax approached. A mind-fix developed, blunting the imaginations of western intelligence personnel. They knew that their vital concern must be the access routes, because unless those were kept open, West Berlin was in trouble, and possibly lost. So the appropriate contingency plans were devised and worked over. If the Russians did such-and-such to interfere with those routes, the Allies would respond in such-and-such a way. If the East Germans presumed to do this-and-that on the routes, the Allies would react with that-and-this. A whole catalogue of responses had been devised to cope with everything from petty harassment to a full Communist blockade.

But in examining Ulbricht's options for dealing with the refugee problem, which was a totally different issue, the analysts had developed tunnel vision. All they could imagine him doing was slapping tight controls on traffic between Communist East Germany and Communist East Berlin, in effect turning *all* of Berlin rather than just West Berlin into a political island. Such a move would not affect Berlin's four-power status, so it was nothing to get excited about.

At the British Mission, Bernard Ledwidge had been told by well-informed Norwegian colleagues based in West Berlin that the East Germans had planned instead to seal off the Soviet Sector from West Berlin the previous weekend, and that the operation had been cancelled at the last minute. But that had seemed like just one more rumour to add to the profusion of rumours in circulation – which, indeed, it was, because at the time Honecker had just received the go-ahead and had a lot of preparatory work yet to do on his massive assignment.

Gaston Koblentz, a resourceful newsman with a habit which infuriated his colleagues of wandering about that city of suspense with a knowing grin, was not prepared to dismiss the idea so readily. He reported in the *New York Herald Tribune* that Ulbricht had been asking Khrushchev to close the border between East and West Berlin – and without delay. But even if that was more than just another rumour, it didn't mean much. Ulbricht wanted the Russians to do a lot of things for him, including handing him all of Berlin on a plate. Flora Lewis reflected prevailing thought in the journalistic as well as diplomatic and intelligence fraternities in West Berlin when she reported to the *Washington Post*, 'No one here expects an effort to shut off the traffic across Berlin at this point.'

That the Russians might permit the East German Communists to split the city in two had, in fact, not been completely overlooked by Allied intelligence, and particularly not by the American Berlin Watch Committee. The job of that standing group, made up of United States Army, CIA and State Department intelligence analysts in Berlin, was to give the first alert in case of trouble brewing. It had examined and discussed the possibility of a move in the middle of Berlin to choke off the refugee outflow, but had dismissed it as too far-fetched to deserve serious attention. It knew something was going to happen 'pretty darn soon', but was not able to say what exactly it would be with any firm conviction.

When John Mapother, an intelligence officer who had been dealing with the Berlin situation in Washington since 1958, was transferred to the city at the end of July, he questioned people there who could have been expected to know whether it was possible for the Communists to throw a cordon around West Berlin rather than around the perimeter of the entire city. 'The answers I got,' he said, 'persuaded me that it would be too much of a problem. There were too many doors and windows to be sealed. There were buildings that opened in East Berlin on one side and in West Berlin on the other side. The conception of sealing the city down the middle was one that people in the know found too difficult to take on board and see as realistic.'

Later, there would be countless people who said they had given advance warning that the Communists would quarantine West Berlin to stop the refugees. Such people were as easy to run across afterwards as they had been scarce on the ground before. There was a flamboyant American newspaper correspondent who had arrived in town the week before and who said later that he had known it would happen but hadn't reported it to his newspaper because he would have endangered the life of the East German source of his information. Martin Hillenbrand, who was directing the operations of the Berlin Task Force, said if there were westerners who knew in advance, 'they must have squirreled that information away because it didn't reach Washington'.

A report in the *New York Herald Tribune* two weeks after the border-closing operation began said that the Communist plan had been known to the Allies since 1958 and had been labelled 'Operation Chinese Wall' by American and West German intelligence agents. The newspaper account said an East German official who had defected to the West had brought with him a document describing the plan – which called first for a barbed-wire barrier to be built on the sector borders, then for its replacement by a cement block fence, and finally for the erection of concrete 'palisades'. It was said that the plan had been reported to United States intelligence officers by Brandt. However, the West Berlin mayor denied that he had any suspicion whatever before 13 August that the East Germans might divide the city. He believed the East Germans would consider it sufficient to introduce 'very severe, very strict controls on travel between the East and West sectors – on every car, every train, maybe introduce passport controls – and tighten controls between East Germany and East Berlin.'

A more thorough partition of the city was within the realm of possibility and discussed as such. It is the job of intelligence analysts to examine all possible options, including those which border on fantasy, but to concentrate on those which appear credible. Splitting the city was not considered credible. John Mapother said, 'There was nothing precise on which we could have acted, nothing you could take into a three-power meeting and persuade everybody that there had to be a unified Allied plan for dealing with it. You'd be asked, "What's your source?" and get cut to ribbons bureaucratically.'

In view of the improbability of what happened, the few people – one CIA operative in Berlin at the time says he knew only two – who did speak up were thought to be fantasists, or self-seeking buncombe artists (of whom Berlin had more than its fair share), or they had their suggestions dismissed as just more of the speculation being churned out by the rumour mill. The senior CIA officer there thought Ulbricht would be committing political suicide if he tried to seal off East Berlin from West Berlin. Others believed he was determined to take control of all of Berlin in due course and wasn't about to settle for only the half of it that was his already.

One man who was convinced the Communists would divide the city, and said so with a passion, was Stephen Koczak at the Berlin Mission. But Koczak was considered, even by other hardliners among his colleagues, to be too obsessed with the Communist menace for his reports on what was likely to happen to be given the attention they later turned out to have deserved. One Mission member who served with him said Koczak had 'a brilliant mind which produced brilliant ideas but because he was thought to feel so strongly about issues generally, other minds closed against his suggestions. When he came up with an original idea, people were as likely as not to think, "Oh, Steve's got one of his notions." ' Koczak's credibility at the time was also damaged by his seriously strained relations with the man whose deputy he was, Thomas Donovan, chief of the Mission's Eastern Affairs Section. Donovan believed a lot of people were getting far too excited by Soviet threats. It was a case of insurmountable personality and policy clashes between two men who were supposed to be working closely together. Both were soon to leave the foreign service, each soured by his Berlin experience.

Another man who declined to dismiss out of hand the idea of Berlin being split in two by the Communists was Colonel Ernest von Pawel, chief of the American Liaison Mission in East Germany. It seemed to him the most rational way for the Communists to deal with the refugee problem. Furthermore, after several years of duty in East Europe, it was his belief that, 'If you think a wall is the least likely option, then that is where I place my bet, because we've never outguessed the Soviets yet.' He pointed out that it would not be the first such wall the Germans had built – they had sealed off Warsaw's Jewish ghetto with a wall during the Second World War. But von Pawel had no evidence to back up the theory.

Nevertheless, there was good reason to take von Pawel's hypothesis and Koczak's conviction seriously, though it wasn't until after the event that tell-tale clues were easier to spot. The clamp-down on cross-border movement during the Evangelical Church Congress the previous month could now be seen as a dry run by the East German security authorities. The so-called *sputnik bahn*, an elevated railway line the Communists had tried to build at great expense in money and labour more than a year earlier, in an effort to provide East Germans in the area with extra public transport which skirted West Berlin, could now be recognized as long-range planning for splitting the city. Western intelligence had picked up reports that unusually large amounts of barbed wire and cement posts were being stockpiled in and near East Berlin. But the East Germans had been talking about major East Berlin construction projects. It was not unreasonable to believe that some effort was being made to launch those projects as a gesture towards refurbishing East Berlin's depressing image. Most of those who nevertheless remained suspicious assumed that the construction materials were being stacked not to split the city, but as part of the expected move to cordon East Berlin off from East Germany.

Dolchstoss (stab-in-the-back) rumours began circulating in West Berlin during the first few days after the barbed wire had been strung. It was suggested that the United States had known the Communist plans in advance, had even been tipped off by the Russians. That, it was suggested, accounted for the absence of any forceful American response. This story was initially spread by the Russians, who told German reporters there was no chance of war because Moscow had informed the Americans of what was coming. The Americans, they said, had understood that it was inevitable, that the refugee exodus had to be halted for the sake of peace and stability in Europe. Having been nonplussed by Washington's mild reaction, some Germans believed it.

Rumours spread that Khrushchev had himself briefed John McCloy about the operation when McCloy had visited him at Sochi two weeks earlier. It was said also that Marshal Koniev, when he held a reception for the chiefs of the Allied liaison missions to mark his arrival in East Germany a few days before the border-sealing operation, had tipped his hand by assuring them that whatever was about to happen would be a purely internal matter for East Germany.

Years later, when Walt Rostow's memoirs reported that Kennedy had told him prior to border operations that the East Germans might have to build a wall to stop the refugees, it was taken by diehards as further confirmation that the Americans had known beforehand. It explained why the President had responded so calmly and at such a leisurely pace. Some Germans remain convinced even today that a deal was made between the Americans and the Russians, that Berlin was sold down the river by its protectors, and that reunification of Germany was thereby made even more remote than it already was. The myth of American betrayal of Berlin may one day be revived to cast a shadow over relations between the United States and Germany.

Erich Honecker did an extraordinary job of organizing the sealing-off of West Berlin. Getting it done without his crash preparations being detected by the West, and with even remarkably few East Germans entrusted with the details until the troops and trucks were ordered to roll, was even more extraordinary. Sometime later, John Mapother got to know an East German army colonel, a defector, who had been commander of one of the troop units deployed on the border that Saturday night and Sunday morning. He said he had not been told exactly what was going to happen until 10.00 p.m. on Saturday night, two hours before the operation commenced.

It was a blitz action in the most daring and pugnacious German military traditions. According to General Maxwell Taylor, appointed by Kennedy to be his personal military adviser because of his reluctance to accept easy answers to tough problems, 'If someone had suggested [it] as a possible course of action to me, I think I would have said it was highly improbable . . . We later reviewed the intelligence that came in during the two weeks preceding [the operation] and found only fragments which have pointed to this event taking place. Movements of engineering material were reported. However, I still can't blame the intelligence people or those of us who had access to the intelligence for not anticipating [what happened].'

Nevertheless, Allied intelligence services did not come out of the affair with their reputations untarnished. They were the natural butt for criticism and ridicule. British correspondent Terence Prittie recalled that just before the border closure he was assured by a senior British intelligence officer in Berlin that 'the present crisis will end in anti-climax after the [West German] elections [in September] . . . This is naturally my own theory . . . but I have a maddening habit of being right on most occasions.'

Most curious was the failure of the West Germans to know what was going to happen. Their intelligence services were reputed to have had first-class espionage networks throughout East Germany. They were widely criticized for failing to forecast what the East Germans would do. General Reinhard Gehlen, the head of the *Bundesnachrichtendienst*, the West German federal intelligence service, insisted later that this was unfair because he had 'received and passed on reports of an imminent sealing of the sector boundary'.

If he did so, those reports were either lost in a bureaucratic shuffle or dismissed as humbug. In any case, West German officials did not pass such reports on to the Allies; nor did Gehlen's men, who had close links with their Allied counterparts, trouble to tip them off. Even among those who believed the Communists capable of the most cunning behaviour, only von Pawel and Koczak are known to have predicted developments more or less accurately, and they did so through logical deduction rather than because of evidence.

The only reasonable excuse for the intelligence failure was the fact that, in conception, the project could be dismissed as a logistical nightmare. But that underestimated the lengths to which the Communists were prepared to go to keep the German Democratic Republic from being bled dry.

Stragglers showed up at the Marienfelde refugee centre early Monday morning, some of them weeping, overcome by the trauma of their escape. Some had made their way across border wasteland flattened during the war which wouldn't be completely secured by the Vopos until later in the day. Several made their escape through cemeteries which straddled the sector boundaries and which also hadn't yet been fully wired off. Two young men made their way to East Berlin from the East German industrial city of Karl-Marx-Stadt and, finding the way to the West they had charted blocked, they stripped down, dived into the Teltow Canal and arrived dripping in West Berlin in nothing but their underpants. A couple with a young daughter crawled to West Berlin through a border-straddling drainage pipe. Some simply used wire cutters to break out in places where they thought they would not be spotted by guards or patrols. These belated escapers employed a mixture of ingenuity and recklessness in their desperation to find a route out. But this was the tail-end of the exodus. From then on, the numbers would dwindle sharply.

By dawn's early light it was clear that the Communists had made good their announcement that border-crossing points would be reduced to only thirteen. Through those thirteen, West Berliners, West Germans and foreigners were crossing from West to East and back again, after having their passports or identity documents examined, and after convincing the border guards that they were not bent on causing trouble and were not carrying subversive literature or contraband. But the only East Berliners and East Germans permitted to cross the other way through the Communist checkpoints were the rare few on official business for the East German authorities. They were not required by West Berlin police to answer any questions or go through any control procedures. There were no restrictions on the trickle of people coming West.

In the tense atmosphere which prevailed, it was uncertain how long foreigners in East Germany would be permitted the freedom of movement no longer enjoyed by East Germans. At the Reuters East Berlin office, Kellett-Long got a telephone call from a Soviet diplomat with whom he had become friendly. 'How are you?' the Russian asked.

'Pissed off,' Kellett-Long replied. 'I don't want to get stuck here.'

'How's Mary?'

'Like me – okay but apprehensive.'

'Tell her not to worry,' the Russian said. 'If worse comes to worst, we will fly her out through Prague.'

If his Russian friend had meant to reassure Kellett-Long, he was only partly successful. It meant that Mary would be safe, but worse might come to worst (war was considered a real possibility) and he might still be locked in there.

Foreigners living in West Berlin were also apprehensive, but we did not suffer the same sense of isolation. However, I found going East to size up the situation even by car, had become an intensely disagreeable experience – the barbed wire, the control posts manned by armed guards, their sub-machine-gun-toting back-ups in reserve not far away, the questioning about destination and purpose, all of this in the centre of one of the great cities of Europe. It triggered the queasy feeling of entering a prison camp.

To people there abruptly cut off from contact with loved ones, what had happened was a matter of profound grief. To those who had been habitual border-crossers – whether for work or pleasure – it was a tyrannical, disorienting intrusion in their lives. To those of us who were observers, transients, passers-by, it was grim and depressing.

To West Berliners as well as East Berliners, it was as if a glacier of a political ice age, having previously come to rest, had suddenly taken a surge forward, smothering what lay in its path. Even words took on a crushed, distorted aspect. A photographer positioning himself to take a picture of the barbed wire and armed guards from the eastern side was stopped by a Vopo. 'This is free Berlin,' he was told. 'Taking pictures here is forbidden.' It was impossible on the spot not to imagine the same sort of barrier being drawn across the middle of New York, and not to dismiss that vision as a frightful hallucination.

In *Passport to Pimlico*, a British movie made a good few years back, people were required to have their passports stamped as they went from one part of London to another. It was a delightful comedy, made hilarious by the absurdity of the notion. Being checked out by the armed guards in the middle of Berlin, being crisply ordered to drive on when I wanted to linger for a close look at what had been done to their side of the sector border, being eyed dolefully by people in clusters a hundred yards into East Berlin as if I had come from some fabled Babylon and would, unlike them, be permitted to return there when I wished, was also absurd. But rather than being hilarious, it was loathsome. It was impossible not to think that, despite their condemnations of fascism, the Communists of East Germany were the true heirs of Adolf Hitler.

To guard against the possibility of popular discontent spilling over into action, armed Vopos were posted in front of all major buildings, and particularly at the Soviet Embassy on Unter den Linden. On side streets near the border, troops were still held in reserve. Their rifles slung over their shoulders, they lined up for breakfast at field kitchens. Tanks, troop-carriers and armoured cars remained positioned in strategic locations, ready to roll if summoned. East Berliners walking by them looked the other way, as if refusing to acknowledge the humiliation they represented.

In an effort to dispel the bitterness felt even by the great number of East Germans who never intended to abandon their homes and jobs but who resented being locked in, East Berlin radio stations broadcast interviews with East Berliners who professed to be delighted with the events of the preceding day. One woman, bubbling with satisfaction, said she was enormously relieved that her young daughter was finally safe from the kidnappers who had been spiriting children away to the West. Another woman said she was grateful that the people of the German Democratic Republic, who had for so long endured the disruption to their lives caused by currency speculators and slave merchants in West Berlin, would no longer be exposed to those wicked elements.

No one in those interviews, or the commentaries that accompa nied them, mentioned barbed wire. Reference was made only to the *massnahmen* – the nameless 'measures' which were transforming the face of the city and life of its people. Not a word was said about Berlin being split in two. Though Vopos near the border had distributed leaflets detailing the new restrictions on travel, no one mentioned on radio in the East that an East Berliner who now tried to go West did so at the risk of his or her life.

There was no announcement that telephone communication between East and West Germany, maintained after phone links between East and West Berlin had been cut years before, had been severed just before dawn, along with postal links, leaving East Germans and East Berliners even more cut off from external contact. There was no analysis in depth of what would no longer be permitted, of how individuals would be affected and might react, of what might still be in store, or of the anxiety to be seen on the faces of people in the streets.

In its columns, *Neues Deutschland* stressed the advantages that had accrued to East Germans overnight: 'Families will now be protected from the enticements of slave traders, peoples' industrial and commercial enterprises will be protected from headhunters, the public order will be protected from criminals, the security of the nation will be protected from warmongers.' On the radio, Gerhardt Eisler confidently forecast that 'one day the red flag of the working class will fly over all of Germany', a comment which, when more widely reported, sent a shudder through West Berlin.

East Berliners who congregated as near to the wire as they were permitted – in some places they were still able to get close – appeared to share none of the relief and satisfaction of the people interviewed on East German radio. They looked on in solemn silence. Many came hoping to catch a glimpse of a relative on the other side of the border. Some of them were refugees who had previously made good their escape to the West but who feared that if they re-entered East Berlin to see kinfolk, even with their new West Berlin identity papers, they would not be permitted to leave again.

There were poignant sights to be seen that morning. An elderly woman broke into a broad smile as she spotted her son on the far side, in the West, and then almost instantly dissolved in uncontrollable weeping at the realization that they could come no nearer. A man in the West held up his wide-eyed, bewildered baby for his parents in the East to see and ridiculously make cooing noises at from too great a distance for the infant to notice. A young man and a young woman, separated by the wire, stood there looking at each other, both their faces masked by profound sadness, calling out things to each other, but too timid to do so loud enough for the other to hear. Others just looked at each other wordlessly.

A few of the Vopos on duty between them kept their eyes focused on the ground or on the far distance, seemingly distressed by this emotionally-charged atmosphere. Others, scanning the weepers, wavers and message-callers on their side of the wire for signs of trouble, seemed vigilant rather than perturbed. They needn't have worried. People standing in the East seemed thoroughly cowed and were easily dispersed when Vopo officers ordered their men to move them on.

But elsewhere in the East, there were still pockets of protest. More than once that day, western correspondents touring East Berlin were told by people that the Americans should tear down the barbed wire. 'Give the goatee [Ulbricht] twenty-four hours to remove it himself,' one man said. 'If he doesn't, then do the job for him.'

The Communists weren't worried about disgruntled or aggrieved individuals. Those who made too much of fuss were hustled away by the Vopos, but so much effort was required to maintain the overall security operation that the police couldn't yet be bothered to launch a systematic crack-down on complainers. That would soon come but, for the moment, attention away from the border was concentrated instead on the workers of East Berlin as they gathered at their work places that morning. That was where there could be trouble. Party activists in the factories and at the construction sites had been instructed to explain in great detail the benefits the people of the Socialist Fatherland would derive from the border 'measures'. Nevertheless, there was deep and widespread unease among the workers.

At lunchtime outside one factory not far from the city centre, some men in a crowd of sullen workers muttered bitterly about what was happening. 'This is no way to treat us,' one man complained, ignoring my presence though for all they knew I could easily have been a Communist informant. 'They didn't have to do it; we are not criminals,' another said. There were no explicit political complaints, but neither did any of those men speak out in defence of the 'measures'. (Meant as a euphemism, that word quickly became something else; it was mouthed with caustic emphasis, as if it were an insult to intelligence.) Mingling with the crowd of workers were two teenagers from the Free German Youth organization who, after a few minutes, went off to report to a Vopo officer nearby, who made notes, presumably for action to be taken later in the day when there would no longer be a group of malcontents gathered together to react when the police singled out the more outspoken ones – the potential counter-revolutionary ringleaders.

Press reports the following day would tell of the arrest of western agents who had tried to foment trouble by stirring discontent among the workers. It wouldn't be long before the people of East Berlin would learn that grumbling in public was a luxury it was now even wiser to do without than before. East Germans would soon have no need of the urgings of the West German Minister Ernst Lemmer to 'refrain from committing reckless acts' which might provoke Communist retribution. They had more potent warnings on their own side of the wire.

Four days earlier, on Thursday, driving out of East Berlin after vainly seeking confirmation from East German government spokesmen of reports that stiff anti-refugee action was imminent, I exchanged pleasantries with a Vopo on duty at the Brandenburg Gate. 'Where are you going?' he asked. I told him I was heading for a café on the Ku'damm for a cup of coffee. He smiled and joked, 'Got room for one more?' But on Monday, some thirty-six hours after the clamp-down had begun, I stopped to be cleared through the gate and that same Vopo, whose double-take indicated he recognized me, stiffly asked for my passport. He looked at it, handed it back, scanned the floor of the backseat of my car for any unauthorized passengers, saluted and briskly waved me on. No pleasantries this time. No smiles. Berlin had a new order, and it bit deep.

The Communists did not want to close the Brandenburg Gate. The gate, like most of the fine old architectural treasures of Berlin, was situated in East Berlin, just a little way in from the British sector. It was the single most recognizable symbol of Berlin and they were reluctant to be blamed for defacing it with barbed wire. But the crowds of angry West Berliners congregating on the far side of the gate were becoming increasingly unruly. If a few thousand of them tried to surge through those monumental arches into East Berlin, they might be uncontrollable. There was no point in taking chances. Things were proceeding too well.

On Monday afternoon, a troop of Vopos marched through the gate to form up shoulder-to-shoulder, still on East Berlin territory, but just west of that magnificent monument; behind them, armoured cars and water-cannon vehicles rolled into position; and behind them, the bales of barbed wire were brought forward. Like most of the rest of the border between the two parts of Berlin, the gate was now being sealed.

If the Communists thought that would disperse the demonstrators on the far side, they were mistaken. They gathered in front of the closed gate in ever larger numbers as the day wore on, despite instructions to the police from the West Berlin authorities to disperse all unauthorized demonstrations near the border. The vision of a clash between unarmed civilians and armed Vopos was a nightmare which seemed about to be transformed into bloody reality as the demonstrators began inching forward. Stones were thrown at the Communist guards, at East German armoured cars in front of the Gate, and at a Soviet bus which arrived for the regular changing of the guard at the Soviet war memorial. West

Berlin police reinforcements were rushed to the spot to press the crowd back, and the West Berlin authorities quickly issued a decree banning all demonstrations within a half-mile of the border.

The consequences of the clamp-down were being felt elsewhere in West Berlin as well. With the cross-border commuters no longer able to get through, West Berlin's labour force was immediately slashed by seven percent. Factory managers took a close look at their personnel rosters to see how badly their production levels would be hit. Skilled and unskilled workers were lost. Service industries were particularly affected. With many chambermaids caught behind the wire, beds in some hotels went unmade and rooms uncleaned. Waiters did not show up for work in some restaurants and in others they had to double up as dish-washers.

The dimensions of personal reaction among West Berliners ranged from the tragic to the trifling. A cleaning woman who worked for an American family collapsed in hysterical weeping because her daughter, who lived in East Berlin, was supposed to undergo serious surgery that day. With telephone communications cut and doubting that she would be permitted to cross the border, she feared she would have no way of learning how her daughter had fared. Less agonizing was the case of a man who worked in West Berlin's old main post office building, which housed the radio transmitting studio used by foreign radio correspondents. He had gone to see his mother in East Berlin the previous week and had left his raincoat there – a chic garment for which he had paid a fancy price in Düsseldorf the previous *Fasching* time. Would a western correspondent, who didn't have to worry about crossing into and out of East Berlin, be kind enough to visit his mother, send his filial greetings and retrieve that precious coat?

Five thousand West Berlin workers, outraged that their city was being chopped in two, marched on West Berlin's Town Hall to demand retaliation against the Communists. Brandt sympathized with them, but urged them not to be provoked into rash action. He said he was in touch with the Allied commandants to press for a strong response. Brandt himself was, for purposes of morale, considering ordering that offices of the Communist SED in West Berlin be closed, and was looking into control of the *S Bahn* which, since the war, had been run throughout the city by the East Berlin authorities. But there was little he could do that would change things now.

The Monday-morning meeting of the Berlin Task Force at the State Department was a well-attended, lively session. All sorts of questions were raised. Was the barbed wire only the first step in a bigger Communist operation, with the next move just around the corner? If so, what was that next move likely to be? Was the border barrier permanent? (In the early hours of the previous day, Reuters had cautiously reported from West Berlin that 'It was not clear immediately whether the borders would be closed for long or perhaps for only . . . until necessary controls had been put into effect.') If the barrier was to be permanent, what were the implications for the viability of West Berlin as a western outpost? How would the confidence and morale of America's allies, particularly West Germany, be affected?

There were no answers to those questions, nor to the question which most troubled members of the Berlin Mafia in attendance: What was the United States going to do? There was much heated rehashing of what had gone before – the President's identification of *West* Berlin, rather than all of Berlin, as America's concern; the signal sent to the Russians that East Berlin was theirs to do with as they liked; the absence of a more forceful response the day before. One participant said that feelings of some in the Task Force 'ran so high, you could cut the tension with a knife'. But with details of the Communist operation still flowing in from Berlin, and with Task Force director Foy Kohler's eyes still focused firmly on the far more serious concern – the fate of the access routes – the approach of the Task Force was less 'What do we do now?' and more 'What will they do next?'

Elsewhere in Washington, there was a similar sense of being upstaged by the Russians. It led to some agonizing on how to recapture the initiative. Robert Amory, Deputy Director of the CIA and a friend of National Security Adviser McGeorge Bundy, recalled:

> Mac and I sat around at first alone early in the morning and he said, 'What the hell do we do now?' . . . I was quite freewheeling, at least with him, and I didn't worry about making policy recommendations. I said, 'Mac, there is one thing you can do right here and now, and that is to vividly enhance your commitment to Berlin. I think you ought to send a cable to Norstad . . . to send another combat team in this afternoon over the autobahn.' Then Taylor came in, and Mac said, 'What do you thing about that, Max?' Max said, 'That's a hell of a bad idea. We're in a dangerous situation here. This would be further maldeployment. Any troops that we have in Berlin will be casualties in the first six hours of fighting. We

can't afford to give up 5,000 good armed men out of the NATO shield [in West Germany] to that.' Mac was more or less on my side and we pressed that all day. But Kennedy decided in favour of Max Taylor and the Joint Chiefs agreed with Max.

General Taylor was worried because the NATO shield was thought to be desperately thin. The American reinforcements promised by Kennedy had not yet reached Europe. Only two out of the twelve West German divisions were combat-ready, and most of the French Army was still in Algeria. American military chiefs were not prepared to take chances that Khrushchev was bluffing when he threatened war if he didn't get his way. Assessing comparative strengths as far as they knew them, they feared they might have no alternative but to go nuclear if it came to armed conflict over Berlin before the American military build-up was complete.

They tended to see the small Allied garrisons in West Berlin not as a political asset, keeping the Communists at bay, but as militarily insignificant, doomed to be lost if things turned hot and being kept out of the true defensive line further west, where they would be able to do much more good in the event of armed hostilities. General Clarke in Heidelberg, who checked the numbers at his disposal as he reviewed his defensive tactics, knew that 'Berlin was not a [militarily] viable community. It could have been taken at any time.' And that was the long and the short of it! The generals dealt with cold military facts: how strong were the forces at their disposal, what could they do if the guns went off, and what could they not do. Trip wires and such stuff was for the politicians. Reinforcing a militarily hopeless position was just plain crazy.

Kennedy's White House aides were equally caught up in a frenzy of calculations about the dangers, so relentlessly stressed by the Russians, of calamitous armed conflict. In a National Security Council memorandum on Monday, Walt Rostow said, 'We should take the view that the weakness and incompetence of the Ulbricht regime is leading to a situation which might trigger a general war unwanted by the major powers. We do not propose to let this irresponsible regime lead us by the nose into war. We [should] therefore [be] asking for four-power negotiations.'

Bundy told Kennedy, 'I find unanimity in your immediate staff for the view that we should take a clear initiative for negotiations within the next week or ten days . . . This opinion is strengthened by the border-closing episode which can be described as one reason more for calling talks – because of the dangerous and explosive weakness it reveals in [East Germany].'

Little thought was devoted in the White House to suggestions that anything be done about the barbed wire. No one suggested that it should be torn down as an unacceptable violation of four-power control. For one thing, it still wasn't clear how long the Communists planned to keep it up. For another, as Bundy said, 'It was apparent from hour one that this was an action on their side of territories sharply staked out.' Bundy told Kennedy, '1) This is something [the Communists] have always had the power to do; 2) It is something they were bound to do sooner or later . . .'

The British felt the same way. Edward Tomkins said, 'We [at the Foreign Office] accepted there was little we could do to stop the Russians from acting in a unilateral manner in their sector,' and there was no doubt that the East Germans were acting with Soviet approval. Not even at the American Berlin Mission, where feelings were more fiery, was there any call for action against the barbed wire. Howard Trivers, political adviser at the Mission, believed that 'if we had crossed the line to remove the barbed wire, I am convinced that [the Communists] would not have sought to resist. They would have moved back 200 or 400 yards and commenced to rebuild the barbed-wire fence there.' If that was also torn down, they would have moved further back again and rebuilt it again. 'We would have been obliged to keep moving further and further into the Soviet Sector.' It was generally acknowledged that if that was the way things developed the situation would soon have become both ridiculous and danger-ous. Allan Lightner said it was later believed that there would have been no resistance when Allied troops rolled over the first barrier built by the Communists, nor would there have been any when they knocked down the second barrier which would then have been erected further back, but that the Soviets would have resisted with overwhelming military force at a third barrier, an encounter from which he could have seen 'nothing but tragedy resulting, certainly a terrible humiliation for the West'.

Even if an Allied move to prevent Berlin from being split had not been resisted, it was feared it could have been the catalyst for the much-dreaded popular uprising in East Germany, for which there were wildly exaggerated expectations. That would have brought Soviet tanks out into the streets, and they might have been tempted to go in hot pursuit if the uprising spilled over into West Berlin, as it so easily could. What would the Allied commandants do then? Could they send their own few tanks (the Americans had only twenty-seven of them in Berlin) to drive the Russians back? They couldn't very well instruct the West Berlin police to push demonstrators for freedom back into East Berlin to avoid such a clash. Nor could they order American, British and French troops to crush anti-Communist demonstrations. Distasteful as it was, Allied interests coincided with those of the Soviet Union in trying to prevent anything happening that might produce such hopelessly unacceptable options.

However, there were possibilities for action. General Taylor, momentarily suspending his military caution, suggested that the Allied commandants notify the Soviet commandant in East Berlin that they were coming over in a body to talk things over, and to make it clear that they were going to enter East Berlin at a point which was not among those designated by the East Germans as open to westerners. They should serve notice that they would use force to cross over if obstructed. But the idea was thought too risky and got no backing in the White House.

If General Clay had been in command in Berlin on 13 August, the situation might have been different. 'This was the place,' he later said, 'where if the commandant in Berlin had acted, even if he had been in violation of his instructions, he would have succeeded and he would have been forgiven and he would have become a very great man. All he had to do in my opinion that night was to have run trucks up and down the street unarmed – unarmed soldiers in the trucks.' No sooner would the wire be put up than it would be run over. Clay was convinced the Russians did not want war and would back down. It was, of course, easy to be bold after the event, but Clay's later performance in Berlin indicated that he might very well have done it the way he suggested it should have been done. But he was not yet there and the barbed wire stood.

Inevitably, various other responses that might have changed things occurred to people afterwards. The Allies could have expanded on General Taylor's abortive suggestion, notified the Russians that the crossing points designated by the East Germans were unacceptable, and set up crossing points of their own. The barrier would have been left in place, but it would have signified western determination to remain in at least partial control of the situation. Or the Allies could have announced they had no intention of obeying the orders of the East German minister of the interior, and intended to send military vehicles through all the border crossings that had been open before, forcing the Russians to show their hand openly.

Another idea conjured up well after the event was for the Allies to have seized upon the fact that the Russians had conspicuously abandoned responsibility for East Berlin. Troops from the three western garrisons would move into a portion of East Berlin and claim it for West Berlin. The idea would have been to bring the Russians back to reclaim it. The Allied troops would then have withdrawn, but a farce would have been made of the East German barbed-wire spectacle.

Even if ideas of that kind had been broached while there was still time, it is unlikely that they would have got past the talking stage. Not only would they have been rejected as heightening tensions, but they would have been seen as showing that the United States was prepared to bully East Germany, while fearing to stand up to the Russians. An indication of how reflexive was Washington's acceptance of the Communist initiative in Berlin was given in a memo from Kennedy to Rusk on Monday, asking, 'What steps will we take this week to exploit politically propaganda-wise the Soviet–East German cut-off of the border . . . The question is how far we should push this.'

Berliners raged and grieved, but what was being done to them and their city meant far less to the President than the awesome fact that he had been prepared for a war in which millions of people, including Americans, might have died, and suddenly it looked like it wasn't going to happen – not yet. The Washington ambassadors of the three western powers and senior State Department officials met and agreed that 'some sort of counter-measures' had to be taken. The Americans gave assurances that Washington's reaction would go beyond paper protests. There was some talk of banning East German commercial representatives from western countries and imposing economic sanctions on East Germany. But no firm proposals were advanced, no agreement was reached, and no sense of urgency was drummed up.

In West Berlin, officials at the American mission who had long engaged – as a matter of policy as well as personal inclination – in cultivating contacts among West Berliners were deluged with calls from prominent local figures who wanted to know what the United States intended to do about the situation. Still banned from making formal statements, they privately took every opportunity to reaffirm America's vow never to abandon West Berlin to the Communists. Edward R. Murrow, head of the United States Information Agency who happened to be in the city at the time, sensed the desperate need there for an American morale-booster. Murrow told the staff at RIAS, 'There is no Berlin crisis. It is Khrushchev's crisis. He has, in the vernacular of our western movies, told us to "Get out of town by noon tomorrow." We do not choose to depart.' Though folksy, defiant and reassuring, it had nothing to do with the barbed wire or the despair Berliners felt as the hours passed and Communist action remained uncontested.

In London and Paris, as in Washington, there was still little to indicate that the Berlin developments aroused much concern. Barely a word on the subject was forthcoming from the Quay d'Orsay. The British pooh-poohed suggestions that economic counter-measures might be considered. They stood by their attitude that the West should match whatever action the Russians took, but not go beyond it in any way that might provoke a stronger Russian action and thus lead to escalations – and so far the Russians had taken action only on their own turf. Though he had been in long telephone consultation with Edward Tomkins of the Foreign Office Western Department, Foreign Secretary Lord Home, vacationing at his Scottish estate, declined to fuel the crisis. He told reporters, 'I hope to do plenty of walking and inhale some good Scottish air to get rid of the Whitehall cobwebs.'

West German government spokesmen said the border closure would have serious consequences for the East German regime. But Chancellor Adenauer, though making some appropriate noises of outrage, devoted most of his energies to running for re-election, his most newsworthy comment of the day being a shabby allusion to the illegitimate birth of his opponent, West Berlin Mayor Brandt.

To the Russians, day two of the operation appeared to have passed satisfactorily. There had been no notable disturbances by malcontents in East Berlin or any of the other East German cities. Whatever problems had arisen had been quickly and efficiently dealt with by the East German security services. The refugee problem seemed solved, only 150 escapers having got through on Monday, many by swimming the fifty yards across the Teltow Canal, along which more stringent security precautions were already being introduced. Nothing had been heard from the Americans, the British or the French. There was no reason for any Soviet objection to the implementation of the next step of the East German operation.

11

Lives, Fortunes and Sacred Honour

ON TUESDAY MORNING, before West Berlin had fully digested what had happened, the East German authorities issued a new decree. West Berliners would henceforth require special authorization if they wished to drive their cars into East Berlin. This measure was said to have been made necessary by abuses of the hospitality of the German Democratic Republic. Some West Berliners were alleged to have used their vehicles to smuggle espionage agents into the East or to disrupt public order.

It was true that some West Berliners had been risking arrest at the border by using their cars for smuggling. But they had not been trying to sneak people in; they had been trying to sneak refugees out, hidden in the trunks of their cars or pushed down beneath rear seats. However, not many had been able to evade discovery by the Vopos, who had become increasingly meticulous in their inspection of border-crossing vehicles. The measure was really a muscle-flexing exercise by the East Germans, firming up the sector border as the frontier of their Communist state, thumbing their noses at the western powers and, having not yet run into problems, continuing to test the limits of western tolerance.

A comparative trickle of refugees continued to get through. Some used documents provided by West Berliners who were still able to pass both ways on foot through the Communist checkpoints by proving their identity. If they took the risk of carrying along extra borrowed or forged West Berlin identification papers, those could be passed on to East Berliners who, if the photos looked anything like them, were then likely to be waved through to West Berlin with a minimum of checking by the

198

Vopos on the border. But the Vopos caught on quickly. Admission and exit procedures for West Berlin pedestrians were tightened and a touch of menace was added. They had to line up at the checkpoints to explain their reasons for wanting to visit East Berlin. Sometimes on their way out they were asked also to provide details of where they had been. What was more, they faced the prospect of being searched. Any East German found to be in possession of West Berlin identification papers faced three years in prison.

The Communists then turned their attention to a conundrum which had done so much to convince western intelligence that Berlin could not be split in two – the rows of sturdy, old, city-centre tenement buildings on the border, situated in the Soviet Sector but looking and opening out on western sectors. The thousands of people who lived in those buildings, almost all of them long-time residents, had always crossed back and forth over the border simply by stepping in or out of their front or back doors. Though they lived in East Berlin, people across the street in similar tenements in West Berlin were their neighbours. Choking off that traffic was a formidable challenge for the East German security officials charged with unconditionally discon-necting the two parts of the city.

When they were able to divert some of their men from duty at the wire, they had the Vopos lock and nail shut the west-opening doors of those buildings to make certain they would not be used as escape routes by residents or non-residents, as several refugees had already done. In one case, a woman living one floor up in one of these buildings answered a knock at her door, opened it and was startled to see a young man race past her without a word and jump from her window into West Berlin.

On Tuesday, the western commandants got around to register-ing their formal protest with the Soviet Berlin commandant, Colonel Andrei Solovyev. Despite the serious violations of the four-power agreements, their protest employed only routine language and made no suggestions that the Allies might consider counter-measures. Nevertheless, the following day Solovyev replied briskly, 'Your protest cannot be taken seriously. As you know, the commandant of Soviet troops does not meddle in the affairs of the German Democratic Republic.'

The Allied commandants knew that to be nonsense. They knew that the Russians were still very much in charge. But Solovyev was telling them that, as far as Moscow was concerned, four-power Berlin was a thing of the past. Not only were the

Communists dismissing western insistence that they could not unilaterally make such a decision, they were making demands, with implied threats, of their own. Annoyed at continuing demonstrations on the western side of the barbed wire, the East German regime announced that West Berliners, for their own safety, should not come any closer than one hundred yards to the East Berlin borderline.

Such gall did nothing to lessen the fury of the West Berliners or their anguish at the absence of any meaningful reaction from Washington. Joachim Bölke, a young journalist on the West Berlin newspaper *Taggesspiegel* at the time, recalled that 'some members of the United States Mission were furious, as I was furious, that it was impossible to get the message through to Washington. We waited from day to day for something to happen.'

But the White House, though still braced for trouble on the access routes, was unruffled by the Berlin developments. It remained convinced that the division of Berlin made no significant difference to the power balance in the city. The Soviet Sector was still the Soviet Sector and the western sectors were still under western control. The President and his advisers were prisoners of western publicity which for years had been dramatically portraying Berlin as 'the divided city', really two cities – one Communist and one free. So, aside from the refugees, nothing was different except, possibly, as columnist David Lawrence pointed out in the *Washington Evening Star*, 'It really means that there now is less chance than before of a shooting war between the Soviet Union and the western democracies.'

Some senior American officials and presidential advisers did not even know that the western powers exercised residual rights in East Berlin – that American, British and French military vehicles drove through the Soviet Sector every day on flag-showing missions, that American officials in Berlin regularly drove in as well without seeking permission, and that they had a right to do so. The Russians, seeking to avoid premature trouble on that point, had instructed the East Germans not to obstruct those vehicles in any way, even after the barbed wire was up. Martha Mautner at State said that she had 'a big fight with a couple of people up the line who didn't quite understand the theology of Berlin. There was an awful lot of cynicism about that theology. But anyone who was involved realized that you had to stick very, very close to it in dealing with the Russians or you'd end up with the shorter side of the salami.'

Mission political adviser Howard Trivers believed, 'The United States government did not push for counter-measures because there were too many people at the top who espoused the view that [the erection of the city-splitting barrier] might be 'good' in the context of overall US–Soviet relationships.' Indeed, Kennedy told his appointments secretary and intimate Kenneth O'Donnell, 'This is [Khrushchev's] way out of his predicament. It's not a very nice solution, but . . . a hell of a lot better than a war.'

As the East Germans, under the vigilant eye of their Soviet 'advisers', escalated the clamp-down step by careful step, the attention of the Berlin Task Force remained focused instead on the likelihood that the Berlin shenanigans were a sideshow for an imminent Russian move to squeeze the West out of the city altogether. Contingency planning for a new Berlin blockade were pored over, debated and updated with exhaustive thoroughness. How could West Berlin's essential supplies situation be improved? Could a 1948–49 style airlift be mounted if necessary? At what stage should force be used to keep the city's lifelines open? What counter-measures should be implemented if the Russians tried to blockade the city again – perhaps taking action along the East German–West German border, perhaps sniping at Soviet interests elsewhere in the world to get them to back off, perhaps going to the brink of war, perhaps going even further.

Minds were still fixed on the threat to the access routes virtually to the exclusion of everything else. Foy Kohler told John Ausland, 'I hope this business in Berlin doesn't take attention away from the crisis,' when a lot of people believed the crisis was already upon them. Upon hearing that veteran diplomat and presidential adviser Charles Bohlen (among others) had described the Communist closure of the border as 'a great failure of the Soviet system', Willy Brandt muttered, 'One more failure like that and we won't be around any more.'

Whether it was a Communist failure or a triumph, the West was baffled by how to deal with it. State Department legal adviser and White House consultant Abram Chayes said, 'We decided in the end that there was no appropriate response, that any response was either over-reactive or under-reactive.' Chayes said the Russian move was essentially 'not an aggressive but a defensive act'.

Marching troops into the Soviet Sector to shoo away the East German guards and dismantle the barrier would, on the other hand, have been seen as an aggressive act against defensive Communist positions, no matter what the four-power agreements said. Presidential military adviser Maxwell Taylor said later that even in retrospect he would not have supported the use of force to keep Berlin from being divided, even though he believed the Russians would have backed away from a direct confrontation. The abortive 'roll back Communism' crusade was no longer part of the American government's foreign policy thinking, and that applied to Communist East Berlin as well as to Communist East Europe. It was also beyond possibility that the necessary agreement could be reached among the Allies for military action by the small Berlin garrisons.

Caught by surprise, the western powers were fortunate not to have had to make a deliberate decision to let East Berlin go by default. That would have been hard to do. That would have generated much friction in their ranks – the West German government could not have agreed to it and survived – as well as causing Kennedy considerable domestic political embarrassment. Being caught by surprise meant that the Allies were not prepared to take retaliatory action against Soviet interests elsewhere with which they might have been able to extract from Moscow something of value from the Berlin affair.* As a consequence, the West had nothing to show for its acquiescence – neither the junking of the Russian demand that West Berlin become a 'free city', nor guarantees over the access routes. At minimum cost to themselves, the Communists were solving the refugee problem which had been doing East Germany colossal damage, which was threatening the stability of the East German Communist state, and for which they had themselves been responsible. It was a trump card the West, still waiting for the real crisis, was tricked out of playing.

Like General Simpson's men on the Elbe a decade and a half earlier, some officials at the Berlin Mission were champing at the bit. Ever since the early hours of Sunday, they had been

*Later in the crisis, having fine-tuned contingency plans for responding to Communist action, members of the Berlin Task Force thought that some of those plans should be tried out in response to Communist harassments. They sought to arouse interest in Washington for surveillance of Soviet ships in the Mediterranean – not doing anything to them, just staying close so that the Russians would know they were being watched. In contrast to Soviet moves, it was a low-level response, totally without conflict potential, just to see how the Russians would react. But when it was put up to the Pentagon, senior officers there began talking about training schedules for the fleet and for the air force and how such activity would divert their forces from their prime military mission, which was to be at readiness at all times to deal with threats to American interests.

struggling to keep abreast of developments – answering a flood of inquiries from Washington and the American Embassy in Bonn, liaising with the British and French Missions, writing and transmitting their reports, reassuring West Berlin officials, fielding countless inquiries from resident correspondents and the army of journalists flooding in from all over, and trying to catch up on lost sleep. Howard Trivers had to leave the hubbub of the Mission compound and go home to draft his (futile) report on possible western counter-measures. Now, they were finally able to take brief breaks from their hectic pace to examine the long-term significance of what they were living through.

Like American Ambassador Walter Dowling in Bonn, Allan Lightner was pleading with Washington for a more substantial response to the situation than had so far been offered. A CIA official assigned to Berlin said, 'Neither I nor the people I was working with had any doubt that the East Germans would pull back in the face of the slightest positive unfriendly reaction from the West.' Mission officials could see no reason why General Watson should not be authorized at least to dispatch troops from his garrison to the border to demonstrate America's armed presence in the city. There could, they thought, also be more energetic diplomatic activity. Washington could issue a tough statement declaring that an acute situation had arisen endangering world peace and demanding an immediate four-power foreign minister's conference, perhaps to be held in Berlin itself. The United States would not be over-reacting, but neither would it be seen, by either its allies or the Communists, as the castrated giant the Chinese and Ulbricht had tried to bludgeon Khrushchev into believing it was. George Muller drafted a memo to that effect and handed it to Lightner. But Lightner regretfully said there was no point in sending it on because, as had been made clear to him, 'Washington is handling this.'

Many felt this was a charitable description of what was going on in the nation's capital. In Berlin, America's low profile was made to seem doubly negligent and misguided when word spread that a Vopo who had jumped the barbed wire reported that he and his comrades had been given no ammunition for their weapons. Their superiors were taking no chances that they might panic and use them if the Americans advanced to tear the wire down. There were doubts about whether this story was true, or whether (as was actually the case at first) it was true only for lower ranks, or, if it had been true at first, whether it was true any longer. The answer to whether the Communist guards had ammunition came on Tuesday when shots were fired at but missed a couple who had jumped into the Teltow Canal and were swimming to the West Berlin bank.

The phased Communist operation had again been taken one step further, with the West looking impotently on. But it was beginning finally to filter through to the White House that, though Kennedy was fortunate not to have a catastrophic war on his hands, he did have a very serious problem in Berlin, and he was making it worse.

Assistant Secretary of State Foy Kohler later conceded that the American government 'did not initially fully anticipate the traumatic reaction of the West Berliners and West Germans.' 'Anticipate' was, however, the wrong word. The fact was that Washington – waiting for the real Berlin crisis – did not recognize the extent and significance of that traumatic reaction for a full three days after it had set in. But there was no mistaking it on Wednesday afternoon, when more than a quarter of a million people, one in every four West Berliners, jammed into the big square in front of the West Berlin Town Hall for a demonstration called by Mayor Brandt in an effort to channel frustrations away from the twin dangers of despair and violence.

The people there were no longer stirred up only by the barbed wire. They were outraged by what the Communists had been able to get away with, but as far as they could tell the future of West Berlin was at stake as well. Were the Communists always to have their way? Was West Berlin, like East Berlin, ultimately destined to be absorbed into Ulbricht's Democratic Republic? Would Vopos one day be patrolling their streets as well?

Anxiety over the absence of tangible proof that the West was prepared to face up to the Communist challenge was fuelled by another shooting incident – sub-machine-gun fire sprayed at a car driven by a middle-aged East Berlin woman who, with her teenaged son in the passenger seat, crashed successfully through to West Berlin despite the installation of concrete obstacles at crossing points to make cars slow down for inspection.

Bitterness about Allied inaction was intensified by the headline of the Berlin tabloid *Der Kurier* – MARSHAL KONIEV TIPPED OFF THE WEST – which gave wide circulation to the rumour that the Russians had cleared the border closure with the Americans in advance. When he saw that story, Brandt's aide Egon Bahr telephoned the American mission and said, 'I need a clear-cut denial within half an hour, otherwise, instead of gathering in front of the Town Hall, there is a danger West

Berliners will gather in front of the American Mission on Clayallee.' Officials of the main 'protecting power' did not appreciate implied threats like that, but they felt very much on the defensive and Bahr was called back with a firm denial in twenty-five minutes.

Not to be outdone as the voice of the people, another West Berlin newspaper, *Bild Zeitung*, complained about West Berlin being left in the lurch by its supposed guardians: THE WEST DOES NOTHING – KENNEDY IS SILENT, MACMILLAN IS OUT HUNTING, ADENAUER SNEERS AT BRANDT. The newspaper then proceeded to do some sneering of its own about the Allied response: 'They speculate. They get in touch. They prepare steps. They try to take a common stand. In the meantime our fellow countrymen are bloodied on the Communist barbed wire!' Some West Berliners suggested sarcastically that the Allies were so upset by what had happened that they might go on a hunger strike.

The placards carried by people in the square for the big demonstration showed how deeply disillusion had sunk in. In addition to those which condemned Ulbricht and the Communists, some were targetted against the West: 'We Were Betrayed!' 'Deeds Not Protests!' 'Quiet, Please. People Are Still Asleep.'

It was to the frustration of his fellow Berliners that Brandt was going to address himself with great care but much emotion. He realized the people of his city needed both reassurance and direction. Their confidence had been badly shaken. They were bewildered, vexed and worried. 'People,' he recalled, 'were afraid something might happen to them. I did not believe that but certain things had to be said.'

West Berlin housewives were already out on panicky shopping sprees, to stock their pantries with non-perishable staples. Already the telephones of moving firms specializing in transport from West Berlin to West Germany were jammed with calls from people making bookings or inquiries. Popular anxiety could not be pooh-poohed or sweet-talked away. Neither could the fury which had several times since Sunday led mobs of young West Berliners to try to rush the barbed wire and tear it down – something their American guardians appeared too timid to do. Only by showing that he shared their anguish could Brandt hope to guide their responses. He was also not totally unaware that his performance could have some bearing on the results of the forthcoming West German elections.

The mayor gave a stirring speech, delivered in his deep,

permanently strained-sounding voice which added to the effect of
his distress and controlled fury. 'Berlin,' he rasped, 'expects more
than words. Berlin expects political action!' He said the prestige
of the Allies and the fate of the western world were at stake. He
warned that Berlin should not be permitted to become 'another
Munich' (where in 1938 Britain and France had tried to avoid a
war by appeasing Adolf Hitler).

Brandt directed the thoughts of the assembled crowd towards
the tribulations of the people in the East. 'Our countrymen in the
Soviet Sector and the Soviet Zone,' he said, 'now carry the
heaviest burden.' He promised those on the other side of the
border that they would not be forgotten and appealed to East
German police and troops to ignore orders that they shoot at
their countrymen.

The mayor revealed that he had written a letter to Kennedy
drawing the President's attention to the anxiety of the people of
West Berlin. In that letter, the details of which were not publicly
revealed at the time, Brandt warned of the consequences of the
failure of the Allies to take action:

> The illegal sovereignty of the government of East Berlin has been
> recognized . . . I consider this a serious turning point in the post-
> war history of this city, such as has not been experienced since the
> blockade. This development has not altered the will to resist of the
> population of West Berlin, but it has succeeded in casting doubt
> upon the capability and determination of the three powers to react
> . . . The Soviet Union has used the [East German] People's Army
> to achieve half of its proposals for a 'free city'. Act Two is only a
> question of time. After Act Two we would find a Berlin which
> resembles a ghetto. Having lost not only its function as the refuge
> of freedom and the symbol of hope for reunification, it will also be
> cut off from the free section of Germany. Then, instead of a
> refugee movement into Berlin, we might see the beginnings of a
> flight out of Berlin. I consider it appropriate in this situation that
> the Western Powers demand . . . the re-establishment of four-
> power responsibility.

Brandt also told Kennedy that the Allies should reaffirm
assurances of their continued presence in West Berlin until
German reunification was achieved. He urged the President to
bring the Berlin situation before the United Nations and to
reinforce the American garrison in the city.

Neither his disclosure that he had written to the President, nor
the letter itself, did anything to endear the Berlin mayor to the
White House. Kennedy was riled that word that Brandt had sent

him a letter had been made public before he had received it. He also objected to being lectured to by the mayor after he had personally devoted so much of his time and energy to the Berlin crisis, and after he had repeatedly given absolute assurances of America's determination to defend West Berlin and Western Europe.

That very day, United States Secretary of the Army Elvis Stahr had frozen in military service almost 100,000 men who were soon due for discharge from the armed forces. Stahr had also alerted more than one hundred army reserve units that they might soon be called to active duty. He had announced that 3,000 more troops would be sent to Europe, and had ordered that the number of combat-ready divisions in the United States strategic reserve be doubled. All this, administration officials said, was hardly a sign that the United States was reneging on its obligations.

It was suggested by some in Washington that Brandt's letter to Kennedy was just a stunt to gain him points in his election contest with Chancellor Adenauer. Adenauer was indeed furious at both the letter and at the fact that Brandt was in the Berlin limelight. Some American newspapers said Brandt – 'a mere mayor' – was trying to dictate American foreign policy, which could not be permitted to concentrate on Berlin to the exclusion of other issues, some of which, like war or peace, were far more important. Some accused him of being a demagogue, trying to stir up the West Berlin crowd – which was unjust because Brandt lived in fear of a violent explosion of anger in the city.

Nevertheless, his letter contributed to the growing realization at the White House and the State Department that a very important aspect of the Berlin crisis had been neglected – the effect it would have on West Berliners and, even more dangerously, on West Germans, who were asking with increasing concern whether the United States could be relied upon to protect them if they too came under pressure from the Soviet Union.

Newspapers throughout West Germany questioned whether, in view of the recent events, the United States could claim to be the guardian of freedom. Was there really an advantage to being linked to the western alliance if this was the best it could do? Little reassurance was derived from a *New York Times* report that the Kennedy administration believed that the long-awaited Berlin crisis hadn't yet occurred. From Bonn, Ambassador Dowling dispatched a warning that further changes brought about in the situation by the Communists, even if they only amounted to tightening the screws in East Berlin, could direct public support in West Germany towards a radical reorientation of their country's foreign policy. A group of West German students sent Kennedy a black umbrella, reminiscent of the one carried by Prime Minister Neville Chamberlain who had knuckled under to Hitler at the 1938 Munich meeting. (When that was reported, a West German pacifist group urged Kennedy to send the umbrella back to them so that they might return it to the students 'in a drastic way'.)

A report from the Berlin Mission, telling of a crisis of confidence developing in the city, could easily have been taken as another of the recurring outbreaks of Berlinitis among the Americans stationed there. Not so easily dismissed was a message from Berlin sent outside regular channels to the President by Edward R. Murrow, in whose judgment Kennedy placed great value. Murrow told the president that the United States was badly misplaying the situation. He said the people of West Berlin had been demoralized by the absence of a meaningful American response to the border closure. He urged that efforts be made to correct the 'psychological climate'.

A call for the United States to derive greater advantage from the situation came also from the man Kennedy trusted most – his brother, Attorney General Robert Kennedy. In a memorandum to the President, the Attorney General pointed out, 'We have been handed a propaganda victory of tremendous dimensions on a silver platter and we are just not taking advantage of it.' He said that if the Americans had done what the Communists were doing, there would be riots and disturbances around the globe. Why, he wanted to know, was American public relations failing to alert the world to the enormity of what the Communists were doing in Berlin?

The Russians had been relieved that the White House had accepted the division of Berlin without making a fuss. But they were aware that pressures were mounting on Washington to adopt a stronger line. Moscow accordingly took steps to avert a change in the American stance. Andrei Smirnov, the Soviet Ambassador to Bonn, paid a well-publicized call on Adenauer to deliver a message from Khrushchev assuring the Chancellor that the Russians had no intention of doing anything to exacerbate the situation. Smirnov urged that the West also refrain from heightening tensions. In a message meant to be transmitted to

Washington, Smirnov told the West German leader that Moscow believed there was no need for anyone to get excited because the danger of war had now receded.

But the signals emanating from Berlin were now stronger than any the Kremlin was sending. It could no longer be comfortably concluded that America's vital interests in the city had remained untouched and untarnished. The crisis of confidence was no longer simply a warning from Willy Brandt; it was real and spreading. Kennedy and his advisers might protest that America's commitment to the freedom of West Berlin was undiminished. They might explain that the problem was purely psychological. They might insist – to the fury of the Berlin Mafia – that in closing off East Berlin the Russians had admitted a failure, not achieved a victory. But it was glaringly obvious that such words did nothing to calm the anxieties of West Berliners and West Germans. America's leadership of the West was being tested. John Kennedy had to pass that test if that leadership was to retain its credibility.

Ironically, it was the timid British who moved first to display western resolve not to be pushed around. While officials in London suggested that counter-measures in Berlin were out of the question because they might distract the world's attention from the barbarity of the Communist action, a detachment of Royal Green Jackets showed up at the Soviet War Memorial in the British Sector near the Brandenburg Gate to enclose the memorial in a barbed-wire cage, with a space left at the rear for entrance and exit.

When it was realized what was happening, a Soviet officer drove through the gate, the Vopos having quickly opened a gap in the wire for him, and angrily confronted the British officer on the spot. He demanded that the fence around the memorial, dedicated to the men who had heroically given their lives in the fight against fascism, be removed immediately. The British officer, resisting a temptation to say simply, 'You're on our patch, mate!', informed him that it was just a precaution to protect the memorial against West Berliners who were enraged by what was happening to their city. Fuming, the Russian officer insisted that his commandant should have been consulted first. But he drove back through the gate to East Berlin and no more was heard about it. When this act was compared to what appeared to Americans to be the determined British efforts to avoid confrontation with the Russians at all costs, a White House official allowed that 'the British come in two sizes.'

Late on Thursday night, West Berlin police on duty near the barbed wire at Potsdamer Platz reported unusual activity on the far side of the barrier. Concrete blocks were being stacked and an extra detail of guards was being deployed. Soon, closely watched by armed Vopos, workmen began shifting the concrete blocks into place just behind the wire. The next phase of the border-closing operation was being launched. The Berlin Wall was being built.

If the Americans, British and French had done nothing about the barbed wire except issue a protest, there was no reason to assume they would do anything about the concrete that was to replace it. Only five days had passed since *Stacheldrahtsonntag* (Barbed Wire Sunday) but now the wire – messy, not completely effective, and needing to be patrolled by far too many guards – was to be make way for a more permanent, tidier fixture.

The dimensions of the Wall were not immediately apparent. Ranging from five to six feet high and topped with barbed wire, the new barrier at first seemed meant only for specific lengths of the border, those which the East German security forces considered most vulnerable to border crashers or to trouble from West Berlin protesters. In fact, preparations for such a formidable obstruction clear along the entire East Berlin–West Berlin frontier had been part of the plan from the beginning, though the Russians withheld final authorization until it was confirmed that a vigorous western response to the earlier stages would not be forthcoming.*

Like the barbed-wire barrier, the Wall was going up safely back from the actual borderline. There was still to be no encroachment on West Berlin, no provocation that might elicit an Allied response. No territorial changes were involved. Having already been locked in, the East German people were merely being locked in more securely. Those still trying to Flee the Republic would have a much harder job of it than before. As the Wall took shape, East German troops could be relieved of border duty and sent back to their barracks. Vopos could be shifted to other duties. Members of the Worker Battle Brigades could be sent back to their factories and offices. The guards still on duty at the border would not have to concern themselves with the antics of

---

*It is still believed by many who were involved with the situation at the time that the Russian fall-back positions included ultimately abandoning a city-centre barrier altogether and reverting to the rejected idea of tight controls between East Germany and East Berlin.

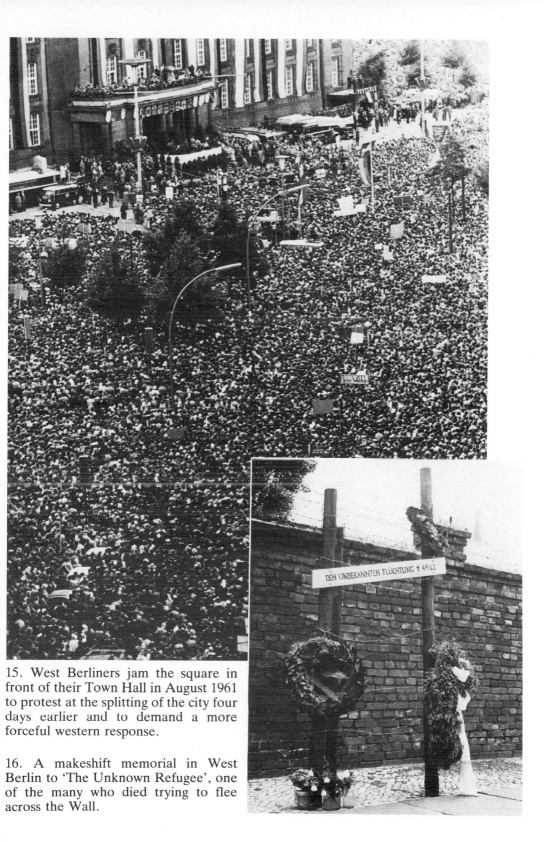

15. West Berliners jam the square in front of their Town Hall in August 1961 to protest at the splitting of the city four days earlier and to demand a more forceful western response.

16. A makeshift memorial in West Berlin to 'The Unknown Refugee', one of the many who died trying to flee across the Wall.

17. British troops escort a boy to school from one part of West Berlin to another through Vopo lines in the rural outskirts of the city.

18. Token American reinforcements arrive in West Berlin to raise morale on 20 August 1961.

19. The Wall runs down the middle of the street in parts of the city. The buildings above are in the West Berlin borough of Kreuzberg.

20. Jeeps with armed American soldiers escort a civilian vehicle through the Communist barrier at Checkpoint Charlie in October 1961, on the eve of the tank confrontation there.

21. American tanks roll up to the Wall to back the right of unrestricted access to East Berlin by Allied officials.

22. American tanks at Checkpoint Charlie during the border confrontation of October 1961.

23. General Lucius Clay.

24. A tense moment at Checkpoint Charlie in the winter of 1961.

25. A rapturous reception in West Berlin for President John Kennedy in 1963. With him are Mayor Willy Brandt (centre) and Chancellor Konrad Adenauer.

26. The graffiti-marked western face of the Berlin Wall.

27. The view from the observation platform overlooking the Wall on the West Berlin side. The watchtower and lightpost rise over the no-man's-land between the Wall and a secondary concrete barrier, beyond which East Berliners are not permitted to approach.

28. Checkpoint Charlie today, manned by British, French and American military police. In the background is East Berlin with the East German checkpoint, manned by Vopos, and slalom barriers to prevent refugees from crashing through into the West in vehicles.

29. On Unter den Linden in East Berlin, less than a mile from the Wall, East German soldiers goosestep in 1985 during a changing of the guard at the Memorial to the Victims of Fascism. Onlookers are mostly West German tourists with one day visas.

demonstrators on the other side of the barrier. It was said that the new barrier would defend the German Democratic Republic from militarists, saboteurs, spies and others bent on undermining socialist construction. For Kennedy, Macmillan and de Gaulle, concrete instead of wire changed nothing. A barrier was a barrier. You had to see the Wall – cold, solid, intimidating, and giving the first, undeniable intimations of dismal permanence – to shudder and share the outrage of Berliners.

But even before reports that it was going up reached the White House, Kennedy had been persuaded that the United States had been made to look impotent in Berlin and that this could have dangerous consequences. Intelligence and Research at the State Department warned that to the extent the 'Soviet manoeuvre' in East Berlin was not successfully challenged, 'it strengthens Moscow's hand vis-à-vis the West on the Berlin question'. Though convinced that America's message to Russia – 'thus far and no further' – was sufficient, the President decided something had to be done to overcome the sense of betrayal felt by West Berliners and to neutralize the paranoid suspicions of the West Germans. He would send General Clay, the hero of the airlift, on an official visit to Berlin, to be the living symbol of America's determination not to be squeezed out of the city. Clay had formally volunteered his services in a brief note to the White House on Tuesday.

However, this presented a problem for the President. Clay was a prominent Republican and had been active in supporting the candidacy of Kennedy's rival, Richard Nixon, in the presidential election campaign. For domestic political reasons, he would have to be balanced off on the trip by a prominent Democrat. On Thursday night, Kennedy called Vice President Lyndon Johnson away from a dinner party and asked him to fly to the city the next night. Johnson was to go with Clay (rather, vice versa) as the President's representative, unequivocally reaffirming by his words and his presence America's reliability and commitment to the defence of the freedom of West Berlin.*

That wouldn't be all. General Clarke in Heidelberg had already been alerted that a battle group of American troops was to be dispatched up the autobahn from West Germany to West Berlin to reinforce the American garrison in the divided city. The

---

*When Johnson stopped off to see Adenauer in Bonn en route to Berlin, the Chancellor pointed out to him a sign reading 'Action, Not Words' carried by an old woman with whom the Chancellor said he himself would want neither.

troops were to arrive in Berlin on Sunday, to be ceremonially received and welcomed there by Johnson.

Saturday turned into a day of almost frenzied celebration in West Berlin. Johnson and Clay landed at Tempelhof Airfield to a ceremonial welcome from local dignitaries and, wherever they went in the city that day, flower-throwing, cheering crowds lined the streets. All signs of demoralization and anxiety vanished as the West Berliners, and the tabloids which had done so much to arouse their fear and trepidation, accepted the visiting Americans as the reassurance they had begun to fear would not be forthcoming. A crowd-pleaser from way back, Johnson got out of the official limousine whenever he could to mingle with the people, shake their hands and accept their jubilant, excited greeting.

Practised political campaigner that he was, the Vice President was in his element. When Kennedy had asked him to go to Berlin, he had at first declined, saying it was too dangerous. He had to be gently informed that he was being ordered to go. According to McGeorge Bundy, 'Johnson approached anybody else's decision about what he should do with the utmost wariness. But once he got to Berlin, he thought it was great.' How could anyone treated like a hero think otherwise?

The crowd which overflowed the square in front of the Town Hall to hear Johnson bring a message from Kennedy was even larger than the one which had filled the square three days earlier to hear Mayor Brandt try to calm their fears. There was a translator on hand to repeat Johnson's words in German, but the crowd often did not wait for the running translation before bursting into loud cheers. People were moved not as much by the words as by Johnson's reassuring presence among them, though the speech was the most stirring the Vice President had ever had the opportunity to deliver:

> To the survival and the creative future of this city, we Americans have pledged in effect what our ancestors pledged in forming the United States – our lives, our fortunes and our sacred honour. The President wants you to know and I want you to know that the pledge he has given to the freedom of West Berlin and to the rights of western access to Berlin is firm . . . This island does not stand alone . . . Your lives are linked not merely to those in Hamburg, Bonn and Frankfurt. They are also linked with those in every town in Western Europe, Canada and the United States, and with those on every continent who live in freedom and are prepared to fight for it.

General Clay spoke also, briefly, but Berliners didn't need words from him to know he was with them in spirit as well as body, and they cheered as clamorously for him as they had for Johnson. The faces of the people who were jammed up against one another in the square were radiant with relief and pleasure. When they didn't peer contentedly up at the balcony from which their illustrious guests addressed them, they glanced at each other, nodding and grinning, as if to say, 'Everything is all right now.' And when the speeches and the playing of the national anthems were done, a magnificent hush fell over the square for the tolling in the Town Hall tower of the Freedom Bell which Clay had brought to Berlin in 1950, after the airlift.

The sound of the bell in those circumstances was profoundly thrilling and the hush which had settled over the 350,000 people assembled there was as soul-stirring as their earlier exultation had been. (Two years later, when Kennedy himself visited West Berlin and received a similarly ecstatic reception from the crowd in the Town Hall square, the dour Adenauer, who had always been suspicious of emotional excess, muttered gloomily to Dean Rusk, who was standing next to him, 'Does this mean Germany can one day have another Hitler?')

The 1,500 men who comprised the First Battle Group of the Eighth Infantry Division of the United States Army, under the command of Colonel Glover S. Johns Jr, had bivouaced at Braunschweig, not far from the East German border, on Saturday night. They had been drawn from forces stationed at the US Army base at Mannheim well back from the border. Under the circumstances, General Clarke felt it was wiser not to spare any of his frontline troops – a decision which revealed how precarious the situation was considered to be.

The battle group was to proceed to Berlin in six columns of 250 men and forty vehicles each. They were to set off through East German at intervals, so that any obstruction along the way would not lead to a snarl-up on the road. The columns were to remain in radio contact with each other. Even more important, they were to remain in contact with General Clarke through a command post near the West German–East German border. And Clarke was to have an open line both to General Norstad in Paris and to the White House.

Before climbing into their vehicles for their trek across East Germany, the men in the battle group were assembled to hear about their mission from Colonel Johns, who would be leading the front column on the journey. The colonel told them that their mission was to protect freedom. The eyes of the world were upon them. They were told they might be stopped. They were not to acknowledge the right of any Russian or East German to question them, inspect their vehicles or demand identification. In accordance with long-standing agreement, the colonel would be handling all of that with a Russian officer when they first crossed into East Germany. They were told that it was unlikely there would be trouble, but that they were, nevertheless, as always, to be prepared.

Although detailed orders had been issued for the operation, the Pentagon had neglected to mention in those orders whether the troops should be armed with ammunition for their weapons during their trip across East Germany. General Clarke took it upon himself to have them issued with ammunition. 'Suppose,' he said later, 'the Russians had tried to stop our men and a reporter had found that the soldiers had not been issued ammo? Wouldn't I have looked ridiculous?'

The decision to send the battle group up the autobahn to West Berlin had not been lightly taken. Several of Kennedy's key advisers didn't like the idea at all. They said that sending Vice President Johnson to Berlin was enough and that daring the Russians or East Germans to stop the battle group as it roared up the autobahn was needlessly tempting fate. Generals Taylor and Lemnitzer thought it was unwise to 'put additional troops in an undefensible area.' But the President was by now convinced that his Berlin gesture had to be comprehensive and convincing. He wanted no more backbiting from the West Germans, or from hardliners in his own entourage, about the failure of the United States to respond forcefully enough to the Soviet challenge. Small though it was compared to the Soviet divisions deployed in the area, the battle group would demonstrate the determination of the United States to maintain its presence in West Berlin, regardless of what the Communists might be inflicting on East Berlin and East Germany.

Kennedy was apprehensive about how the Russians would react. *Time* magazine quoted a White House aide as saying on the eve of the operation that 'talking to Kennedy was like talking to a statue. There was the feeling that this mission could very well escalate into shooting before morning.' The President was worried enough to have United States air and ground forces in Europe put on the alert, and to instruct his military aide, Brigadier General Clifton, to remain personally in touch with

developments from the situation room at the White House right
through Saturday night Washington time – when the battle group
would be traversing East Germany – and to wake him if it ran into
difficulties.

As it turned out, there was a problem almost immediately.
Through an agreement made years before which the Allies had
long since regretted, the Russians were authorized to make a
headcount of western troops heading for Berlin through East
Germany. However, when, according to standard procedure, the
Russian officer on the East German side of the border made the
headcount of the troops while they were still in their vehicles, the
number did not tally with the manifest. After a recount, which
also did not tally, Colonel Johns, who wanted no delay, had his
men fall out so that they could be more easily counted by the
Russians.

Having 'amicably resolved' this difficulty, his column moved on
to Berlin to be followed by the others. Colonel Johns' remedy
would cause problems later. Never one to pass up a chance to
turn a one-time gift into standard operating procedure, the
Russians insisted from then on that American troops in trucks
heading for Berlin up the autobahn dismount to be counted.

The rest of the journey for the battle group was uneventful. All
other traffic had been cleared from the autobahn and Vopos were
stationed on all the bridges under which the troops passed. Each
of the battle group columns was escorted front and rear by jeeps
of the East German army and was thus compelled to travel no
faster than twenty-five miles an hour which, along with rest
breaks en route, meant that Colonel John's front column did not
get to Berlin until half past noon, by which time Lyndon Johnson
had been out again, happily mingling in the streets with Berlin
crowds and giving out not only handshakes but also ballpoint
pens as mementoes of his visit. The Vice President was extracted
from this enjoyable duty by West Berlin police and his secret
service entourage and whisked away to the crossing point from
the East German autobahn into West Berlin, just in time to take
the salute as Colonel Johns and his men rolled into town.

Word of the imminent arrival of the battle group had been
widely publicized. Thousands of West Berliners congregated near
and around the reviewing stand that had been hastily erected for
Johnson, Clay, Brandt, Watson and other dignitaries who, with
the help of an army band and the cheering populace, were to turn
the arrival of the troops into a triumphal occasion.

The troops went straight to McNair Barracks to be fed (though because of the pace of events some had to go hungry till that night) and to be formally addressed by Johnson, who told the men: 'All the resources of the mightiest nation in the world stand behind you.' At 5.00 in the afternoon, by which time the last column of the battle group was completing its journey down the East German autobahn, West Berlin was treated to the first American military parade through the centre of town since 1945. The battle group rolled right down the Ku'damm. Again the streets were jammed with people; again they cheered, and some cried. They threw flowers, which some of the soldiers tucked into their helmet straps. Colonel Johns said it was the most remarkable reception he had experienced since the liberation of Paris from the Germans.

Less dramatically, a British military train rolled into town carrying eighteen armoured cars and sixteen scout cars to help beef up the British garrison. Macmillan had resisted American pressure to send a token force of troop reinforcements but, as with the American battle group, it was the gesture rather than the details that mattered. By nightfall on Sunday, a full week after the barbed wire was first stretched across the sector border, West Berliners felt they had good reason no longer to fear exposure to a Communist take-over.

'Flashpoint Berlin' continued to exist on a plateau of excitement and drama. For correspondents who flocked in from all over the world, it was a stirring news story. The pictures and details of the Wall as it grew, and of the divided city coming to terms with its new existence, were grist to any editor's mill – people still lining up at both sides of the barrier to wave at each other where they were able to make visual contact, shouting greetings and weeping; the heavy hand of the police state tightening its grip on East Berlin; the West Berliners, who seemed to inhabit another universe, daintily dipping forks into hunks of chocolate truffle gateau at Kempinski's on the Ku'damm, while refugees not fifteen minutes away gambled with their lives to slip or crash out of Germany's first workers' and farmers' state. Just about everywhere a person turned in the city, there were the makings of an image rich in human or political significance.

Of special political significance was the fact that what had previously been a Berlin problem had been transformed by the Russians into a West Berlin problem. The Communists made no secret of their confident expectation that the western powers, and even the West Germans, caught up in their corrupt materialistic pursuits, would soon lose interest in the outpost city on which they were spending a fortune in grants and subsidies. West Berlin, they predicted, would wither on the vine. Business and industry there had already been badly hurt by the absence of the *grenzgängers*, now locked in behind the Wall.

West Berlin was having to adjust to a new set of circumstances. Influential Americans were no longer coy about saying publicly and without apology that the western powers could not have been expected to do anything about the Wall, and even that the border closure to stop the refugees may not have been such a bad thing after all. Syndicated columnist Joseph Alsop, a hardliner bowing to accomplished fact, pointed out in dozens of newspapers across America that, 'the western nations have no more obligation to the right of jail breaking for the East Germans than for the Poles, or the Hungarians, or the wretched Chinese . . . If western nerves remain steady, and if Khrushchev is convinced the West means business [in standing by its commitments] there is hope for a good outcome.' The emphasis on steady nerves was important because barely had Vice President Johnson reported to the President on his mission* than the Russians were once again making menacing gestures. In a note to the United States, Moscow warned that it might find it necessary to take action against what it called the misuse of the air corridors through which West Berlin had been supplied during the blockade. This drew a vigorous warning from the White House that no such interference would be tolerated.

That had no bearing on the change of circumstances in East Berlin. To indicate that they were impressed by neither the Johnson–Clay visit nor by the arrival of the battle group, the East Germans proceeded with the next phase of their border-closure operation. Five of the twelve remaining crossing points in the city were sealed. Of the seven still open, the East German interior minister decreed that four were to be for West Berliners and two for West Germans. Only one would be for Allied personnel and

---

*There had been a less publicized aspect to the Vice President's Berlin visit. He had insisted that Mayor Brandt, who had other things on his mind, arrange that stores which were closed be opened for him on Saturday night and Sunday so that he could acquire palpable mementoes of his trip to the frontline city. The store managers were summoned from their homes so that a selection of shoes for Johnson to choose from – two pairs of each because his feet were different sizes – could be delivered to the Berlin residence of Ambassador Dowling, where he was staying, as well as a Royal Porcelain china service and a collection of ashtrays to be handed out to friends.

other foreigners. In addition, it was announced that West
Berliners would no longer be permitted into East Berlin merely
by showing their identification papers. They would require
special permits. Still testing the limits, the East Germans warned,
more firmly than before, that people in West Berlin were not to
approach closer than one hundred yards to the sector border.

This last decree was finally recognized by the western powers
as, literally, going too far. Everything else had happened in East
Berlin. Now the East Germans were presuming to assert control
over part of West Berlin. The western commandants reacted
immediately and uncompromisingly. In addition to lodging the
standard protest with the Soviet commandant, they moved troops
to the sector border to show, as British troop commander
Brigadier Goff Hamilton said, that they had 'no intention of
being told where the west sectors begin and end.'

Troops of all three western powers were deployed right up
against the Wall. American tanks rolled to within several feet of
the East Berlin demarcation line. Armoured cars of all three
garrisons patrolled up and down along the western side of the
Wall, and machine-gun nests were set up well within one hundred
yards of the line. It didn't change things in East Berlin, but it
showed the Russians that, for the moment at least, whatever they
still wanted to do would have to be done within the confines of
East Berlin.

The following day, three American army buses carrying
soldiers from the newly-arrived battle group for a sightseeing tour
of East Berlin were halted at the Friedrichstrasse checkpoint,
where Vopos demanded to inspect the identity papers of the men
on board. The convoy captain flatly turned them down. American
Provost Marshal Colonel Robert Sabolyk was quickly summoned. He told the Vopos, 'These buses are going through in
thirty minutes. If they are held up, we will know what to do about
it.' When the buses started forward again, after the Vopos had
had a chance to get instructions from higher up, no move was
made to stop them. Later, an East German water cannon sprayed
two American soldiers standing just west of the Wall, but stopped
immediately when an American officer drew a tear-gas grenade.
It was apparent in both cases that the East German guards had
been instructed to take some liberties, but not to push the Allies
too far, which did not prevent them that day – eleven days after
the operation had begun – from shooting dead an East Berliner
trying to swim to the West across the Teltow Canal. It was the
first recorded killing of a would-be refugee.

As reports came in of more people being cut down while fleeing, a Vopo who went West said that, despite orders, he and many of his fellow policemen only pretended to aim at escaping refugees. They did not wish to be murderers and deliberately fired their weapons wide of the mark. Nevertheless, though bullets missed some of those who fled, the number of casualties – shot dead or wounded or drowned trying to swim to freedom – grew, particularly after Vopos and Grepos were brought in from Saxony to replace East Berliners on border duty. Saxons had a reputation for being less inclined than Berliners to agonize over disagreeable orders. It was thought they would be less reluctant to shoot people breaking the law by breaking for freedom.

Meanwhile, the Wall continued to be extended, to creep along the border like an insidious growth, taking on an even more nightmarish aspect when, on Bernauer Strasse where the buildings were in the Soviet Sector and part of the street was in the French Sector, the doors and windows of the tenements were totally bricked up – though not before some refugees escaped through them. At least one of them tried but failed: fifty-nine-year-old Ida Siekmann threw a mattress out of her window into the West and, after agonizing indecision on the window sill, jumped after it, hitting the concrete sidewalk instead. She sustained injuries from which she died before reaching hospital. Another woman would later be caught in a squalid tug-of-war between Vopos trying to drag her back through the window of her border apartment and West Berlin firemen in the street below, who were trying to pull her down. The firemen finally won that cold war in miniature.

The West Berlin fire department stood ready to dispatch men with safety blankets whenever word came that someone had appeared at a window in a border tenement not yet fully bricked up, ready to leap into the West. The Vopos became aware of it and took action to discourage them. There were several incidents in which someone seemed ready to jump, the firemen were alerted by people in the street below and rushed to the scene and spread the blanket, only to be bombarded from above with paint or stones. Later, all the East Berlin border buildings were forcibly evacuated, their residents were housed elsewhere, the entire border area was levelled, and the ever advancing Wall crept along to rise where people had once lived.

As the summer wore on and refugees continued to dribble through, makeshift look-out towers, much like those on the East German–West German frontier, were erected along the inner-city border to give guards a clear view of unauthorized persons making for the Wall. Sections which foot patrols could not adequately cover were turned into free-fire zones, within which anyone spotted could be shot without question or warning. Shots were heard along the Wall at night, often followed by screams of pain. Tall grass growing near the border was trimmed to deny fugitives a place to hide until they could attempt an escape at nightfall. Frogmen strung barbed wire in border waterways and patrol boats were sent cruising along those waterways to swoop on swimmers who had managed to evade the wire. Despite these precautions, people continued to get through.

A professional photographer gained permission from an officer at the Wall to take press pictures of the guards defending the Democratic Republic against the slave traders and militarists. As he clicked away, he backed toward a border crossing, then turned and raced across. One man put together bits and pieces to fashion a home-made American army uniform, in which he walked through a checkpoint without being challenged. Another did the same with the uniform of a Soviet officer. A man crashed through the Wall in a five-ton dump truck, his wife at his side.

A woman brought flowers to the men at a border crossing, handed them over with praise and thanks, then ran towards the West. A Vopo sergeant on duty raced after her, waving his pistol and shouting, 'Stop! Come back! I'll shoot!' – effectively preventing his colleagues from taking aim. They both soon checked in at Marienfelde. After that incident, and after reports of guards being bribed to let people through had appeared in the western press, East German newspapers announced that several Vopos had been approached by people offering money to let them Flee the Republic, but had quickly arrested those who had tried to corrupt them. It was impossible for people to know whether that was true, or only an effort to discourage would-be bribers.

The more ingenious or daring the escape, the more it was evident that the escape hatch was effectively closing and that the East German security forces could begin cracking down in earnest on dissident and obstructive elements which, prior to 13 August, had been undermining the construction of the socialist state. Those in the East who openly criticized the erection of the Wall did so at great risk. East German newspapers explained that it was no crime to use 'workers' fists' to teach badly-needed lessons to such people. Squads of Communist vigilantes moved about serving out rough justice to 'enemies of the people'. It was decreed that persons 'endangering public safety and order' could be moved from their places of residence and assigned different jobs.

Work conditions in the factories and on the farms, difficult before the Wall, became increasingly onerous. In an effort to make up for lost production, workers were required to meet inflated output quotas. There were work rehabilitation camps for those considered to be malingerers or who failed to volunteer for special work details, and for those who were reported to be subversives. Kangeroo courts were called into session to try people accused of defaming the state and its leaders, or of assisting spies or slave traders in the West – a convenient, blanket charge which served when nothing more specific could be found. The prisons were soon jammed with people who objected to the Wall and to the subsequent police crack-down and who said so, either defiantly or without realizing who was listening. Meetings were called all over East Germany – in factories and in village squares, in community centres and sports halls – to congratulate the regime for its 'anti-fascist, anti-militarist measures'. Local people knew it was advisable to attend such gatherings. With everything under control, socialist planners could finally begin working out programmes for trying to create the kind of economy and society they pined for.

That many East Berliners pined for something else was evident despite the police-state atmosphere, and not only in the continuing escape attempts and the general mood of dejection so conspicuous in the streets of East Berlin. Frustrated refugees with their suitcases and expressions of despair were no longer to be seen in the hall of the Friedrichstrasse railway station. They had long since trudged off home to come to terms as best they could with the way of life they had sought to put behind them. But that station remained an extraordinary place.

East Berliners were not permitted through the control booths there to go West on the trains which stopped at Friedrichstrasse, but it was the only station in the East open to visitors arriving from West Berlin. There were armed guards in abundance; people travelling to and from the West had to submit to a careful screening procedure to see that they did not carry forbidden literature and were not on the list of excluded persons, and to make certain that those leaving were not East Germans trying to fake their way through to the platform where West-bound trains stopped.

All that was remarkable enough at a city-centre train station. Even stranger was the character of the new shift of East Berliners loitering in the station hall and just outside it. They could not entertain hopes of making a sudden break through the guard positions; escape there was totally out of the question. Some were there because they expected visitors from the West whom they could no longer meet half-way and who, like myself, could pass through Vopo controls by showing personal documents. Some East Berliners hung around the station because the sight was as extraordinary to them as it was to me. But many were there because that station, and the West-bound trains they were forbidden to approach, were the closest they would ever again get to whatever material and spiritual rewards they longed for on the other side of the Wall.

12

The Rogue Symbol

A S REPORTS of the crackdown in the East filtered through, the
euphoria generated by the weekend's proceedings in West
Berlin proved remarkably short-lived for many there. After the
cheering had stopped, after Johnson and Clay had gone home,
after the battle group had settled in at McNair Barracks, the facts
of the case came even more chillingly to the surface than before.
West Berlin leaders, who had been too busy and too choked with
rage and anxiety until then to study the terrain soberly, started to
do so and finally grasped what suddenly appeared to them to be
the full significance of what had happened at the border.

Though pleased with the arrival of the American troop
reinforcements and the friendly tone of a Kennedy message
hand-delivered by Johnson, Willy Brandt was pained by the
dismissive contents of this reply from the White House to his own
controversial letter. 'My own objection,' Kennedy had written,
'to most of the measures which have been proposed – even to
most of the suggestions in your own letter   is that they are mere
trifles compared to what has been done.' Remarkably, Kennedy's
words stating the obvious were even more disturbing: 'This brutal
border closing evidently represents a basic Soviet decision which
only war could reverse. Neither you nor we, nor any of our
Allies, have ever supposed that we should go to war on this
point.'

No one could deny that, but Brandt now saw that his hopes for
Germany had been built on an illusion. He had never expected
or wanted anyone to go to war to reunify Germany, but it was
now clear for the first time that, for the Americans and the other
Allies, questions of reunification were 'either rhetorical or long-

range'. That was proved by their acquiescence to the division of Berlin. It was an unnerving, unsettling revelation. When Edward Tomkins flew over from London in September, Brandt did not seem to him to have a firm idea of what he wanted done. But his disillusionment would, in time, have momentous consequences for Europe and for East–West relations.

As for the Johnson–Clay visit, it made Egon Bahr realize immediately afterwards that 'the Wall was like a terrible traffic accident. The victim is taken to the hospital, operated on, wakes up after surgery, and is taken to his room where friends are waiting. They tell him he is lucky he didn't lose his life. Then his friends go away and he discovers that one of his legs has been amputated.' East Berlin was gone; taken away.

Little encouragement for West Berliners was drawn from a comment extracted from Macmillan by reporters who had pursued him onto the eighteenth green at Gleneagles Hotel in Scotland, where he had gone to get in some golfing before returning to the cares of London town. 'Nobody is going to fight over Berlin,' the Prime Minister said confidently, as if dismissing the city as not worth fighting over. Then he added, 'I think the thing has been got up by the press.' The British leader clearly wasn't overly upset by developments.

But in West Berlin, personal and public priorities were transformed overnight. To Manfred Rexin, then a young Berlin Social Democratic Party activist, Adenauer and the domestic policies of his Christian Democratic government in Bonn had earlier been the nemesis. Instead, the overriding menace had suddenly become Ulbricht and the possibility that he might have his way with West Berlin also and inflict on it the police-state controls to which East Berlin was being subjected.

A wave of concern about the city's future swept through the western sectors. Sealed off from East Berlin and East Germany, West Berlin would no longer be able to fill the role that had kept it viable deep behind Communist lines. It could no longer be the 'beacon of liberty in the red sea', 'the haven for refugees from tyranny', 'the shop window of freedom'. It was now no more of a showcase of democracy than Munich or Hamburg or, for that matter, Chicago, where garrisons of troops did not have to be maintained to keep the Russians out. Would the protecting powers still consider it worthwhile garrisoning forces in so exposed an outpost, given the circumstances which now prevailed? Had West Berlin become redundant? Situated well inside East Germany, it was still the 'frontline city'. But its continuing allegiance to western values had become a defiant gesture rather than an effective advertisement for the failure of Communism.

For the people of West Berlin, that gesture remained crucial. Their freedoms and their way of life were at stake. For others far away from the Wall, whose primary focus was on the danger of nuclear holocaust by miscalculation, the value of the gesture could become questionable. Was it wise, for both diplomatic and military reasons, to meet the Soviet international challenge in a patch of land behind Soviet lines? Had West Berlin been transformed from an asset into a liability? Many in the rest of the world couldn't grasp what all the fuss was about. Upon first hearing of the division of the city Indian Prime Minister Pandit Nehru, a champion of self-determination for oppressed peoples, commented that the East Germans were legally justified in closing the sector border. He had to be informed of the legal as well as the human aspects of what had happened before he changed his mind.

There was a question also about whether people in West Germany would be prepared to sustain West Berlin in its new circumstances. Like big cities everywhere, it had been renewed and kept vibrant by a constant transfusion of new blood – new people from the provinces and lesser cities, from West Germany as well as East Germany. Now, as Walt Rostow asked, 'Could West Berlin, walled off, remain a city worthy of a young man's investing his life?'

An announcement by Dean Rusk that there would certainly be negotiations with Russia over Berlin, probably in September, once more nourished suspicions that the United States was desperately anxious not to do anything that might provoke the Russians. It again aroused the endlessly recurring suspicion that Washington would be willing to give even more ground in Berlin than it had already. Kennedy told Rusk he wanted 'a stronger lead on Berlin negotiations.' It was rumoured (without foundation) that the United States might be prepared to close down the American-run RIAS radio station and perhaps reduce the recently-enlarged American garrison in return for paper guarantees from the Russians on West Berlin's independence and on the access routes – though as they had already shown, the Russians couldn't be trusted to honour agreements and would continue to nibble away at the western presence until it was all gobbled down.

Reading the despairing cables coming in from Bonn and Berlin of popular sentiment and fears there, Kennedy was convinced that West Germans and West Berliners needed a daily fix of reassurance, but it was beneath the dignity of the American government to provide this. However, a message from Adenauer made him realize this was no time for petulance. The West German Chancellor warned that, in the absence of a more convincing reaction to the Communist exploits in Berlin, neutralist notions were spreading in his country. He said they could fundamentally endanger the future of the western alliance. The West may have hedged before, but now, said the Chancellor, counter-measures were essential to revive morale.

The problem for Kennedy remained the same – what counter-measures? Those which were proposed were either too trivial – like cutting off cultural links with East Germany and perhaps ruling out western attendance at a forthcoming East German trade fair – or too great – like economic sanctions, which were being held in reserve as one of the planned responses for when the Soviets fulfilled their threat to move against the West Berlin lifelines. It would be foolish to provoke Soviet action with a move planned as a counter to it.

Washington had been coming to the conclusion that West German pronouncements were meant primarily for public consumption and were not meant to be taken seriously. A paper prepared by the Historical Studies Division of the State Department later showed that the demands for action made publicly by Bonn were far stronger than those formally recommended by West German officials at Allied meetings. Adenauer publicly urged economic counter-measures, and even hinted at a possible economic blockade by the West against the entire Soviet bloc. But when it came to talks at Allied gatherings where counter-measures were to be actually drawn up, the West Germans made no requests for such extreme action. It was, for example, suggested that West Germany might abrogate its trade agreement with East Germany, but Allan Lightner learned that this proposal 'went over like a lead balloon when it was discovered that Adenauer was very much opposed to it.' It was believed in Washington that the Chancellor's public demands for stiff counter-measures were part of his effort to offset Brandt's Berlin advantage as election day drew closer.*

*Shortly after the launching of the border-sealing operation, Adenauer had foolishly suggested at an election rally that the Wall was being built by the Communists to help Brandt get voted in as Chancellor. No one believed that was even remotely true. Instead, it permitted Brandt to score an election point by saying, 'The old gentleman [Adenauer was eighty-five years old] really cannot grasp what is going on any more.'

Nevertheless, Kennedy accepted as genuine the warning about the possible danger of neutralism spreading in West Germany. He had, in fact, done so even before receiving Adenauer's letter. Reports from the American Embassy in Bonn had issued similar warnings. There was, however, no reason to believe that the West Germans were anything but deeply committed to western values and profoundly anti-Communist, so Kennedy wasn't going to be panicked by Adenauer into precipitate action. But it was something he believed he had to take into account. He had already sought an answer to questions about West German confidence in America and had found one, though not one he liked overly much. He would send General Clay back to Berlin to take up residence there as his personal representative in the city.

There were two reasons why Kennedy was reluctant to pick Clay for the job. For one thing, the general was known to be a strong-willed, impulsive man, not prepared to accept orders gracefully if he did not agree with them. McGeorge Bundy warned Kennedy, 'Clay will be a burden to you if he takes a line more belligerent than yours.' Also, Clay's Republican Party connections automatically associated him with several prominent Republicans who had been sharply critical of Kennedy's Berlin stance. After Kennedy's return from Vienna, Richard Nixon had charged that his administration was plagued with a 'Hamlet-like psychosis which seems to paralyze it every time decisive action is required,' and he had later called Kennedy's dispatch of the battle group to Berlin an 'empty gesture' which Khrushchev might see 'as weakness rather than strength'. Republican National Chairman William Miller charged that the administration was displaying a 'general attitude of appeasement'.

But Kennedy was tired of being distracted by the relentless, nagging nervousness of West Germans, West Berliners and American hardliners from finding out whether Khrushchev was prepared to talk sensibly about disarmament, as well as about Berlin. Not expecting simple answers from Moscow, he was convinced there had to be a dialogue with the Russians, if only to find out where they stood. He didn't intend to be kept on a leash by Teutonic fears and frets. The West Berliners trusted Clay as they trusted no other outsider. If his arrival in their midst as the President's personal representative didn't finally reassure them and the West Germans of his reliability, nothing short of declaring war on the Russians would.

*

Claims in the West that the Berlin Wall illustrated the failure of Communism may have done nothing to allay anxiety or boost drooping spirits in West Berlin, but they were not without a solid grounding in reality. The fact that Communist rule was unable to compete for the minds of people where there was a free choice was a deep embarrassment for Communist leaders. Nowhere was this more keenly felt than in the Kremlin where, despite his ferocious speechifying, Khrushchev was still unable to provide convincing proof to the Soviet hierarchy that he was making progress toward the fundamental goal of booting the western powers out of Berlin. It was just not happening, and there was nothing to indicate that it was going to happen.

Feeling in Russia remained strong that the Allied powers had no business being in the divided city, scene of one of the most historic Soviet triumphs in the 'Great Patriotic War'. Soviet hawks exploited Khrushchev's Berlin frustrations to back their incessant calls for increased military strength to match that of their American adversaries. That meant diverting expenditure from other programmes and projects and pumping it into escalated military spending, concentrating especially on the costly development of advanced nuclear weaponry. Hoping to shield the sagging Soviet civilian economy from the ravages of military priorities, Khrushchev was reluctant to comply. He said it was not his intention 'to saddle the [Soviet] people with unnecessary hardship'. But his had been a losing battle ever since Kennedy had publicly and unequivocally committed the United States to the defence of the western presence in Berlin.

As the Wall wound inexorably around the western sectors, the Soviet leader was faced with a dilemma. Having expected the Americans to succumb to his rocket-rattling and obligingly tiptoe out of Berlin, taking the British and French with them, he found that he had been forced deeper and deeper into an expensive confrontation he had never expected or wanted the Soviet domestic economy to finance, and in which there was no guarantee of success. He was now too deeply committed to resist hardline pressures on budgetary priorities. He had no choice but to cave in and divert even more domestic resources to the Soviet confrontation with the American superpower.

Despite his personal assurance to Kennedy that the Soviet Union would not be the first to break the moratorium on nuclear testing, and though the United States and Britain had sent clear signals that they were interested in negotiating an extension to the test ban, it was announced on 30 August that the Soviet Union had resumed nuclear testing in the atmosphere. A Soviet

Government statement said, 'To discourage an aggressor from criminally playing with fire we must let him know and see that there is in the world a force . . . ready to repulse any challenge to the independence and security of peace-loving states and that the weapon of retribution will smite the aggressor in his own lair.' Defending the move, Khrushchev told visiting left-wing British members of parliament Sir Leslie Plummer and Konni Zilliacus that it was to shock the West into serious negotiations over Berlin. He explained that the tests were being resumed 'to cool the hotheads in the capitals' of the western powers. Kennedy's reflexive response was an earthy Anglo-Saxon expletive. Presidential aide Arthur Schlesinger put it differently: 'I fear that Khrushchev has decided to make the USSR the embodiment of terror and power in the world in the expectation that all "lovers" of peace, terrified of war and recognizing the futility of trying to alter Soviet policy, will concentrate their energies on making the West give way over Berlin.'

Ever since taking office, Kennedy, like Khrushchev, had been under pressure to resume nuclear testing. He himself had insisted during the election campaign the previous year that the Republican administration which preceded his had permitted a 'missile gap' to develop between the United States and the Soviet Union, with the Soviet Union taking the lead in nuclear capabilities. His critics said he knew it wasn't true. Whether he did or not, after taking office and gaining access to confidential information on comparative military strengths, no more was heard from him about a Soviet nuclear lead.

However, a battery of American military experts, foreign affairs analysts and professional cold warriors had maintained a barrage of warnings that the Soviet progress in nuclear weapons technology was such that the tests had become essential. The Joint Chiefs of Staff urged the President to let them begin again, as did the Joint Atomic Energy Committee of Congress. A public opinion poll indicated that Americans backed a test resumption by a two-to-one majority.

Fearful of triggering a tit-for-tat escalation in testing, Kennedy had resisted such pressures. He did sanction preparations for new underground tests, partly to avoid being completely upstaged by his domestic critics. But he held back from actually authorizing even those 'clean' tests. Aside from the danger of launching a new nuclear race, he felt that to let them begin would complicate his exhaustive efforts to pin down acceptable conditions for negotiations with the Russians. Now the complications were there anyway. What was at stake was far more serious than Berlin.

Kennedy immediately huddled together with his chief aides to work out an appropriate response to the Soviet action. The suggestions included the immediate detonation of a test device – to show that the United States wasn't unprepared for whatever the Soviets had in mind – and even knocking out the Soviet test site with one well-placed nuclear bomb. But Kennedy wasn't going to be stampeded into an impetuous reaction. He labelled the Soviet move 'a threat to the entire world' and issued a statement saying that the United States would do whatever its national interest required. He said the Russians were testing 'not only nuclear devices but the will and determination of the free world to resist such tactics and to defend freedom'. A week later, after publicly and fruitlessly offering the Russians an opportunity to renew the test ban, he privately gave the green light for the resumption of underground testing by the United States.

In London, Paris and other major capitals, anti-nuclear movements which had long been heavily tinged with anti-Americanism found that the Soviet decision placed them in the unfamiliar position of demonstrating against the Soviet Union, though not with the ferocity they reserved for anti-American demonstrations. Those they were able to resume once the United States began testing as well.

The new Soviet tests – 'atomic blackmail', Kennedy called them – triggered a new wave of nuclear-phobia across the United States. The Director of the Office of Civil Defence Mobilization had already publicly appealed for additional funds to promote American awareness of nuclear dangers. That did nothing to ease fears. Nor were people comforted by blueprints prepared by civil defence officials for backyard and cellar nuclear shelters which could be made of concrete, steel or even earth. These would cost only $150 and, it was claimed, would prove as effective as those which a new crop of entrepreneurs who had set up 'survival stores' were offering for sale at prices ranging from $1,500 to $50,000. Advice was widely given on how to stock the shelters to survive in them until the danger of radioactive contamination had lessened: two weeks supply of food and water, first-aid kit, flashlights, battery radio, periscope, chemical toilets, sanitary napkins, deodorants, games for kids.

Magazines and newspapers printed maps showing the lethal fall-out areas of nuclear explosions. A map in *Time* magazine showed that within an area of up to one mile from ground zero everything would be vaporized; shelters would provide no protection. Within a five-mile radius of ground zero, heat radiation would incinerate virtually everything. Radioactive particles would be scattered over 150 miles from ground zero. People were quoted as saying that if there was a nuclear attack, they'd rather die when it happened than survive to live with the consequences.

Nor were the Russians spared nuclear anxiety. Sorenson says that Khrushchev's son-in-law, Aleksei Adzhubei, told him a joke circulating in Russia about advice to Russians on how to deal with fall-out: 'Question: What should I do if a nuclear bomb falls? Answer: Cover yourself with a sheet and crawl slowly to the nearest cemetery. Question: Why slowly? Answer: To avoid panic.'

Kennedy tried to make avoiding panic a guiding principle. He had been threatened and lied to by Khrushchev on the nuclear issue and he was sorely tempted to respond dramatically. However, he delayed authorizing atmospheric testing by the United States until the following spring, after his efforts to gain agreement from Moscow for restoring a test ban had failed. At the same time, he pressed ahead with constructing a flexible-response military strategy and capability so that the United States would never again find itself in a position where it's only credible reaction to a military challenge would be to go nuclear.

National security experts in Washington drew up a programme to provide guidance for graduated moves in a crunch. First, there would be representations through diplomatic channels, followed, if necessary, by conventional military measures, and finally the escalating use of nuclear weapons. In discussions with the British, French and West Germans, American officials underplayed the nuclear options which, in the words of one American official, 'were not very attractive'.

Nevertheless, to reassure Americans and to signal Moscow that the United States would not be intimidated by the rattling of nuclear weapons, Assistant Secretary of Defence Roswell Gilpatrick did some weapons-rattling of his own in a speech 'cleared at the highest level':

> . . . this nation has a nuclear retaliatory force of such lethal power that an enemy move which brought it into play would be an act of self-destruction on his part. The United States has today hundreds of manned intercontinental bombers and many more medium bombers capable of reaching the Soviet Union, including 600 heavy bombers and many more medium bombers equally capable of intercontinental operations because of our highly-developed in-flight refuelling techniques and world-wide base structure. The

US also has six Polaris submarines at sea carrying a total of ninety-six missiles, and dozens of intercontinental ballistic missiles. . . . We have a second strike capability which is at least as extensive as what the Soviets can deliver by striking first. Therefore, we are confident that the Soviets will not provoke a major nuclear conflict.

Those words did little to dispel the atmosphere of dread which the Berlin crisis had spawned and which the nuclear testing had thickened. John Ausland, who was more knowledgeable than most about the chances of armed conflict, said he was very much afraid that a shooting war would break out – until he was told by a Pentagon officer whose judgment he respected that if things reached a danger point, 'All we have to do is put the Strategic Air Command on alert and the Russians will freeze.'

Government agencies and military commands are creatures of habit. They have standard operating procedures, and deviations from these raise eyebrows, raise hackles and raise hell. Even before General Clay set off for Berlin to take up his job as President Kennedy's personal representative there, it was obvious that he was a wild card introduced into a game in progress and that the rest of the deck wasn't taking kindly to the idea.

At the State Department, Dean Rusk was worried that Clay would go beyond merely being a symbol of American commitment. Martin Hillenbrand feared that the general, who had been out of government service for several years, didn't understand that times had changed since his determination to stand by the city had made hash of the Soviet attempt to blockade Berlin. Hillenbrand believed he 'was not quite aware that we now had to consider a different framework for action than that which prevailed when we had had a nuclear monopoly'. Ambassador Dowling in Bonn resented the dispatch of Clay to the city. He took it as a criticism of his own performance as official head of the American Mission in Berlin, which was not an unreasonable interpretation to put on it.

If Clay had thought the 'West Point Protective Society' would gather around him, he was soon disabused of that expectation. The Pentagon did not take kindly to the idea of the White House plucking a general out of military retirement to supersede active-service generals in the field. Both General Norstad and General Clarke were offended by the Clay appointment and the trouble they were sure it would cause in the workings of the chain of command. Norstad passed word along to the White House that he believed Clay's presence would complicate an already complicated administrative set-up. Years later, Clarke, who declined even to acknowledge that he had once been a student of Clay's at West Point, said with some bitterness, 'I never did find out what [Clay's] status was.'

Nor was Clay's appointment happily received by those of Kennedy's White House aides who believed that – though the situation remained precarious – a rapprochement with the Russians over Berlin was possible, provided neither side did anything to aggravate the situation. Clay's presence in the city, with the blessings and authority of the American President, could hardly be interpreted as a bid to calm things down.

Though a shy man personally, and though leaving an impression of great modesty in casual encounters, in action Clay had a swashbuckling manner and a fierce temper. He believed with a passion that he knew more about both Berlin and Soviet tactics in Germany than anyone else. He intended to teach the novices in the White House, the State Department and the Pentagon how to deal with the situation. Having faced down the Russians during the blockade, he was convinced that the only way to handle them was not to give an inch, and that they regarded any concession as merely an invitation to demand more. He also firmly believed that the Soviet Union would always back down when the United States did something that could be overcome only by the use of force.

Clay regarded himself not simply as the President's special representative, instructed to 'report, recommend and advise'. He came to the city believing he would take charge of American policy and action there. He had firm ideas about what had been happening and what should be done about it. Those ideas, which had not been discussed in any great detail before he had left for Germany, tended not to coincide with those of the President. The White House was sending Clay to Berlin to reassure the Berliners; he was going there to take on the Russians.

According to one State Department official, when Clay went to Berlin to deal with the problem there, 'he *became* the problem'. That was, of course, hyperbole. But it was true that the general's actions and messages in the following months repeatedly caused the White House much concern and some grief. McGeorge Bundy, viewing the situation from the White House, saw Clay as '. . . difficult. At least once a week, he would send a cable saying if A, B and C didn't happen or if the current instruction or intent to do D and E should persist, he couldn't answer for the consequences.'

One day during the crisis, someone who had been in the State Department at the time of the blockade asked Bundy, 'Have you begun to get the weekend cables from him yet?' He explained that when Clay had been in charge of the Berlin situation during the airlift, it had always seemed that on Friday, at the end of a long, hard week, he would gather the week's frustrations, cable them back to Washington, 'if not with the intent, certainly with the consequence that it spoiled our weekend'.

There were, no doubt, many moments during Clay's 1961–1962 tenure in Berlin when Kennedy regretted having sent him there. According to Bundy, however, it remained for the most part at 'a level of mutual irritation much lower than a loss of confidence by the President'. That was just as well for Kennedy, because the President's freedom of action in dealing with Clay was limited by international and domestic political considerations. Even if he had wanted to, he could not have fired the general without disagreeable repercussions.

When the general arrived in Berlin on 19 September (two days after the West German elections in which Adenauer retained the chancellorship but was compelled by the gains made by Brandt's Social Democrats to form a coalition government with the smallish Free Democratic Party), he was again given a hero's welcome by cheering crowds. For many, Clay's return once again neutralized fears about the future. Had he been recalled by Kennedy, Berlin's shaky morale would have been totally shattered, and the repercussions in West Germany would have been momentous.

Aside from that, if Kennedy had permitted an open breach to develop between Clay the Republican on one side and his own Democrats on the other, Berlin policy might have been turned into a political free-for-all in Washington. The result was that Clay, never one to be intimidated by authority anyway, was in a position to treat with little deference signals from the State Department and the White House in Washington, from the American Embassy in Bonn, from General Clarke in Heidelberg, and from General Norstad in Paris that he watch his step as he set about trying to regain the initiative for the United States in the Berlin showdown. Clay was to do things of which they all disapproved. One Berlin Task Force member recalled, 'He was a loose cannon. He was a prima donna putting on an act and we were a bureaucracy trying to run a long-term, complicated operation.'

Geoffrey McDermott, the British minister in Berlin, was not

alone in having little doubt that Clay was not merely second guessing when he told Lyndon Johnson that if he had been in Berlin on 13 August American tanks would have rolled that day (though Clay later said it was trucks rather than tanks that he would have sent across). Some believed he would have had the the barbed wire brushed aside because they knew he was a man of action, others because they thought him reckless and impetuous. He certainly wasted no time in proving one or both of those views to be accurate. Upon arriving in Berlin, he asked General Watson to have a concrete wall built on a military training range so that his troops could practise knocking it down. Bitter at the criticism for inaction unfairly directed at him personally by some West Berliners – 'Why blame me; I didn't build that blasted Wall!' – Watson was pleased to comply. Clay then ordered the resumption of United States military patrols on the autobahn in East Germany, suspended years before when the Russians caused problems for them. The general also immediately took on the nagging problem of the village of Steinstücken.

Steinstücken was officially part of West Berlin, but was separated from it by a narrow neck of East German territory. To get to West Berlin proper, the people of Steinstücken – a community of some 300 families – had to cross Vopo lines. The Vopos had harassed them even before 13 August, but that harassment had grown severe since the building of the Wall. It was apparent that the East Germans were preparing to lay claim to the village and that western officials, fearing a dangerous escalation, couldn't figure out how to deal with the situation. It was a small, vulnerable place, over which it was hardly worth risking war.

Clay immediately set about trying to sort that problem out. He told General Watson to send two companies of troops up to the border to punch a hole through to Steinstücken. When General Clarke, who happened to be visiting Berlin from his Heidelberg headquarters, heard about it, he was both astounded and outraged. Profoundly aware of the West's hopeless military position in Berlin, Clarke asked Watson whose idea it was. When Watson told him it was Clay's, Clarke asked him pointedly, 'Al, don't you know who you work for? Don't you know who writes your efficiency report.' Watson knew. The troops, already assembled for the operation, were ordered back to their barracks. 'Afterwards,' Clarke said, 'I called Norstad on the phone and told him what I had done. Norstad said, "Thank God you were in Berlin." '

Clay was not so easily discouraged. Denied the troops to open a corridor to Steinstücken, he ordered up a helicopter and flew off to the village to assure the people there that the United States considered them to be under the protection of its military garrison, which wasn't exactly the kind of reintroduction to Berlin the White House had planned for him. The East Germans called it 'a warlike move'. Others felt the same way. The British served notice to Washington that they weren't at all satisfied that the dangers of an armed clash over comparative trifles were fully appreciated by the President's personal representative in Berlin.

Clay ignored the fuss. The following day, he dispatched another helicopter to the village, this time carrying military policemen, three of whom stayed behind to establish an American presence there. Again, the East Germans were furious and, when seven refugees from East Berlin who had taken refuge in Steinstücken were flown out, they threatened to open fire on helicopters flying that route. It was an empty threat. No shots were fired and the Steinstücken problem, which had previously caused some anguish and much befuddlement, was seen to have been briskly resolved – though not everyone in Washington was overjoyed with the means employed.

The White House and the State Department had been trying to fix on a way to signal Moscow that, while standing firm, the United States wanted to tone down the level of tension in Berlin. A speech being drafted for delivery by Kennedy to the United Nations General Assembly a few days later would reaffirm America's commitment to the freedom of West Berlin, but also recognize 'the historic and legitimate interests of others in assuring European security'. Yet here was Clay stirring things up over a tiny bit of territory nobody had even heard of before. Kennedy had even greater reason to wonder whether he really should have sent Clay to Berlin a few weeks later, when it seemed that the general was on the verge of provoking an armed clash between America and Russia in the middle of Berlin over what looked like another triviality.

The control post set up by the Americans in a prefabricated shack on the western side of the border at Friedrichstrasse was designated Checkpoint Charlie.* It was the only crossing point for surface traffic which Allied personnel and civilians and other

*Checkpoints Alpha and Bravo were at either ends of the autobahn through East Germany.

foreigners entering East Berlin were permitted by the Communists to use. (The crossing point at the Friedrichstrasse subway train station, which could be used by non-Germans as well as Germans, was a mile down the street in East Berlin.) Checkpoint Charlie was manned by American – and later also by British and French – military police. As a precaution, military and other official Allied personnel registered at the checkpoint when entering and leaving the East.

On the night of 22 October 1961, after checking in at the checkpoint, Allan Lightner, the senior American civilian official in Berlin, drove with his wife into East Berlin. They were going to a performance there by a visiting experimental Czechoslovak theatre company whose performances had attracted widespread critical acclaim. Several officials of the Allied missions in West Berlin had already gone across to see them, but the Lightners did not get far.

On the Communist side of the crossing point, their Volkswagen was stopped by a Vopo officer who asked to see their passports. In accordance with established practice and instructions for official American personnel, Lightner and his wife refused to show them. Their car bore official United States licence plates which, as far as the Americans were concerned, were adequate identification when crossing into East Berlin.

If any problem arose, official American personnel were to demand the presence of a Soviet officer. Under no circumstances were there to be dealings with East German officials. That would have been tantamount to diplomatic recognition of East Germany, as well as recognition of East Berlin as part of East Germany.

Despite Lightner's demands that they step aside, the Vopos would neither let his car pass their checkpoint without passport inspection, nor fetch a Soviet officer. When, after sitting there for half an hour, Lightner tried to spurt forward in his vehicle anyway, he was slowed by the zig-zag obstacles at the checkpoint and his car was quickly surrounded by Vopos. He was told he would not be permitted to enter East Berlin without showing his passport, no matter how long he sat there.

From the very start, the American military policemen who manned Checkpoint Charlie, one hundred yards across the border from the Communist checkpoint, had observed the incident. The MPs reported what was happening to Lieutenant Colonel Sabolyk, the provost marshal, who immediately informed General Clay. Clay instructed Sabolyk, who was about to rush there anyway, to make for the scene to try to sort things out. A platoon of infantrymen, four M-48 medium tanks and two armoured personnel-carriers were ordered to Checkpoint Charlie as well. The East Germans were not meant to misunderstand the message Clay was sending.

It was too late for the theatre in East Berlin, but much more was now at stake. Sabolyk's first move was to try to persuade the East Germans at the checkpoint to let the Lightners through without further hassle. When they refused, insisting that all civilians had to show their identity papers when entering the German Democratic Republic, the provost marshal asked Mrs Lightner to get out of the Volkswagen and return to the American Sector. She declined to do so until told that General Clay had ordered her back in view of what was about to happen.

Once she had been escorted back through Checkpoint Charlie by an American officer and was clear of the scene, two squads of four American troops each, led by a lieutenant and all with M-14 rifles at the ready, moved forward, took up positions on both sides of the Lightner car and, with Lightner at the wheel and alone in the vehicle, escorted it past the Communist checkpoint into East Berlin. The East German guards, though scowling, made no effort to obstruct this procession. Lightner drove about two blocks, cruising very slowly so as not to outdistance his escort, and then returned to West Berlin.

Joined there in the Volkswagen by Mission press officer Albert Hemsing, he turned his car around and drove back into East Berlin, unescorted by the troops. When the Vopos again insisted that he and Hemsing show their passports, Lightner signalled with his hand and the troops came forward again to escort him once more past the grim-faced East German guards. Lightner later said, 'If the East Germans had tried to stop us . . . say by shooting one of us, we would have had to kill all of them . . . All hell would have broken loose.'

As the incident approached its climax, Howard Trivers, the political officer at the American Mission, arrived at the crossing and spotted Major Lazerev, the acting Soviet political adviser, standing at the border between the American and East German checkpoints. He walked over and asked him what was going on. Lazerev seemed perplexed. He said that he was sorry about the incident. He said that the Vopos (who hadn't realized they were dealing with a senior American official) had acted improperly and that 'remedial measures' would be taken. Though the East Germans had earlier tried, unsuccessfully, to get other American officials to show their passports for inspection at the border, they had taken that next step in the phased border operation without clearing it with the Russians. They were quickly and sharply ordered back into line. When Lightner again tested the border that night, he was able to drive right through without being obstructed and without having to summon up his armed escort.

However, rarely missing an opportunity to turn a chance incident into an advantage, the Russians took a closer look at what had happened and decided that the the unauthorized East German manoeuvre was, perhaps, not such a bad idea. The East Germans were, after all, claiming sovereignty over East Berlin and were, therefore, well within their rights in demanding to see Lightner's passport. It was consistent with everything that had been happening and everything they had been saying ever since the first bale of barbed wire had been unrolled on the border. Independent initiatives by Ulbricht were not to be encouraged, but the passport ploy was worth another try. It would be one more step toward consigning Berlin's four-power status to oblivion. The following day, with Soviet approval, the East Germans formally announced that only Allied military personnel in uniform would be permitted to enter East Berlin without displaying their identity papers. Western civilians, even if they had official status, would be required to show their passports.

Given advance notice that the East Germans would personally involve the American minister in an undignified border squabble, it is likely that the State Department would have issued instructions that there should be no quibbling over the issue. Washington had already repeatedly shown itself reconciled to Communist jurisdiction over East Berlin and its boundaries. Howard Trivers was of the conviction that, 'Had it not been for General Clay's presence in Berlin at that time, there is little doubt that the American military and civilian authorities in Berlin would have been obliged to crawl back ignominiously . . .' When Kennedy was first told of the incident – with Lightner's intended destination in East Berlin misreported – the President is said to have snapped, 'We didn't send him over there to go to the opera in East Berlin.'

But Clay, taking full advantage of his position as the President's personal representative, was operating on a totally different wavelength. He placed great importance on the fact that, by long-standing agreement to which the Russians were a party, Lightner had as much right to move about freely in East Berlin as in the western sectors of the city. The general was a devout adherent of the theology of the Berlin situation in which unrestricted access to the East for Allied personnel, the refusal to show passports, and other seemingly trivial observances were symbols of the entire structure of established relationships, a structure which would collapse – jeopardizing the American position – if the symbols were disregarded.

Clay's understanding – rather, his misunderstanding – was that he had been sent to Berlin to make certain no more ground was lost there to the Communists. In the Lightner incident, reaction had to be forthcoming immediately or not at all. The general had sized up the situation and had acted on his own initiative. Now, as he made his plans for his next move, he realized he needed strong, solid backing. The State Department was already showing nervousness about the use of the troops in the Lightner incident. There were toes he had to step on or, at least, to step around. He performed that manoeuvre by invoking the authority conferred upon him by virtue of being the President's personal representative. He put through a call directly to Kennedy – who in an unguarded moment had told the general to contact him directly if he ran into any problems – and explained what he had in mind.

He was going to challenge, with a show of military force if necessary, the East German decree that only Americans in military uniform could enter East Berlin without showing their papers. He told the President that if the Communists weren't stopped, they would continue to nibble away at western rights. The general said that it was humiliating for the United States to feel obliged to obey the instructions on border crossing issued by the regime of a third-rate power it did not recognize. He said something had to be done to counter ever-growing Communist audacity or there would be no end to it.

Kennedy, who needed no lectures on defending American interests, was not convinced that the issue of passports on the East Berlin border was the right issue on which to make a stand. Besides, the Russians appeared to have been sending signals that they wanted to cool things down. But, aside from distrusting such signals, Kennedy liked and respected Clay. He was grateful that, despite being a political opponent, the general had taken on for the administration, at considerable personal inconvenience, what very likely would turn out to be a thankless assignment. There was also the simple fact that he needed Clay in Berlin. The tiresome necessity to sustain morale in West Berlin and West Germany remained. He had heard reports of the backbiting the general had endured from people he believed should have been backing him and he did not want to risk provoking him into throwing up the job in disgust. So Clay got the go-ahead he requested from the President, and the Berlin crisis entered a new phase.

On the morning of Wednesday 25 October, with American officials, military police and correspondents milling about and a crowd of some five hundred onlookers held well back on the western side, two young American military police officers, looking overly-stylish for the occasion in their civilian clothes but very military with their crew-cut hair styles, drove through Checkpoint Charlie in a civilian Opel sedan bearing official American licence plates. When they were halted by the Vopos on the East Berlin border for refusing to show their passports, they turned back to Checkpoint Charlie and picked up a waiting escort of three US Army jeeps carrying battle-ready soldiers, conspicuously clutching their rifles. With one jeep in front and two behind, the sedan drove without stopping through the Communist checkpoint. The East German guards made no move to obstruct them.

This was, however, not going to be a one-shot affair. A half-hour later, ten American M-48 tanks and three armoured personnel-carriers rumbled up to the border and took up positions near Checkpoint Charlie. With tension rising, journalists – and a pretzel seller who had managed to slip through to peddle his wares to tank crewmen – were shoved by military police into the adjacent Hallo Bar ('Hungarian Specialities') and Café Koeln, from which some climbed to the roofs to observe the proceedings. There followed a succession of tests of the East German claim to jurisdiction at the crossing point. Each time an official American civilian vehicle was stopped by the Vopos, the combat-ready jeeps were sent in to escort it. Each time that happened, the Vopos stepped grudgingly aside as the jeeps rolled up.

With the Americans driving in and out, flouting the East German regime's passport decree, Ulbricht's claim to sovereignty looked very flimsy by nightfall. It was the most significant setback the Communists had experienced since the border sealing operation had begun. The Russians, who had sent their embassy's military attaché and political adviser through Checkpoint Charlie to reconnoiter American armoured strength and positions at the border, weren't at all happy about it. This was to have remained an East German operation, but on Thursday night, after further successful American probes of the border crossing, thirty-three

Russian tanks rolled into East Berlin and parked in a lot not far from the Brandenburg Gate. It was the first appearance of Soviet armour in the city since the East German uprising of 1953.

On Friday, the Russian commander, who had been awaiting orders from Moscow, sent ten of those tanks down the Friedrich-strasse and positioned them facing the border, a little more than one hundred yards from the ten American tanks deployed there. For the first time ever, American and Russian tanks faced each other, if not in anger then certainly not as friends. Both the American forces in Berlin and the Soviet forces in East Germany had been put on full alert.

General Clay, at an emergency operations centre set up at US headquarters on Clayallee, was in direct communication with the American commander at the checkpoint, Lieutenant-Colonel Thomas Tyree. Tyree had had his tank crews load cannon shells into their gun racks, ready for firing. The machine-guns atop the tanks were at half-load. But Tyree recalled, 'My major concern at the time was not to prepare my men for a firefight, but to make sure something unexpected did not occur, such as a nervous soldier accidentally discharging his weapon.' He was, however, prepared to send his tanks into East Berlin if necessary to protect the vehicles dispatched by Clay across the border to affirm the American right of unrestricted access to East Berlin.

People around the world worried and waited as word was fed back from Checkpoint Charlie on what was and was not happening. One of the news agencies paid a huge sum for exclusive use of the telephone in the apothecary right on the borderline. All the other correspondents played catch-as-catch-can with the phones in the cafés. As always, rumours abounded. *Es geht los um drei uhr* – It's going to happen at three o'clock. (What's going to happen?) General Clay is on his way to the border to direct the operation personally. (What operation?) Lieutenant-Colonel Sabolyk has slugged a Vopo. (Firmly denied by the provost marshal.) With the tanks virtually snout to snout and word of their encounter flashing around the world, a lot of people in a lot of places were getting very anxious – though not at the checkpoint where, after the first hour or so, it had begun to seem like a game, especially with the pretzel seller back and making a small killing unloading his stock to the soldiers and others standing around doing nothing in the middle of a city street.

The British, whose mission personnel had already been showing their passports to the Vopos when crossing into East

Berlin, wanted to know why the Americans were engaged in such military posturing 'over an essentially minor issue'. Kennedy also wondered what the point of it all was. He telephoned Clay, who assured the President that the Russians did not want war over Berlin any more than he did, and that there would be no shooting. Despite his qualms, Kennedy told Clay he had his full support. But over at the State Department, Foy Kohler told his staff, 'I think we've had enough of this.'

The Russians felt the same way. On Saturday morning, under orders directly from Moscow, the Soviet tanks withdrew from their border positions, sixteen hours after they had arrived there. A half-hour later, the Americans did the same. As far as Clay was concerned, the operation had served its purpose – to show that it was the Russians who were still in charge of East Berlin and not the East German regime. 'The fiction,' he said, 'that it was the East Germans who were responsible for trying to prevent Allied access to East Berlin is now destroyed. The fact that the Soviet tanks appeared on the scene proves that the harassments which were taking place . . . were not those of the self-styled East German government, but ordered by its Soviet masters.'

Whatever moral victory was scored was, however, soon to be diluted by (unpublicized) instructions from Washington that American civilian officials should refrain from entering East Berlin for the time being. After Clay's triumph on the issue, they couldn't very well begin showing their passports to the Vopos, and the State Department wanted no new Berlin confrontations to damage chances of getting talks going with the Russians.

The growing divergence between Clay and Washington was as yet not widely known; and few people knew that General Clarke in Heidelberg was asking, 'What in the hell did Clay think he was doing? You don't spit in the face of a bulldog.' Clarke viewed both the operation and the hijacking of his troops and tanks by Clay without his even being consulted with great resentment. Asked later by historian Honoré Catudal, 'Would we have retreated if the Russians had used force to try to turn back our armed escorts into East Berlin?', Clarke, tough soldier that he was, replied, 'I would hope so.'

West Berlin's military vulnerability also coloured the views of General Norstad in Paris. In command of Allied forces in Europe, he was furious at being completely excluded from prior knowledge and planning of the confrontation with the Soviets. NATO had drawn up detailed plans for when and how military forces would be deployed in the Berlin dispute. Those plans had been approved by the various NATO powers after lengthy consultations. There was nothing in them which covered Clay's manoeuvre at the checkpoint which, as his critics pointed out, put the United States in a position where it might have had to back down in the face of far superior firepower. The question was: After you bring our few tanks to the Wall, what do you do next if the Russians either do not show up or do show up and just stay there? Norstad not only had not been consulted on the operation, he had not even been officially informed. He sent an angry cable to Berlin which concluded, 'I will not be ignored!'

However, West Berliners were delighted that the Americans had demonstrated in the streets that they were prepared to defend them, by force if necessary. And the Russians could see that they could no longer expect that the changes they wished to impose upon the situation would draw only routine protests from the United States.

13

Endgame

THERE WERE now three alien presences in once-proud Berlin –
the Allied presence, the Russian presence as represented by
the Communist regime, and the Wall. Though there were – and
would be for a long time – gaps where concrete had not yet been
substituted for barbed wire along the border, the Wall had
quickly replaced the Brandenburg Gate as the symbol of the city.

Sounds of gunfire east of it each night testified that more
people were attempting to escape than the comparative few who
were succeeding. During the day, people in the West brought
chairs to the Wall to stand on and peer across, trying to spot loved
ones on the other side. Not permitted close enough to do the
same, people in the East stood where they could, squinting,
hands cupped over eyes, scanning the top of the Wall, now
capped with barbed wire, for a familiar face. On both sides,
elderly men and women, forlornly trying to make contact, wafted
white handkerchiefs back and forth as if transmitting coded
semaphore messages laced with sorrow. People held up placards
on which they had written greetings or family news in the hope
that they could be read on the other side.

Worries about the viability of West Berlin after the Wall were no
longer academic. Fearful of the future, 300 people, on average,
were leaving the city every day to settle in West Germany where
the attractions remained considerable – statistics showed there
were six unfilled jobs for every unemployed person there. The
new exodus was helped along by circulation-grabbing headlines in
the popular press asking 'Is West Berlin Now Being Sold Out?'
West Berlin newspapers were full of advertisements of real estate
for sale. Businesses as well as individuals and families were

abandoning the frontline. Many people who were not yet leaving were nevertheless 'putting a foot' in West Germany – buying property if they could afford it and taking soundings for jobs. Some married couples and families who had not long before debated on whether to leave their homes in East Germany now debated on whether to leave West Berlin as well.

Inducements were devised to keep people from going. Income taxes were cut for West Berliners. Cash bonuses were paid to low income workers. Substantial tax and other financial advantages were offered to businesses. Large loans were offered to young marrieds. No effort was made to play down the fact that a young West German man could gain himself an exemption from being drafted into the army by moving to West Berlin.

One night, a young woman knocked on our door to offer us money. It was, she explained, *zitter geld* (fear money). Every resident of Berlin was being given a reward simply for being there! – one hundred marks for an individual; in a family, one hundred marks for the husband, fifty marks for the wife and each child. But the drift out of the West Berlin continued.

The city was being hurt in other ways as well. The Hilton, once fully booked every day, was half empty. Businessmen from afar saw less reason to visit Berlin and fewer journalists were sent to the city to cover a story that was beginning to grow stale. Correspondents reporting from Berlin found that their stories about Wall shootings, Communist demands, Allied protests and local morale problems were having a tough time competing for space in their newspapers and on television and radio news programmes. The world's concerns had moved elsewhere.

In Bonn as well as Berlin, political scientists, sociologists, financial specialists and other experts were put to work to come up with ways of convincing West Berliners that there was no reason for them to desert the city. Such studies were undertaken by the Americans as well. There was no sense in keeping a garrison in the outpost city if the people they were there to protect went astray.

Despite persisting rumours, the possibility that Berlin would be abandoned by the West played no part in continuing discussions in Allied capitals on how to defend the access routes. In Washington, in addition to the unceasing deliberations of the Berlin Task Force and the studies undertaken by the Pentagon and the National Security Council, political–military exercises were held at Camp David to give additional substance to thinking on what the Russians might do, and how the West might respond in an escalating conflict.

Those participating in these 'war games' were divided into the Control Team, the Blue Team (representing the United States) and the Red Team (representing the Russians, East Germans and other Warsaw Pact nations). At the start of the game, Control would set the stage with a scenario covering the development of a crisis situation – for example, not only a blockage on the access routes, but also related developments in East Germany, West Berlin, Moscow and Washington. The Blue Team would then describe how it would react; the Red Team would respond to the ensuing situation, and the Control Team would project the situation forward from their responses to present a new crisis. A game would last three days, after which Control would offer a critique.

It was not a way of formulating policy. It was primarily an exercise in close reconnaissance of the terrain. Players found it easier to understand the thinking of the Russians when put in the position of taking decisions as if on their behalf. Players representing the United States found it helped to expand their thinking; hypothetical positions they were taking proved more vulnerable than they had imagined they would be.

It proved a useful exercise also because participating players, often men who had been dealing independently with the Berlin problem, got to know each other better. The sessions were, however, not without heated clashes. At one point, the normally mild-mannered Henry Kissinger exploded in anger at what he considered a foolish move by a member of the opposing team. At another point during one of the game sessions, Carl Kaysen, who was on McGeorge Bundy's staff at the White House, issued a gratuitous condemnation of the State Department, its personnel and its procedures. Taken aback, John Ausland said, 'Carl, the Soviet Union is the enemy, not the State Department.' Kaysen fixed him with a stern look and responded, 'I'm not so sure.'

Even before the tank confrontation at Checkpoint Charlie, the Russians, stopped dead at the Wall, had begun reviewing their Berlin tactics. In September, Mikhail Kharlamov, head of the Soviet foreign ministry's press division, had told presidential press secretary Pierre Salinger that Khrushchev was prepared 'to consider American proposals for a rapprochement on Berlin'. A week before the Lightner border incident, to the barely concealed fury of Ulbricht, Khrushchev had told the Twenty-Second Congress of the Soviet Communist Party in Moscow that the western powers had finally shown 'some understanding of the German problem and are disposed to seek a settlement of . . . the question of West Berlin on a mutually acceptable basis.' Therefore, the Soviet leader said, the deadline he had previously set for signing a peace treaty with East Germany 'was not really important'. He told visiting Belgian Foreign Minister Paul-Henri Spaak, 'Berlin is not such a problem for me. What are two million people among a billion Communists?'

Mikhail ('Smiling Mike') Menshikov, the unsmiling, hardline Soviet Ambassador in Washington, was replaced by the personally more agreeable Anatoli Dobrynin, who was said by western intelligence services to be less hawkish in his approach to East–West differences. Ulbricht continued trying to force Khrushchev's hand. There were no less than twenty-four incidents in the closing months of 1961 involving detention, harassment or damage of American military vehicles in East Berlin. West Berlin police on the border were equipped with rifles and automatic weapons after Vopos, who had been equipped with such weapons since 1948, had persistently fired into the western sectors after fleeing refugees. But faced with Allied firmness on West Berlin and the American military build-up in Europe, the Russians, though still deeply affronted by the continuing western presence in Berlin and while not abandoning their objectives, were stepping back to re-examine the possibilities. The Americans were doing the same.

When Gromyko went to the United Nations General Assembly in New York towards the end of September, he met there with Dean Rusk for 'exploratory talks'. If no progress could be made towards ending the Berlin dispute satisfactorily, Kennedy hoped at least to trap the Russians into a protracted dialogue while the western defensive build-up in Europe was completed. Rusk said, 'Westerners usually like to rush to agreement while Russians like to wait it out and hope to gain an advantage that way. But we decided we'd just talk, talk, talk. We'd talk just as long and just as repetitively as Gromyko would.'

At the same time, indications began to appear that the United States was preparing to offer concessions – though not over West Berlin – if comparable concessions could be extracted from Moscow. Apparently acting under instructions from the White House, no less a hardliner than General Clay, while briefing some American correspondents, said with a steely grin that West Germans would have to come to terms with the new situation and 'recognize the reality of the existence of two German states'. This was such a remarkable turn-about for the general that UPI's Joe Fleming, who knew him well, asked him twice if that was what he really meant to say. It was, and when it was reported the storm of outrage in West German official circles was so intense that Clay was quickly instructed to declare that he had been misquoted and that the United States still firmly backed reunification for Germany. However, Senator Hubert Humphrey, a leading Democratic Party figure and close political ally of the President, spoke in Washington of 'give and take on both sides'. After visiting East and Central Europe, Senator Claiborne Pell suggested that, no matter what Adenauer was saying, most Germans did not care all that much about whether their country was reunified, implying that most Americans didn't either, and that facts were facts and had to be recognized as such.

When he visited Berlin the following February, the President's brother, Attorney General Robert Kennedy, reassured people there that they were not alone. 'An armed attack on West Berlin,' he told them, 'is the same thing as an armed attack on Chicago, New York, London or Paris. You are our brothers and we will stand by you.' But he also made it clear that, though the Wall was an atrocity, no miracle was going to bring it down. A new situation had been created, he said, and the West had to reconcile itself to it. Remaining unsaid but clearly implied was what Willy Brandt knew already – no matter what the official position, American acceptance of the division of Berlin ratified its acceptance of the division of Germany.*

Despite the feelers put out by the administration, the fact was that Kennedy, while prepared to discuss the future of Germany with the Russians, was still not willing to recognize East Germany. He told President Urho Kekkonen of Finland, whom the Russians were trying to use as an intermediary, that the United States was not going to associate itself with the Soviet-imposed division of the country and 'thus weaken our ties to West Germany and their ties to Western Europe'. As for Soviet offers of guarantees on the access routes in return for Allied conces-

---

*The Attorney General was accompanied on that trip by his younger brother, Edward Kennedy, later to be senator for Massachusetts. The youngest of the Kennedy brothers took the opportunity to visit East Berlin, entering by way of the Friedrichstrasse railway station, where his passport was checked and his photograph was taken for the Communist press. The East German news agency ADN later boasted that Edward had 'respected in every way the sovereignty of the German Democratic Republic'. When the reports reached Washington, Foy Kohler telephoned Allan Lightner and told him the President wasn't at all happy about this and wanted him to do what he could to stop publicity on Edward's visit. He feared it might hurt his brother's political career.

sions, Kennedy told Kekkonen that the Russians were 'asking us to make concessions in exchange for which they will give us what we already have . . . We would be buying the same horse twice.' Negotiations would have to be serious, not a matter of one party taking and the other required to give.

The French, declining to agree to what would be essentially a superpower dialogue with themselves merely looking on, remained adamantly unimpressed with the whole idea; and Adenauer, resenting suggestions from Washington that he would soon have to face up to the reality of two Germanies, was increasingly suspicious of Kennedy. Backed only by the British, who were even more anxious for negotiations than he was, the President was increasingly exasperated with Paris and Bonn. He told French Ambassador Alphand that he was weary of the French habit of offering objections to talks with the Russians while doing little to contribute to the western military build-up in Europe, which was the only alternative. He warned that the Allies would have to 'come along or stay behind'. That was an empty challenge. The last thing he wanted to do was achieve the Russian objective of splitting the western alliance. It was, moreover, soon apparent that though the Russians might be willing to talk, their objectives remained unchanged. They were not interested in negotiations which might involve concessions of any kind on their part. Only a western cave-in would suffice. Pressure towards that end had merely been suspended until a more suitable moment. That moment was not long in coming.

Barely had the sounds of the 1962 New Year's celebrations faded out than Gromyko suggested to Ambassador Thompson in Moscow that the Soviet Union would not object to the continued 'temporary' presence of western forces in West Berlin, provided Soviet troops could be stationed there as well. It was an unabashed bid to turn West Berlin into the four-power city that all of Berlin had previously been. It was immediately, unequivocally rejected. The Russians were, however, now again ready to shift their efforts away from fruitless diplomatic exchanges to exchanges of a more palpable kind. Once more, their actions were influenced by the position of General Clay, but in a different way.

Clay had flown off to visit Washington early in January. A State Department spokesman called it a 'routine consultation' and denied reports that the general had returned to Washington to protest at being hemmed in not by the Communists, but by his own side. The patrols he had reintroduced along the autobahn in

East Germany had been removed so as not to exacerbate the situation. General Watson, through whom Clay had been able to bring out the troops and tanks when needed, was ordered in no uncertain terms to clear all future American military moves in Berlin with General Clarke, who still refused to acknowledge that Clay had any special authority. Clay was being turned into the mere symbol of America's commitment to Berlin that President Kennedy had initially intended him to be.

When he got to Washington, Clay protested to Dean Rusk that General Watson – meaning he and Watson – had to be given enough latitude to deal with emergency situations on the border; such things, he said, could not be directed from afar. He warned that the muzzle that had been fitted on him was an invitation to the Russians to begin nibbling away again at the western presence in the city. He was angry that his cabled complaints from Berlin had been ignored.* He had protested to the White House, but had discovered that his difficulties with the State Department and the Pentagon were not nearly as high on President Kennedy's list of priorities as he thought they ought to be.

In Washington, he did get to see the President for an hour. When he returned to Berlin and was questioned by his aides about what the President had said, he told them that, in view of the senior position in the business world from which he had taken leave to go to Berlin (he was chairman of the Continental Can Company), Kennedy had spoken to him about the problems the administration was then having with the steel industry, which was pushing for inflationary price increases. As McGeorge Bundy has said, 'President's talk about what's on their mind.'

A fundamental problem was that Clay, who had firm ideas on what should be done, was playing a unilateral game, while everybody else was trying to sustain a carefully, sometimes painfully, worked out multilateral Allied holding operation. The contradiction was too sharp to be overlooked. The same was to some extent true of the United States Embassy in Bonn, which was to be sharply reprimanded for sending messages proposing unilateral American moves. These, in the words of one Berlin Task Force member in Washington, 'just didn't fit in'.

---

*The tone of Clay's telegrams had grown increasingly abusive and increasingly offended people in Washington. Some of the resulting exasperation with Clay rubbed off on Allan Lightner. Though the telegrams began 'From Clay', because he was minister at the Mission many of them were signed 'Lightner', though Lightner had been making strenuous efforts to get Clay to tone down those messages and not to send the more abusive ones at all.

Clay's visit to Washington earned him nothing more than an infuriating pat on the back and word that he should go back to Berlin and carry on the good work he was doing. He was incensed, but realized that if he quit in a huff and refused to go back it would do more damage to the American position and West Berlin morale than he believed was being done by the administration. When he returned to Berlin, to their befuddlement, he shunned people at the British Mission there. They had been used as a scapegoat by Washington. Clay had been told that their complaints about his behaviour, at a time when Allied unity was essential for East–West negotiations, were part of the reason for the changes being made.

With no further American challenges to the passport-showing requirements on the sector border, with the American autobahn patrols which Clay had reintroduced removed, with the American tanks which he had kept positioned 300 yards from the sector border now drawn back well away from the Wall, and with various minor acts of harassment on the autobahn from West Germany eliciting mostly routine protest notes, it soon became apparent to the Russians that Clay was being roped in. The significance of this was, however, unclear to them, and they decided to find out what it meant by resuming suspended efforts to elbow the West out of Berlin.

This time, there was to be a major and direct challenge to the Allies – a move against access routes which Kennedy had vowed to keep open by armed force if necessary. The air corridors between West Germany and West Berlin, which had been used to decisive advantage against them during the Berlin blockade, were to be the stage for the renewed Soviet campaign.

On 12 February 1962, the Russians announced that they were reserving the corridors at certain times each day for use by their own military aircraft. They followed that up with an announcement that they were reserving certain altitudes for their own use. They then insisted on certain changes in flight procedures. They backed up their words with actions more dangerous than any so far seen in the crisis.

Soviet jets took to buzzing western commercial aircraft in the corridors. They also dropped strips of metal foil along their routes to disrupt the safety radar of the planes. For a time, searchlights east of the sector border were directed at western aircraft coming in to land at Tempelhof in an effort to blind the pilots. A CIA operative ironically suggested that, since Washington was still insisting that Berlin was a four-power city, the

American command should send a patrol of troops into the East to arrest the people operating the searchlights and bring them back to West Berlin for trial.

The safety of the civilian airliners flying daily through the corridors to Berlin became a serious concern, which was the Soviet purpose. At one point, the director of British European Airways wanted to suspend flights because of the danger. He had to be spoken to very firmly by Lord Home, who was awakened at 2.00 a.m. one morning to deal with the situation, before changing his mind. But there were grim faces in the western foreign ministries as the Soviet harassment of the defenceless aircraft continued. It was feared that all that was needed was one accident for the situation to become irretrievable. John Ausland said, 'When they started fooling around with the air corridors, it was hard to see how we would get out of it without some sort of shooting.' The situation also caused friction between the United States and Britain.

Although General Clay's characteristically bellicose suggestion that American jet fighters be sent through the corridors to demonstrate Allied determination to keep them open had been rejected by General Norstad, the British feared that the United States, with its countless contingency plans, would be provoked into defiant gestures which might increase rather than lessen the dangers, and they said so. At one stage, Foy Kohler took aside Lord Hood, the minister at the British Embassy in Washington, and gave him a stiff lecture on how timid the British were. The Foreign Office in London felt obliged to draft a long telegram to the embassy explaining in detail how that charge should be answered by giving chapter and verse on how unwavering and firm the British had been throughout the crisis.

Though it posed a greater danger, this new Soviet exercise was, in a decisive way, a more difficult undertaking for Moscow than the building of the Wall had been. In the case of the Wall, aggressive action – to tear it down – would have had to have come from the Allies. In the air corridors, aggressive action – stopping Allied aircraft from getting through – had to come from the Russians. Despite the dangerous harassment of flights, Moscow wasn't prepared to risk the consequences of making a plane crash. Though some voices in Washington continued to urge stronger action, the Allies demonstrated their determination not to be budged by doing no more than putting fighter aircraft at bases in West Germany on ground alert, flying military transport planes through parts of the western air corridors which the

Russians claimed to be reserving for their own use, and maintaining normal, uninterrupted civilian air traffic to Berlin.

The Soviet action in flirting with disaster so angered the normally imperturbable Rusk that he wanted to cancel an East–West disarmament conference in Geneva but, in view of the importance attached to the subject, the White House urged him to go through with it. The meeting achieved little, but Rusk was treated to a remarkable display in the Swiss city – the most vigorous dressing down to which he had ever seen Gromyko exposed, delivered by the British foreign secretary. Using language of which Rusk had never thought so courteous a man capable, Lord Home told the Soviet foreign minister exactly what he thought of a government which could order steps that might make civilian airliners crash. The unqualified determination of the West not to back down on this issue persuaded Moscow that a totally different approach to the Berlin problem had to be devised, and harassment of the air corridors soon tapered off and then stopped altogether.

Once more Soviet moves against the western presence in Berlin were suspended. There were still recurring harassments of Allied traffic on the ground access routes and in East Berlin, but they were comparatively minor, and once more tensions eased. The files on contingency plans for counter-measures were stuffed back into the filing cabinet and General Clay seized the opportunity to withdraw from the frontline city without damaging West Berlin morale or the American image. He had no wish to remain a powerless symbol.

When it was announced that the general was going home, the American mission was deluged with frantic calls from West Berliners who believed that his departure was a frightening omen. The general tried to assure West Berliners that they were safe from a Communist take-over. Like the US Cavalry in western movies, he promised to return if he was needed. But, though three-quarters of a million people jammed the Town Hall square to say goodbye to him, he was unable, nor did he try, to reconcile them to the existence of two Berlins.

By then, Clay had long since been shorn of the power to go his own way, and West Berliners had gotten over the worst of their fear and trembling about the future of their portion of the divided city, so it no longer mattered much to the White House, the State Department or the Pentagon whether he stayed or went. Kennedy was relieved and grateful that he went home without public complaint or accusation. After his departure, Dean Rusk and most of the others whose nerves the general had rattled by his actions came to the conclusion that he had served his country and the Allied cause far better than they had imagined at the time. Feisty and insubordinate, he had demonstrated that it wasn't necessary to let aggressors have everything their own way. He had held the fort while everyone else figured out what the problem really was and how to deal with it.

A full year after their city had been divided, Berliners were still trying to reconcile themselves to their new circumstances. On 13 August 1962, the first anniversary of the sealing of the sector border, thousands of West Berliners, mostly youths, converged on the Wall for angry commemorations of the day when their fellow Berliners had been trapped behind barbed wire. Stones and beer bottles were hurled into East Berlin as tempers flared. Vopos responded with tear-gas grenades. More than twenty West Berlin policemen were injured before the crowds were brought under control. It proved only a curtain-raiser for the explosion of popular wrath two days later, when two young East Berlin construction workers tried to escape to the West over the Wall not far from Checkpoint Charlie. One got over as bullets whizzed around him. But the other, eighteen-year-old Peter Fechter, was shot as he tried to pull himself over the barbed wire atop the Wall. He fell back into the East and lay there bleeding and moaning. The seeming indifference of the armed East Berlin guards who left him there slowly dying infuriated West Berlin. That anger was by no means softened by a report that an American lieutenant on duty nearby, when asked to do something, said tactlessly, but in accordance with his orders, 'It's not my problem.' A West Berlin tabloid carried a paid advertisement saying, 'West Berliners accuse American Commander General Watson of being an accomplice to murder.' For the first time in West Berlin, there were shouts of 'Ami Go Home!' and American army jeeps were booed while on patrol.

But anti-American feeling was, for the most part, limited to a comparative few embittered individuals. It was far outweighed by recognition that without the presence of the Allies, particularly the Americans, West Berlin was lost, and by fury against the East German Communists who ordered that fellow Germans be shot down. Anti-Communist riots erupted west of the Wall for the next three nights. Soviet vehicles riding through West Berlin were stoned. One Soviet car, on its regular flag-showing tour of West Berlin, was chased by a crowd of Berliners and had to drive into an American military compound to ask for an escort, which was provided. When the bus carrying troops for the changing of the guard at the Soviet War Memorial in the British Sector had its windows broken by stones, the Russians took to bringing their men across in armoured personnel-carriers. The Allies immediately protested. In response, the Russians, weary of Allied protests in the city, simply abolished the office of the Soviet commandant in East Berlin.

The Allies, nevertheless, told the Russians that they would not tolerate the appearance of Soviet combat vehicles in West Berlin. They were told also that, instead of using Checkpoint Charlie to reach their War Memorial as they had been doing for many months, they should send their memorial guards through a crossing point closer to it. Apparently because they did not wish to make an issue of their war memorial, the Russians acquiesced to these instructions without further fuss, though Kennedy had been deeply worried that it might lead to a new and dangerous confrontation.

In fact, the Russians soon appeared once again to be calling a momentary 'time out' over Berlin. Though they declared, 'It is necessary at long last to liquidate the occupation regime in West Berlin,' the Soviet news agency *Tass* announced that Moscow would make no further Berlin moves until after the American mid-term elections in November. Washington welcomed the respite, but began bracing itself for the long-awaited final showdown on the access routes – the *real crisis* – after election day, just two months away. Not much significance was attached to the fact that the *Tass* announcement coincided with a visit to Moscow of a Cuban delegation which had gone to Russia to sign an arms agreement.

On 16 October 1962, Nikita Khrushchev summoned Foy Kohler, who had by then become the American ambassador in Moscow, to the Kremlin. Dismissing reports widespread in America that the Soviet Union was engaged in a major arms build-up in Cuba as exaggerated, the Soviet leader expressed his admiration for the United States and its President, and added his voice to the chorus of Soviet assurances – Ambassador Dobrynin had chimed in with one as well – that Moscow had no intention of doing anything that might embarrass Kennedy on the eve of the congressional elections.

Two days later, Soviet Foreign Minister Andrei Gromyko called at the White House in Washington and sternly told

Kennedy there would finally have to be a 'normalization' of the Berlin situation. Gromyko once more served notice that his country would sign a separate peace treaty with East Germany if the western powers were not prepared to co-operate, and would not be deterred by American threats. But the Soviet foreign minister also made a point of reiterating to the President that Russia was putting Berlin on hold until election day.

Kennedy briskly informed Gromyko that the United States still had no intention of reneging on its commitment to West Berlin. But the President didn't trouble to spend much time on the subject. Moscow knew the American position well enough. Nor did Kennedy have much to say about Gromyko's assurance that Moscow wanted to spare him possible electoral embarrassment over Berlin during the following few weeks. Of far greater concern for the President were accelerated Soviet arms shipments to Cuba, about which the CIA had first reported to the White House several weeks earlier. Gromyko assured the President that the United States had no reason to be bothered by them. He said that only defensive weapons were being sent and that surely the American superpower didn't have to worry about being threatened by tiny Cuba.

Gromyko did not know, and was not at that time told, that Kennedy knew he was lying. High-flying U-2 reconnaissance aircraft had brought back photographic evidence that the Russians were installing offensive nuclear missiles in Cuba which had the capacity to devastate large parts of America. The recklessness of Khrushchev's move was frightening. The attempt to deceive the United States – to the extent of having the Soviet foreign minister tell the President a brazen lie on crucial security matters – was outrageous. The threat to the American mainland was intolerable.

On 22 October, Kennedy went on nationwide television to tell the American people and the world what was happening, and to announce his response. A United States naval blockade of Cuba would be set up to prevent any more offensive weapons getting through. 'This quarantine,' the President said, 'will be extended, if needed, to other types of cargo and carriers. We are not at this time, however, denying [Cuba] the necessities of life as the Soviets attempted to do in their Berlin blockade of 1948.' Kennedy declared further that if any nuclear missile was 'launched from Cuba against any nation in the western hemisphere' it would be regarded as 'an attack by the Soviet Union on the United States, requiring a full retaliatory response upon the Soviet Union'.

By then, the American Strategic Air Command's nuclear-armed

B-52 bombers had been put on full airborne alert. Jet fighters had been moved to bases in Florida, as had more than 100,000 troops. America's intercontinental ballistic missiles had been primed for firing. Almost two hundred United States Navy vessels were deployed in the Caribbean, ready to board and inspect any ships that might be carrying nuclear missiles to Cuba, and to turn back those found to be doing so.

At the United Nations in New York, the Soviet delegate, who denied that his country was mounting a threat to American security, said the United States was putting millions of lives at risk. British philosopher Bertrand Russell cabled Khrushchev that his 'continued forebearance is our great hope' and cabled Kennedy that there was 'no conceivable justification' for the action he was taking. In London, crowds of demonstrators gathered in front of the American Embassy in Grosvenor Square to shout their protests and try to break through police lines. That scene was duplicated in Paris and in the capital cities of many other countries. The homes of American diplomats were bombed in Montevideo and there were anti-American riots in Rio de Janeiro. Countless people feared that the world was trembling on the brink of disaster.

It wasn't only foreigners who were frightened. Dean Rusk greeted Under Secretary of State George Ball the morning after Kennedy's announcement with congratulations that 'You and I are still alive.' Admiring a beautiful sunset in Washington, Secretary of Defence Robert McNamara wondered how many more he would be permitted to enjoy. In Moscow, military leaders declared threateningly that the Soviet Union would not permit itself to be pushed around, and Khrushchev warned that Soviet submarines would sink any vessel trying to interfere with trade with Cuba. In Berlin, Francis Meehan, who is now ambassador to East Germany but was then at the American Mission, seeking ways to relieve his anxiety and the growing tension, said to his wife and children at their Berlin home, 'Let's all go out and rake some leaves.'

Whatever their fears or expectations, Macmillan and de Gaulle, alerted in advance, had given their unqualified support to Kennedy's move, as did the member nations of the Organization of American States. Adenauer did as well, after agonizing over whether the Russians would seize the opportunity to move against Berlin. But no such fears were felt by those who believed with General Clay that when faced with firm resistance the Russians would back down. In Berlin, Joachim Bölke said,

'When I heard that Kennedy had stopped those ships, I knew the Russians would pull back. It was too dangerous for them. I said to my colleagues [at the *Taggesspiegel* newspaper] – who felt the same way – "That ends the Berlin crisis. We have survived it." '

At the State Department, the Berlin Task Force could not afford to adopt so casual an approach. It shared Adenauer's anxieties. The situation was ideal for a renewed Soviet move against Berlin. America was distracted elsewhere. The smell of catastrophe was in the air. Once more, the various Berlin contingency plans were trotted out. Once more, the Task Force went into round-the-clock session. Once more, LIVE OAK command outside Paris prepared for the worst. And once more, the western garrisons in the divided city were put on the alert.

In the White House too, Berlin was, according to Ted Sorenson, 'first on everyone's list' as the likely target for Soviet retaliation. A special subcommittee of the group of Kennedy's most valued advisers was formed to duplicate the workings of the Berlin Task Force and monitor Berlin developments during the missile crisis.

As it turned out, no significant problems over Berlin developed. One comparatively minor incident occurred at a Soviet autobahn checkpoint over the processing procedure for an American convoy. It was soon resolved, but the American Mission in Berlin, attuned as always primarily to local circumstances, urged that, now that the Kremlin was preoccupied with Cuba, the situation should be exploited to force a showdown on processing procedures. It was, however, pointed out to the Mission by the State Department that the United States was at that moment also up to its eyeballs in the Cuba crisis, and that there was no point in adding an unnecessary dimension to it.

On 28 October, six days after Kennedy had announced the Cuban blockade, Khrushchev beat a clumsy retreat. He announced that the missiles, which the Russians had so strenuously denied were there, would be dismantled, crated and shipped back from Cuba. No other nuclear weapons would be sent to replace them. In desperation over Berlin, Khrushchev had tried and failed at a demeaning deception. The implications of his humiliation, and that of the Soviet Union, would reach much further than the Caribbean.

When word had earlier been scattered like buckshot that Russia would put off further action on Berlin until after the American congressional elections, Khrushchev had expected to have his missiles in place in Cuba by election time. He believed they would then become an American election issue and that he would be able to use them for a proposed trade-off on Berlin. Defence Secretary Robert McNamara later told Congress:

> Their stationing of nuclear-armed ballistic missiles in Cuba was directly related to [the Soviet Berlin] agenda. The psychological if not the military threat that these missiles would have posed to our own homeland was apparently the trump card which Mr Khrushchev intended to play in the next round of negotiations on the status of Berlin.

There was talk during the crisis of Khrushchev angling for a trade-off of the missiles in Cuba for American Jupiter missiles in Turkey. But though the missiles in Turkey were obsolescent, the suggestion was rejected by the White House. It might have been taken by America's allies as indicating Washington's readiness to sacrifice their defence interests to protect those of the United States. In any case, it was Berlin that Khrushchev was after. His missiles in Cuba were to be the key to the removal of the western garrisons from Berlin. West Berlin would fall first under Soviet influence, and then under Soviet control. The heroic victory of the Red Army in conquering the city in 1945 would finally be consummated.

By responding so vigorously and unequivocally to the Cuba challenge, Kennedy had, however, demonstrated the shortcomings of Soviet military capabilities and determination. What was more, the Russians now had to live with the likelihood that Kennedy, having shone brilliantly in his management of the Cuba crisis, would respond with equal vigour and control to any further efforts to squeeze the West out of Berlin. He had finally redeemed himself for the Bay of Pigs. As was clear even in the Kremlin, Khrushchev had behaved with dazzling recklessness in committing Soviet prestige so far from home against a power his military forces could not match. As a last gasp of the Kremlin's shattered Berlin ambitions, Gromyko, meeting with Rusk shortly after the Cuba episode, hinted that the Soviets might be prepared to trade Russian dominance in Cuba for West Berlin. But it was a feeble try and Rusk told him the United States wasn't interested. Not long afterwards, visiting East Berlin, Khrushchev told his unhappy hosts that the existence of the Wall reduced the need for a separate peace treaty.

There were further incidents of harassment on the western access routes and further fulminations from the East German Communists – who continued to denounce West Berlin's links with West Germany as a militaristic provocation, and to condemn the Allied lifelines as an encroachment on the sovereignty of the German Democratic Republic. But the end of the Cuba missile crisis had effectively spelled the end, also, of the Berlin crisis.

Since 1958, Khrushchev had tried everything to snuff out the western presence in the city – ultimatums, smiles, promises that West Berlin's independence would be guaranteed, harassment of Allied access routes, and nuclear threats. But the western garrisons were still mockingly in place, smack dab in the middle of Communist East Germany. Whatever hopes and plans the Kremlin had entertained for West Berlin were now shelved. Soviet diplomacy, shaken by the enormity of Khrushchev's abortive gamble, went into a period of rest and rehabilitation.

However, the Berlin Wall – grey, bleak and forbidding – remained in place. It became a tourist attraction. No visit to Berlin was complete without a look at it. West Berlin – walled in but accessible from the West – remained an island of defiance in a Communist sea. It continued to draw ritual visits of solidarity from Western leaders, who climbed viewing platforms – which had been built to enable people to peer over the Wall in wonder and dismay at the armed guards on the far side, at the watchtowers and the death-strips.

John Kennedy paid his personal respects to West Berlin a few months after the Cuba missile crisis. He looked at the Wall and over it and then stood on the balcony of West Berlin's Town Hall, overlooking the square which would later be named after him, to offer the hundreds of thousands of West Berliners who had gathered there to cheer him an eloquent tribute and a promise that they would not be forgotten:

> There are many people in the world who really don't understand, or say they don't, what is the great issue between the free world and the Communist world. Let them come to Berlin. There are some who say that Communism is the wave of the future. Let them come to Berlin. And there are some who say in Europe and elsewhere we can work with the Communists. Let them come to Berlin. And there are even a few who say that it is true that Communism is an evil system, but it permits us to make economic progress. *Lasst sie nach Berlin kommen.* Let them come to Berlin . . . All free men, wherever they may live, are citizens of Berlin and, therefore, as a free man, I take pride in the words '*Ich bin ein Berliner.*'

Over the next two years, the two prime movers in the Berlin crisis were removed from the scene. John Kennedy was cut down by an assassin in Dallas a few months after his Berlin visit. The following year, Khrushchev – a victim of his failure in Berlin as much as anything else – was ousted from the leadership of the Soviet Union and made to tiptoe into obscurity. The peace treaty to formally conclude the Second World War, which he had been turned into a diplomatic ploy and a threat, was never signed, neither with East Germany nor West Germany. As far as legal documents are concerned, the armies of Adolf Hitler may have surrendered unconditionally a long time ago, but the Second World War is still not over.

Changes in Berlin followed. A secondary wall was built to keep people in the East from approaching the border Wall and reduce still further the small number of escapers. A deep trench was dug between them for the same purpose. More watchtowers were built along the Wall and more lightposts were put up to keep it illuminated through the night. Dog runs were installed and death-strips were extended. Maintenance of the Wall, and the refinements around it, became a main priority of the East German regime.

Though East Berliners were still not permitted West, arrangements were in due course made for West Berliners to obtain visas to visit relatives in the East again. Welcome though that was, it could not eradicate the image of the barrier between the two parts of the city, or the fact that East Germans were still being killed trying to get through it. Nor could it relieve Willy Brandt of the disturbing conviction that he had made a huge mistake in believing that the Allies, and particularly the Americans, would actually strive for the reunification of his country. He did not believe that the failure of the western powers to prevent the division of his city could be glossed over by reference to the dangers of nuclear conflict, frightening as those dangers were. If they could not prevent the division of a city, how could they be expected to do anything about the division of a country?

For Brandt – who had wanted 'energetic steps' taken by the West the day the Wall was built, who reviled and despised the police-state behaviour of the East German regime, who had wanted nothing to do with Communism or its practitioners – the Wall was a turning point that would prove of momentous significance for Europe and the world when, a few years later, he became West German foreign minister and then Chancellor. The seed of his *Ostpolitik* (Eastern policy), his reaching out for reconciliation with East Germany, was planted when the barrier was lowered across the middle of Berlin on Barbed Wire Sunday.

Brandt concluded that the reunification of his country, if such a thing was possible, would have to wait. Some form of contact first had to be established between the two parts of the German nation. He said, 'We had to look for new ways to alleviate the split – and leave the rest to the future.'

Egon Bahr, who went with Brandt from Berlin to Bonn and also became a prominent figure in West German politics, said, 'We had to adjust to reality. Since we could not break through the Wall, we had to start negotiations, not with the Americans, not with the Soviets, but with those damned East German Communists, to get visas to cross the border.'

The turn-about in West German policy initiated by Brandt was seen by his critics as an unforgivable sell-out to Communist tyranny. But it led to an easing of international friction in Europe. In 1972 – fourteen years after Khrushchev's first Berlin ultimatum to the Allies – the four powers which had conquered Germany in the war, and the two German states which had sprung from that defeat, reached agreement on the future status of West Berlin. While it was not to be considered an integral part of West Germany, it was agreed by all concerned that it would retain close and undisputed economic, cultural and political links with the West German state. The western access routes through East Germany would be unimpeded. The continued presence of the three western garrisons in West Berlin would no longer be disputed.

The international status of the German Democratic Republic was upgraded; the United States granted it diplomatic recognition two years later. Its Communist leaders were less than happy to agree that control of West Berlin remained beyond their grasp. But Khrushchev's successor, Leonid Brezhnev, still struggling to make sense of the Soviet civilian economy, and Richard Nixon, Lyndon Johnson's successor as President of the United States, trying to extricate America from Vietnam, were relieved that a less strained, less precarious East–West climate of relations in Europe had replaced the discord which had clouded the atmosphere for so long.

Though the agreement was widely welcomed, not everybody was satisfied with the details. When they heard that there would be a reference in the final communiqué only to the 'western sectors of Berlin', rather than to all the sectors or to just 'Berlin', American officials who had been involved with the crisis from the beginning were amazed that Nixon and Secretary of State Henry Kissinger had agreed to the distinction. One of them cabled the

American delegation that 'we worked too hard on this to give it all away in a communiqué.' His protest and those of others were ignored and he was left believing that it would 'come back to haunt us one day'. The West had never been willing to sign an agreement with the Russians concerning only West Berlin, with East Berlin removed from the equation: it was a violation of the theology of Berlin. The fact remained that West Berlin was (and is) still one hundred miles inside Communist East Europe and the access routes were (and are) still potentially as vulnerable as they always had been.

For the West, the Berlin Wall symbolized the failure of Communism to endure without recourse to force and repression. For Communist ideologists, it represented a necessity as they guided people along the rugged road to what they believed would be a better society and a more fulfilling life. For Communist bureaucrats and officials, it meant being able to call upon the police to guarantee that the requirements of the party and the state were met, without the danger of driving the workforce into exile.

But to many East Berliners and East Germans, the Wall was just concrete and kalashnikovs, and it was confinement for reasons they could not accept, under rule to which they objected, in a place where they no longer wished to be. Confronted with the armed might of a system in which even a few unguarded words could earn them jail sentences, most of those who felt that way resigned themselves to circumstances and grew grudgingly reconciled to being fenced in.

For some, however, though they had enough to eat, places to live and jobs of work, the situation was unendurable. Whether in search of freedom or the comparative luxuries which life in the West could provide, or a more rewarding future than they believed Communism had to offer, people found ways to get past the Wall – at the risk of being imprisoned if their intentions were revealed, or of being shot if they were caught in the act.

In the beginning, before the Vopos tightened their border-control procedures, it was easier. One man drugged his three small children with sleeping pills and, with his wife, carried them to a less well patrolled stretch of the barbed wire in a rural section of the city. There, he snipped the wire with wire-cutters and held the ends apart while his wife carried their children through, and then he followed. Fourteen people took command of an East German excursion boat on the River Spree and forced it to dock in West Berlin so that they could step ashore there and seek sanctuary. An engineer had friends in the West lift him across the border by means of a huge construction crane, which reached over the the Wall to pick up the improvised basket in which he stood.

When the barrier was first being built, look-outs were posted at night in West Berlin apartments overlooking the area while escape helpers hauled two long ladders to the Wall. Propping one of them up against the western side, they climbed up, snipped the barbed wire at the top and dropped the other ladder down to rest against the eastern face of the Wall. In accordance with prearranged instructions, refugees would sprint forwards from the eastern side to climb up and over into freedom.

Twenty-five people fled aboard a commuter train, driven by a refugee, which sped through from East Germany into the British Sector. Another escaper fitted out the rear of his van with armour plate, lined part of the sides with poured concrete, and crashed through a border checkpoint in a hail of gunfire. Others neglected such precautions and tried to ram their unfortified vehicles through checkpoints. Some succeeded; others had their bodies riddled with sub-machine-gun bullets before ploughing into obstructions erected to stop them.

Tight, closed compartments were ingeniously fitted into the cars of some visitors from West Germany who were not barred from entering and leaving East Berlin. Refugees secreted inside them were spirited through checkpoints at great risk to both driver and escaper. West Berlin university students formed what they waggishly called the 'Travel Bureau Incorporated' to organize escapes through various channels and along various routes for, among others, many of the 450 of their fellow students who had resided in East Berlin and had been trapped there when the border was sealed.

The most dramatic escapes were under the Wall through makeshift tunnels. Some, dug soon after the Wall was built, were comparatively short, subterranean passageways, which only dipped under the border barrier. One was started in the basement of an East Berlin home and clawed out by a group of men who took turns at taking sick leave from work to get on with the job. A look-out mounted at an upstairs window of the house signalled the approach of border guards in the area by switching off the tunnel lights. When it was finished, twenty-eight people, ranging in age from eight to seventy-one, crawled through it to the West.

Another tunnel, through which 150 people escaped, went from

a building on the western side to a cemetery in East Berlin, where its entrance was concealed by a gravestone. It was discovered by the Vopos when a woman fleeing with her infant drew the gravestone back into place after she had entered the tunnel, but left the baby carriage standing empty nearby.

The most ambitious tunnel, 145 yards long, was dug over a period of seven months by a group of West Berliners, mostly college students (some of them aspiring engineers), who gave up a term's work to get on with the job. It was started in the cellar of a West Berlin building near the Wall and by sheer luck came to the surface again in a deserted cellar in East Berlin, into which the first tunneller emerged with an automatic weapon at the ready. Like most who worked on other tunnels, they had already sent couriers who possessed West German passports into East Berlin through the Communist checkpoints, to make contact with the East Berliners who were to be brought to the West through the tunnel – relatives, close friends of the tunnellers, and others they could trust. It was a worrying matter for all concerned because it was known by then that the East German security services had penetrated some of the tunnel-building groups in West Berlin.

When the digging was done and the tunnel was ready, arrangements were made for the escapers to converge calmly on the East Berlin tunnel mouth by ones and twos, carrying nothing that might arouse suspicion. During the actual escape, a mother crawled past a son – one of the tunnellers – she had not seen in months. He did not reveal his presence to her for fear of noise that might be heard above. Fifty-seven East Germans escaped through that tunnel before it was discovered by a Vopo. He was shot dead by a tunnel guard, who was then able to scamper back to West Berlin before other Vopos arrived to fire blindly into the tunnel and flood it with tear gas.

Dozens of tunnels were started, mostly from the West. Most were too ambitious and had to be abandoned. It soon became evident that the urge to dig a tunnel and bring people out did not suffice. Expert assistance and careful planning was needed, as well as suitable equipment and materials – timber to prop up tunnel roofs, excavation tools, trucks to haul away displaced earth, electricity for illumination. To finance all of this, money was needed; in one case funds were provided by NBC, which thereby acquired the right to film the operation for television.

Some of the tunnels were intricate, lengthy conduits, planned over a long period of time, which involved dozens of volunteers enrolled in what James O'Donnell has called the 'Berlin Institute of Tunnelology'. In many cases, the tunnels had to be dug deep to get under the pipes and cables which criss-crossed the city. The tunnellers had to cope with the danger of flooding (many of the tunnels were flooded and abandoned before they could be used), detection and betrayal. At least five of the tunnellers were shot dead by East German police. Several others were caught and imprisoned.

Most of the tunnellers were dedicated individuals trying to rescue relatives or friends, or motivated by a belief in human liberty and/or a hatred of Communism. Their efforts became a fashionable, noble cause which attracted the full-time commitment of many young people in West Berlin. But so anxious were some East Germans to go West that shady entrepreneurial elements were soon lured into tunnelling operations by the prospect of commercial gain. In some cases, large sums of money were demanded of would-be refugees or their relatives in the West. To this day, 'escape arranger' advertisements can be seen pasted to the railings of observation platforms overlooking the Wall in West Berlin: 'Emigration Arranged from the German Democratic Republic, Unconventional, Discreet and Reliable.'

Some people who offered services of this kind soon after the Wall was built were from West Berlin's criminal community. They sometimes took the money and abandoned the refugees. In some cases, it is believed that they actually betrayed their clients to the Vopos. It is rumoured that criminal elements are still in the 'escape arranging' business. But it is also said that, for the huge fee they charge for their services – between 50,000 and 100,000 west marks – they do what they offer to do and actually manage to get people through the Wall.

As East German security precautions grew more sophisticated and as the no-go area on the eastern side of the Wall grew larger, tunnels had to be so long to get from safety in the West to secrecy in the East that they no longer became practicable propositions. People had to find other ways to get out and other directions for their escape. And they did, but in much reduced numbers – to Scandinavia across the Baltic Sea from the northern shore of East Germany, or by demanding exit visas when staging embarrassing sit-ins in West German embassies in other Communist East European countries to which East Germans are permitted to go on vacation. There have been several cases in which East Germans have stolen the passports of visiting West Germans – sometimes after flagging down their cars on East German roads –

and have used them to get through the Wall, leaving their victims to try to convince the Vopos that they did not connive in the escape. At times, visiting West Germans did connive in such escapes. There was also a notorious case in which a young man in West Germany proposed marriage to a West German girl, took his fiancée to East Germany, supposedly to meet his family, then stole her passport and used it to bring his lookalike girlfriend out of the East, leaving the West German girl to find her way out as best she could.

Many escapes have been made by individuals permitted access to the Wall – members of the East German security forces. More than five hundred Vopos, Grepos and soldiers have fled to West Berlin since it was erected, some by scrambling over the barrier, some by dashing through a checkpoint, some by other routes. (More than four times that number have fled directly to West Germany.) An East German coast guardsman recently cruised his patrol boat across a border lake to West Berlin while the other members of the crew were taking a coffee break ashore. As a precaution, foot and motorized guards patrol the Wall in pairs. Partners are continually changed so that would-be escapers among them would not be able to count on friendship to save them from bullets in the back if they tried to make a get-away while on Wall duty.

Every so often, the East German authorities issue a number of exit visas in an attempt to defuse discontent – and to earn money, since the West German government has periodically handed over what amounts to ransom payments in exchange for people being permitted to leave. According to several West Berliners who regularly visit family and friends in East Berlin and East Germany, those visas are obtained by no more than a fraction of the number who would head West if they could. That impression appears to be confirmed by the fact that, though living and working conditions for East Germans and East Berliners are now greatly improved, the Wall remains very much in place to keep them from straying. A dud street light in East Berlin can take four months to replace, but the slightest crack in the Wall is repaired instantly.

Even the most grotesque situation becomes normal if you live with it long enough. For Berliners, the Wall is now, therefore, normal. No one likes it and even the Communists make no effort to glorify it. But the Wall no longer arouses the passions it did when it first rose in the middle of the city to divide families and friends and keep people from their jobs. Berliners have reluctantly accepted it. Most do not even think of it any longer, even though it has turned the story of Berlin into a tale of two cities, and even though it represents a profound and disturbing commentary on the nature of our times.

14

Last Look

THERE IS a museum now at Checkpoint Charlie – an old, shabby building, the last house on the street before the border no-man's-land begins. Inside, in a hodgepodge of cluttered wall displays of photos and words, the story of the barbed wire, of the Wall, of the escapes that succeeded, and of some that failed, is thrown at the visitor without subtlety, without sophistication. At first it seems misconceived, distasteful, unwieldy, a mistake. But it is not. It captures with great fidelity the anguish and the terror, the desperation and despair which the building of the Wall begot.

The checkpoint itself, in the middle of the street, is still manned by American, British and French military policemen, some of them young enough not to have been born when the Wall was first built. On the East Berlin side of the border, the Vopo checkpoint is now equipped with parking spaces for the tourist buses that come through and must undergo thorough inspection, including underneath and in the luggage racks, before entering or leaving. The Vopos in the prefabricated huts at the checkpoints have lists of banned persons which they scan carefully before permitting a visitor to buy a visa for five west marks and requiring him to change another twenty-five into non-exchangable east marks. All must pay for the privilege of passing through the Wall from one part of Berlin to the other. How long it takes to be cleared through depends on the size of the crowd seeking entry, the mood of the Vopos on duty, and the international situation. It is possible to be processed in five minutes or, even when there is no great crowd waiting, to have to wait an hour or more. A visitor is left with the feeling that it is East rather than West Berlin that is walled in. It is still an

270

unpleasant experience, if only because of the realization that East
Berliners can be shot for trying to come the other way.

But not far from the crossing point is Platz der Akademie. This
square was once considered the most beautiful in Berlin. Until
just recently it was a collection of stately war ruins. Now it is
being renovated. The German Cathedral, the old Huguenot
Cathedral, and the theatre there are being meticulously restored.
It is part of a long-term project to beautify some long-neglected
sections of East Berlin. Even in its unfinished state, it is an
agreeable sight and goes some way towards relieving the irritation
of being gone over by the Vopos at the border.

At a café, I share a small table with an East German engineer,
a cultured, articulate man. He says I have come to East Berlin too
soon. There is a lot of building and rebuilding going on, not only
of the fine old monumental structures in the downtown area, but
of new apartment houses, hotels, restaurants, sports centres.
'Much is being done here,' he says. 'Come back in ten years. It
will all be *different* then – or,' he says, as he gets up to leave,
'maybe not.'

At the Museum of German History, the ground floor of which
is devoted to what has transpired in East Germany since the
Second World War, history is strikingly selective. There is not a
word about barbed wire or the Wall or about the mass exodus of
refugees which preceded it. The four or five items devoted to
that critical moment in post-war German history deal only with
the defence of the Socialist Fatherland and the foiling of the
nefarious intentions of warmongers and slave traders to undermine the German Democratic Republic.

In another section of the museum, I am caught up in a flurry of
playful, blue-bloused kids from the Communist Free German
Youth organization. When they learn I am an American, they
cluster around laughingly and ask if I have been to Chicago or
Arizona, before they are hushed by a porter for being too noisy.
An American diplomat who was once stationed in East Berlin
and who did some travelling in East Germany said that while East
German officials are as suspicious and uncommunicative as
Communist bureaucrats can be anywhere, 'Sometimes I had the
impression that the East German people like us better than the
West Germans do.'

The people I speak with – ask for directions, ask the time of
day, ask about a particular book in a bookstore, or briefly pass
the time of day with over a watery beer at a street stall – are
polite, agreeable, easy going. But there is a pervasive drabness

about them. It's hard to understand. Then it becomes clear – it's the uniform absence of liveliness or stylishness in the clothes they wear, as if all were backdrop extras in a movie, meant never to attract undue attention.

At the Centrum department store in Alexanderplatz, much is explained. East Berlin's major peoples' emporium is well stocked with clothes and everything else a department store should have. But strangely, for a country which has risen since the Wall to occupy a very respectable position on the world table of national economic performance, the place seems like a large Woolworths. Some of the stores around Alexanderplatz and on Unter den Linden display high-priced, interesting ceramics, high-quality leather goods and other speciality items – and have credit card stickers on their windows to indicate that western customers are their target market. But there is nothing at East Berlin's main department store to compare with the quality of the goods available not only in West Berlin, but also at the unmarked, government-run store on Clara Zetkin Strasse in the East, where only hard foreign currencies may be used to buy imported goods – from camembert to après-ski gear – denied ordinary East Berliners whose relatives in the West have neglected to send them gifts of money. Building for a glorious future, they are short-changed on current material rewards for their labours – and have been since the war ended more than four decades back.

East Berliner: 'We don't lead such a bad life here. Food is cheap. Rents are low. Medical care is free. There is no unemployment. I earn a good salary, but there aren't too many things to buy. All the good things we make are reserved for export. My brother lives in West Berlin. He does all right. He comes to see me now and again, but I cannot go to see him. We drift apart. Our children hardly know each other.'

West Berliner: 'I go into East Berlin three or four times a year – to see my mother. It is not far but it is an expensive trip. I am not a rich man. In addition to having to exchange twenty-five west marks for twenty-five worthless east marks each time, and not being able to change them back when I leave, I try to bring my mother little things that are ordinary for us but are luxuries over there – real coffee, different kinds of spices, a good salami, things like that. If my other relatives over there know I am coming, they also expect me to bring them something. East Berliners think all West Berliners have a lot of money. My sister lives in East Berlin.

But I never see her any more. She is married to a Vopo and he is not allowed to have any contact at all with people from the West.'

The crosstown subway train between the Gesundbrunnen station and Kottbusser Tor, both in West Berlin, passes six stations without slowing down or stopping. Those stations are in East Berlin and have been sealed since 13 August 1961, when the barbed wire was being rolled out along the sector border. Some of them are brightly illuminated, others dimly lit. If you look closely as they whizz by, you can see armed Vopos posted in each of them to make certain the train doesn't slow down to pick up someone who has managed to get into the station and who might be trying to Flee the Republic. Each day, tens of thousands of West Berliners travel back and forth to work or play *under* East Berlin. For most, it is the only contact they have with the other part of their partitioned city. They make that contact without so much as looking up from their newspapers or interrupting their conversations, as if it were just a bit more subway tunnel to be chugged through before they can get off the train when it reaches West Berlin and come to grips again with Berlin's special brand of reality.

Manfred Rexin: 'Shortly before the Wall was built, I visited Jerusalem and looked at the wall that stood at the time between the Jewish and Arab sections of the city. I thought such a thing could only happen in a place where the people on the two sides had different cultures, different ethnic backgrounds, different languages and hated each other. Here in Berlin, we were one people, one culture, one background. I never believed it could ever happen here.'

East German Communist: 'Do you think I am blind? I hate the Wall! It is ugly. But we had no choice. We were losing so many of our best people – engineers, scientists, specialists of all kinds, and so many of our young people who were still wet behind the ears and had no idea of the kind of world we were trying to build. Without the measures we took, we never could have got as far as we have.'

West Berlin school teacher: 'The Wall is the price we pay for Hitler and the Nazis. I am afraid it will take a war to bring it down. The Wall is monstrous but it's better than a war.'

American Foreign Service officer: 'I didn't think so at the time, but now I believe we should have torn down the Wall right away. The sight of the Allies coming in would have so confused and disorganized the Communists that they would not have been able to regroup to build the Wall further back, like we said they would at the time. It would have been such a major event that the world's attention would have focused on the issue. There wouldn't have been a war. The Russians didn't want war and we certainly didn't. There might have been East–West talks that could have led to solutions to problems we have had to live with ever since.'

Sir Frank Roberts: 'Shortly before the Wall was built, at a party in Moscow, Frol Kozlov, the Soviet Deputy Prime Minister, told me, "The situation is not dangerous. After the war a line was drawn across Europe. We would have liked it to be further west. You would have liked it to be further east. We will make trouble for you and you will make trouble for us. We will find it easier to make trouble for you, in Berlin as everywhere else. But there will be no risk of war." '

James O'Donnell: 'The Wall lurks like an iceberg in German–American relations. One day in the future, maybe around the turn of the century, a master demagogue of the quality if not the politics of Joseph Göbbels will arise and will implant the lie – already believed by many in Germany – that the cynical Americans sold the Germans down the river to the Russians on 13 August 1961.'

Postscript

Office of the Attorney General
Washington DC

MEMORANDUM
August 17, 1961

TO: The President
FROM: The Attorney General [Robert Kennedy]

One of the great problems and deficiencies in the Berlin planning is in the propaganda field. This deficiency has been brought to a head by the action of the Communists in closing down the border between East and West Berlin.

I am sure that there has been a tremendous reaction across the world to these events in Germany. But it is a reaction that has flowed from the natural course of events; there has been very little, if any, stimulation from the United States or, as far as I can see, from any of our Allies. We have been handed a propaganda victory of tremendous dimensions on a silver platter and we are just not taking advantage of it.

Assume the tables were turned and we were responsible for what the Russians have just done. The hue and cry, the riots and disturbances around the world, would be echoing and re-echoing at this very moment. American embassies would have been stoned; American flags outside the United States Information Agencies would have been torn down. World leaders would be making statements and putting out pamphlets denouncing you.

None of that is now happening for our side – as a matter of fact, just the opposite. Mikoyan arrives in Tokyo two days ago and

275

instead of being greeted by rioters, he receives flowers and talks of peaceful coexistence and gets away with it.

Foy Kohler says the explanation is that the Russians have the Communist Party apparatus and they can call on their people around the world to foment trouble. We don't have anything that is similar and that is why we don't do anything. I just don't believe that that's the answer.

We have friends, contacts and connections through business, labour, universities, all across the world. We as well as our Allies have representatives in every country of the world. We have the mechanism in my estimation to get the job done but we just have not utilized it.

Allen Dulles [CIA] says that he has spent ten years forming groups that can perform these kinds of functions. To me they sound more like paper organizations than anything else. I have seen no evidence of activity on their part.

Kohler and the people in the State Department are against almost every kind of idea that you bring up in this area. The result is that we are still sitting around doing nothing.

I think we should take some action and do it immediately.

First, we should establish an organization that can be called upon over a period of the next ten years to handle our propaganda operations. When I refer to propaganda I do not mean just the activities of the USIA and the Voice of America. They are undoubtedly in good hands under Murrow. However, the effect of this operations needs study. How many people listen to VOA broadcasts, etc. But I think we should be taking greater steps to stimulate activity among students, university professors, labour leaders and businessmen. This is just not being done at the present time and I don't think that there is an adequate organization established to do it.

Therefore, what I would suggest, to take advantage of what is happening in Berlin as well as for the long-range study purpose, is that we immediately establish a small group to handle and direct this whole propaganda effort. This group would be similar to the one that you have studying intelligence. I would have people from television, radio, newspapers, advertising agencies, a labour leader like Walter Reuther, maybe a businessman like Sam Meek who has business offices across the world, and maybe one or two university professors. They would make a report with recommendations to you on the broad propaganda field which would include a study of USIA, VOA, the impact of these mediums, the effectiveness of our present operations around the world.

Together with its long-range assignment of assessing our efforts in this whole field, I would suggest that they be given the responsibility of immediately stimulating activities and general interest in the Berlin situation among various groups and important leaders including our Allies around the world. (Obviously in much of this they would work through present government structures such as the State Department.)

To assist this over-all committee in this endeavour, I would form a number of subcommittees to carry out specific functions:

(a) Labour leaders to make contacts in South America, Africa and Southeast Asian countries to be sure there is adequate information among their counterparts as to what is happening in Berlin, what the Russians are doing there now, and what our position is vis-à-vis the Soviet Union. This could be done by trips to those various countries of some of our own labour leaders as well as contacts in other ways.

(b) Businessmen's contacts around the world could certainly be utilized in the same effort. Obviously in some areas of the world American businessmen could not be out in front but there are many areas where they could and should be used. Allen Dulles does some of this but this could be increased.

Furthermore, and probably most important, we should also see there is a campaign amongst students and university professors. This would necessitate personal contacts and an organized campaign. It should be started immediately. This over-all committee I suggested could come up with some recommendations in that field also.

This would be just a start. But a start is what we need.

POLITICAL–MILITARY GAMES
DURING THE BERLIN CRISIS

INSTRUCTIONS FOR RED AND BLUE TEAMS

The point of departure is a 'scenario', prepared in advance, which carries events from the present to a future date. It is intended to be plausible, but not necessarily more plausible than a dozen alternative scenarios might be. It is designed to provide a climactic starting point, presenting each side with a pressing need for decision . . .

Certain military assumptions regarding available forces and their status will be provided to Red and Blue. Each will be provided appropriate intelligence about the other's military situation . . .

The game proceeds in a sequence of policy-planning stages. Each team evaluates the situation, identifies the principle strategies available to it, and determines a course of action. The course of action must be responsive to the anticipated actions of the other teams; that is, it should contain *contingent* moves as well as definitive moves, and specifies the response to alternative foreseeable moves by the adversary . . .

The Blue Team represents (or plans on behalf of) the United States government, the Red Team represents the government of the Soviet Union. The Blue Team does not control or represent the NATO Alliance. The Red Team 'controls' satellite governments – and in particular the GDR – to the extent it can be presumed to in reality. The Control Team will determine the actual behaviour of other countries or of dissident elements within, say, the GDR.

278

Control superimposes such events as are outside the control of Red and Blue – eg, third country behaviour, accidents or acts of God, outcomes of chance events . . . The teams are to develop the best strategies they can that are consistent with American and Soviet objectives . . . The teams are not directed to confine their attention to Berlin, or to Germany, or to Europe . . . Strategic forces or events and interests outside the theatre may become a dominant preoccupation. Control will use its unseen hand to keep actions from becoming too diffuse, but, in principle, Red and Blue are deciding national strategy in a crisis, not just local or regional strategy . . .

Control will 'leak' intelligence to Red and Blue, both intelligence of its own invention about the variables under its control, and intelligence about actions determined by the teams.

DRAFT SCENARIO (Game at Camp David, early September 1961)

The time is _____, Oct. 1, 1961. These are principal events leading up to this time.

The sealing-off of East Berlin in mid-August was followed by striking evidence of unrest and disaffection in East Germany. Large-scale arrests of alleged foreign agents, saboteurs, trouble-makers, and would-be escapees were reported throughout East Germany. Protests against food shortages were reported to be widespread and taken as an indication of general discontent. In many cities, East German police were conspicuously unenergetic in enforcing repressive measures against disorderly groups of protestors. Increasing numbers of police and military personnel defected into West Berlin and asked asylum. Substantial reshuffling of top GDR military personnel was reported. Simultaneous appearance of an 'underground' news sheet in several East German cities indicated organized resistance, its news reports of arrests, acts of sabotage, food shortages, personnel changes, and other isolated events were quick and reliable, indicating a high degree of organization and good communication.

Charging that West Berlin was the centre of such illegal activity, the GDR cut telephone communication with West Berlin on September 15, widening the 'no-man's-land' between East and West Berlin by closing up buildings, and stopped entry from West Berlin into East Berlin of all except Allied military personnel. September 20: apparently tipped off, GDR police doubled their security guards around the West Berlin perimeter and rolled up unprecedented numbers of armoured vehicles. At dark, evidently by prearrangement, mobs formed in East Berlin at several points only a few hundred yards from West Berlin; a number of fires broke out in the vicinity, explosions were heard, and the mobs moved quickly toward the barricades separating East and West Berlin. At all points but one, barricades, tear gas, and water pressure were successfully used to stop and disperse the mobs; but at _____ the crowd tangled with police at close quarters, searchlights were destroyed, and in the confusion several persons made it across the barricades. A GDR tank broke its way through the barricade in apparent pursuit but, having opened a swathe, pulled off to one side; the crew escaped to West Berlin. Several score East Germans made it through the gap before GDR tanks moved in to close it. Most of the crowd escaped back into East Berlin in the confusion; several score were arrested.

September 21, another GDR tank on border duty crashed the barricade, and the crew defected. Ostensibly firing on the tank and plugging the gap, several additional border guards defected. The night of September 21, Soviet armoured vehicles replaced East Germans along the East–West Berlin border. During the following week, GDR military units in the area west and south of Berlin were reported being separated from their armour and most vehicles; many units were moved eastward and replaced by Soviet troops.

The night of September 28 riots broke out in a dozen East German cities. GDR troops sent in to support the police defected in several instances, joining the uprising, took up defensive positions, and used local radio stations to call for general revolt. Before dawn, Soviet troops were in motion to isolate all GDR army units; by early morning, numbers of GDR troops through-out the country had joined the uprising. In most instances they retreated into the nearest city or town, joined or initiated rebellion, assumed defensive positions, and denounced the Soviet occupation, calling for Western help. Widespread sabotage of transport and communication links slowed the Soviet counter-measures; and on September 29, large numbers of GDR MIG 15s straffed USSR airfields in East Germany and fled to the West, many of them crash-landing in open fields across the western border.

September 30 all was confusion. Most cities in East Germany, with the notable exceptions of East Berlin and Magdeburg, appeared either to be in rebel hands with GDR military units collaborating, or else to be without effective government. Soviet army units were moving slowly to cut off and surround a number of cities; Soviet troops appeared to be in command of all airfields, but extensive sabotage to aircraft and POL [petroleum, oil and lubricants] had occurred at most fields, some of it by defecting armed aircraft. In _____ Soviet troops had begun a 'Budapest-type' invasion of the city. The night of September 30, identical announcements were repeated over and over on most radio stations in rebel hands.

The USSR – the announcement reported – had reinstituted a crushing re-occupation of what was to have become the German Democratic Republic. It had reversed the movement toward GDR independence, reinstituted repressive measures, and attempted to disarm GDR military forces. Instead of a 'peace treaty', military occupation of the worst sort had been resumed. Spontaneous revolt had become organized, but it had no more chance than in Budapest to hold out against Soviet military might.

The Soviets were already using fire, tanks, and aircraft to massacre the people of East Germany. Only help from the West, within hours, could prevent the bloody suppression of East German self-determination. The West, and especially Germans west of the iron curtain could not this time shirk their civilized obligations to intervene and demand Soviet withdrawal. The alternative is disaster at Soviet hands.

. . . a rebellious GDR army force, approximately in regimental strength, evaded Soviet encirclement and reached the border southwest of Gera. There it overcame Soviet border guards, demolished barriers, and took up defensive positions on the border itself. A patrol made contact with West German military units in the area and asked for support to keep the border open.

In East Berlin, absolute round-the-clock curfew reigns.

It is 1.00 a.m., October 1, 1961.

Acknowledgements

WHILE WRITING this book, I was fortunate to meet and speak with many people with special insight into the Berlin crisis, some casually, some at greater length. I am grateful to them all and particularly to the following for granting me interviews: John Ausland, Egon Bahr, Joachim Bölke, Willy Brandt, McGeorge Bundy, Lieutenant Colonel Michael Burkham, Major Peter Cutler, Arthur Day, William Fulbright, Martin Hillenbrand, Adam Kellett-Long, David Klein, John Kornblum, Sir Bernard Ledwidge, Lothar Loewe (by telephone), John Mapother, Karl Mautner, Martha Mautner, Francis Meehan, George Muller, Nelson Ledsky, James O'Donnell, Manfred Rexin, Sir Frank Roberts, Dean Rusk, Polizei Oberkommissar Dieter Seidel, Richard Smyser (by telephone), Sir Edward Tomkins, and Colonel Ernest von Pawel (by telephone.)

I am much obliged also to Allan Lightner for troubling to make and send me a tape recording of answers to questions I sent him, to Mary Kellett-Long for permitting me to quote from her Berlin diary, to Honoré Catudal for permission to quote from material he gathered while researching his study of American government decision-making processes in the lead-up to the crisis, and to the following for their assistance: Carlotta Anderson, Cynthia Efird, Suzanne Forbes and the staff of the John Fitzgerald Kennedy Library in Boston, Rainer Hildebrandt, Edward Harper, Joerg Henschl and the staff of the Press Office of the Berlin *Senat*, Tom Homan, Polizeihauptkommissar Rainer Schmidt, Clyde Taylor who prodded me into reliving the crisis, Joachim Trenkner, and Dr Bernd von Waldow. I am grateful most of all to my wife, Barbara Gelb, for everything.

Notes

Text references are indicated by a page number followed by a phrase in italics.

Chapter 2 – THE STAGE IS SET

7. *From the day* . . . Walter Bedell Smith, *Eisenhower's Six Great Decisions.*
8. *Not until the campaign ended* . . . Omar Bradley, *A Soldier's Story.*
11. *entirely coincides with the plan*: Dwight Eisenhower, Cornelius Ryan, *The Last Battle.*
11. *Who will take Berlin* . . . Ibid.
12. *The Russian armies will* . . . Winston Churchill, *Triumph and Tragedy.*
13. *George Kennan recalled* . . . George Kennan, *Memoirs 1925–1950.*
13. *for battles fought and won* . . . James Gavin, *On to Berlin.*
14. *I can handle Uncle Joe* . . . Ibid.
14. *in no condition to offer balanced judgments* . . . Robert Murphy, *Diplomat Among Warriors.*
15. *I told the Supreme Commander* . . . Harry C. Butcher, *Three Years with Eisenhower.*
15. *If the Americans launch a major attack* . . . Ryan, op. cit.
17. *Every soldier I know of* . . . James Gavin, op. cit.

Chapter 3 – DISCORD IN THE RUINS

18. *Craters, caves, mountains of rubble* . . . Willy Brandt, *My Road to Berlin.*
19. *It is vital now* . . . Churchill, op. cit.
20. *They illegally occupy* . . . Jean Smith, *The Defense of Berlin.*
20. *We went to Berlin* . . . Frank Howley, *Berlin Command.*
22. *Howley was left with the impression* . . . Ibid.
22. *Why are you Americans* . . . Ibid.
22. *Even at the first meeting* . . . Gregory Klimov, *The Terror Machine.*
24. *We were quite willing to start off* . . . Lucius Clay, *Decision in Germany.*
24. *dreams of a happy collaboration* . . . George Kennan, *The New Yorker*, 25 February 1985.
26. *To the man in the street* . . . Wolfgang Leonhard, *Child of the Revolution.*
29. *He had publicly accepted blame* . . . *New York Times*, 24 July 1948.
31. *We stay in Berlin* . . . Richard Collier, *Bridge Across the Sky.*
31. *When the full dimensions* . . . Harry S. Truman, *Years of Hope.*
36. *People who had devoted their lives* . . . Carola Stern, *Ulbricht.*
39. Refugee statistics compiled by the Ministry for All-German Affairs of the Federal Republic of Germany.

Chapter 4 – ULTIMATUMS AND DEPARTURES

41. *The international Communist movement* . . . John Foster Dulles press conference, 26 November 1958.
43. *If you want war* . . . Jack M. Schick, *The Berlin Crisis.*
43. *situation abnormal* . . . President Eisenhower's press conference, 28 September 1959.
44. *Yugoslav ambassador* . . . Veljko Mikunovic, *Moscow Diary.*
44. *rights we have* . . . President Eisenhower press conference, 27 April 1960.
46. *The Soviets choose* . . . Henry Kissinger, *The Observer*, London, 21 December 1985.
54. *I walked past the open door* . . . Mary Kellett-Long, *Berlin Diary.*
65. *Meeting of Warsaw Pact leaders* . . . Honoré Catudal, *Kennedy and the Berlin Wall Crisis.*

Chapter 5 – COLLISION IN VIENNA

69. *Llewellyn Thompson now believed a showdown* . . . Catudal, op. cit.

71. *All officers, especially marshals* . . . Oleg Penkovsky, *The Penkovsky Papers.*

74. *though you really can't reach* . . . Author's interview with Dean Rusk.

75. *It must not be tolerated* . . . Smith, op. cit.

76. *He looked not only anxious* . . . Nikita Khrushchev, *Khrushchev Remembers.*

77. *shaken and angry* . . . *New York Times*, 15 November 1964.

77. *Harold Macmillan said* . . . Harold Macmillan, *Pointing The Way.*

77. *Kennedy looked kind of tired* . . . Transcript, oral history interview with Peter Lisagor, John F. Kennedy Library, Boston, Massachusetts.

77. *I just want you to know, Joe* . . . Montague Kern, Patricia Levering and Ralph Levering, *The Kennedy Crisis.*

77. *if we're going to start a nuclear war* . . . Kenneth O'Donnell and David Powers with Joe McCarthy, *Johnny, We Hardly Knew Ye.*

81. *I hear you bastards* . . . Hugh Sidey, *John F. Kennedy, President.*

84. *It would not have been to our advantage* . . . Author's interview with McGeorge Bundy.

85. *Once the United States* . . . National Security Files, JFK Library.

86. *The fundamental reason* . . . Ibid.

87. *for God's sake* . . . Author's interview with David Klein, note-taker at the meeting.

88. *absurd contingency planning* . . . Macmillan, op. cit.

88. *he could not conceive of himself* . . . Charles de Gaulle, *Memoir of Hope.*

88. *Manchester Guardian* quoted in *The New Leader*, 26 June 1961.

89. *This view seemed to be confirmed*: *The Times*, London, 11 August 1961.

Chapter 6 – THE CRISIS LOOMS

93. *We should re-screen* . . . National Security Files, JFK Library.

93. *report on levels* . . . Ibid.
94. *formed the impression* . . . Robert Slusser, *The Berlin Crisis of 1961.*
95. *The historic truth is* . . . Ibid.
95. *All I ever hear from your people* . . . Kenneth O'Donnell, et al., op. cit.
96. *Washington bureaucrats will* . . . 'Crisis Management,' by John Ausland and Colonel Hugh Richardson in *Foreign Affairs*, January 1966.
96. *a bowl of jelly* . . . Arthur Schlesinger Jr, *A Thousand Days.*
97. *He's imprisoned by Berlin* . . . Ibid.
97. *saturated himself in the problem* . . . Theodore Sorenson, *Kennedy.*
98. *the United States could threaten* . . . Transcript, oral history interview with Dean Acheson, JFK Library.
99. *It seemed to us* . . . Transcript, oral history interview with Charles Bohlen, JFK Library.
99. *bleak choices* . . . Schlesinger, op. cit.
100. *Kennedy Plan for Central Europe* . . . National Security Files, JFK Library.
100. *We didn't have the negotiating alternative* . . . Transcript, oral history interview with Abram Chayes, JFK Library.
101. *Let me tell you* . . . Author's interview with Sir Frank Roberts.
101. *If Khrushchev restrains himself* . . . Schlesinger, op. cit.
102. Opinion Poll. *US News and World Report*, 19 July 1961.
102. *If we mobilize* . . . National Security Files, JFK Library.
104. *What's wrong with that God-damned department* . . . Charles Bohlen, *Witness to History.*
104. *According to Martin Hillenbrand* . . . Author's interview with Martin Hillenbrand.
105. *With all the changes and clearances* . . . Sorenson, op. cit.
110. *Ted, if you want to make that speech perfect* . . . Author's interview with James O'Donnell.
110. *There was an 'Oh, my God' feeling* . . . Author's interview with Karl Mautner.
110. *It's Berlin I want to talk about* . . . Author's interview with McGeorge Bundy.
114. *The drain of workers* . . . Khrushchev, op. cit.

Chapter 7 – BRACING FOR THE SHOWDOWN

118. *Everyone from the Task Force*: Author's interview with John Ausland.

119. *It was made clear* . . . Author's interview with Karl Mautner.

120. *to settle jointly with interested parties* . . . Slusser, op. cit.

121. *They were often on the road* . . . Author's interview with Colonel Ernest von Pawel.

127. *I argued that* . . . Walt Rostow, *The Diffusion of Power*.

128. *should not feel constrained* . . . Report on *Military Power and the Cold War*, prepared for the Department of Defence by the Rand Corporation, February 1961.

128. *A Russian-speaking British officer* . . . Author's interview with Lieutenant-Colonel Michael Burkham.

131. *There has never been* . . . *New York Times*, 6 August 1961.

131. *Fulbright said later* . . . Author's interview with Senator William Fulbright.

132. *Khrushchev is losing East Germany* . . . Rostow, op. cit.

133. *It became more and more obvious* . . . Erich Honecker, *From My Life*.

133. *Wolfgang Leonhard has described how docilely* . . . Leonhard, op. cit.

137. *Purpose of Moscow 3–5 August meeting* . . . National Security Council files, JFK Library.

137. *I do not propose* . . . Quoted in Schlesinger, op. cit.

Chapter 8 – SOMETHING FUNNY AT THE BORDER

139. *If I were you* . . . Author's interview with Adam Kellett Long.

140. *Adam is getting tired* . . . Mary Kellett-Long, op. cit.

141. *food supplies on hand* . . . Author's interview with George Muller.

141. *At 4.00 p.m. that Saturday* . . . Honecker, op. cit.

142. *Thurow thought it was* . . . *Die Geschichte einer Grenzkompanie des Ringes um West Berlin*, Ministry for All-German Affairs of the Federal Republic of Germany.

142. *Something funny is going on* . . . Author's interview with George Muller.

144. *at the American military liaison mission* . . . Author's interview with Colonel Ernest von Pawel.

144. *I strongly advise you* . . . Author's interview with Adam Kellett-Long.

147. *After checking with the British military police* . . . Author's interview with Sir Bernard Ledwidge.

149. *Minister Allan Lightner of the American Mission* . . . From Allan Lightner's tape recorded answers to author's questions.

149. *There seems to be something going on* ... Author's interview with Richard Smyser.

150. *Soviet 19th Motorized Rifle Division* ... National Security Files, JFK Library.

152. *It was realized the mission* ... Author's interview with George Muller.

Chapter 9 – 'WHY DIDN'T WE KNOW?'

156. *Surprise, when it happens* ... from Thomas C. Schelling's foreword to *Pearl Harbor – Warning and Decision* by Roberta Wohlstetter.

158. *No one knew what was happening* ... Author's interview with Sir Edward Tomkins.

161. *It was hard to remain calm* ... Author's interview with Willy Brandt.

162. *If all the commandants do* ... Author's interview with George Muller.

162. *Scanning the troubled faces* ... Willy Brandt, *People and Politics*.

167. *In Washington, Berlin Task Force duty officer* ... Author's interview with John Ausland.

169. *Embarrassingly, the most detailed report* ... Author's interview with Lothar Loewe.

170. *It was exceedingly difficult* ... Howard Trivers, *Three Crises*.

173. *Time was not of the essence* ... Author's interview with Dean Rusk.

173. *Kennedy himself did not feel* ... Author's interview with McGeorge Bundy.

175. *partly because the Americans have got very excited* ... Macmillan, op. cit.

176. *Returning from vacation* ... Author's interview with Arthur Day.

176. *Around 3.00 p.m.* ... Author's interview with James O'Donnell.

Chapter 10 – POSTMORTEM

179. *At the British Mission* ... Author's interview with Sir Bernard Ledwidge.

180. *pretty darn soon* ... Author's interview with Lieutenant-Colonel Ernest von Pawel.

180. *the answers I got* . . . Author's interview with John Mapother.

180. *they must have squirreled* . . . Author's interview with Martin Hillenbrand.

181. *very severe, very strict controls* . . . Author's interview with Egon Bahr.

184. *the present crisis will end* . . . Terence Prittie, *Willy Brandt – Portrait of a Statesman.*

184. *received and passed on reports* . . . Reinhard Gehlen, *The Service – The Memoirs of General Reinhard Gehlen.*

192. *Mac and I sat around* . . . Transcript, Oral history interview with Robert Amory, JFK Library.

193. *We should take the view* . . . National Security Files, JFK Library.

193. *I find unanimity* . . . National Security Files, JFK Library.

194. *It was apparent from hour one* . . . Author's interview with McGeorge Bundy.

194. *We [at the Foreign Office]* . . . Author's interview with Sir Edward Tomkins.

194. *if we had crossed the line* . . . Howard Trivers, *Three Crises.*

195. *This was the place* . . . General Lucius Clay. Transcript, oral history interview, JFK Library.

196. *What steps will we take* . . . National Security Files, JFK Library.

Chapter 11 – LIVES, FORTUNES AND SACRED HONOUR

200. *some members of the United States Mission* . . . Author's interview with Joachim Bölke.

200. *a big fight with a couple of people* . . . Author's interview with Martha Mautner.

201. *The United States government did not push* . . . Trivers, op. cit.

201. *This is [Khrushchev's] way out* . . . Kenneth O'Donnell, et al., op. cit.

201. *State Department legal adviser and White House consultant* . . . Transcript, oral history interview with Abram Chayes, JFK Library.

202. *Presidential military adviser* . . . Transcript, oral history interview with General Maxwell Taylor, JFK Library.

202. *Later in the crisis* . . . Author's interview with Arthur Day.

203. *Washington is handling this* . . . Author's interview with George Muller.

204. *did not initially fully anticipate* . . . Foy Kohler, *Understanding the Russians.*
204. *I need a clear-cut denial* . . . Author's interview with Egon Bahr.
205. *People were afraid something might happen* . . . Author's interview with Willy Brandt.
209. *the British come in two sizes* . . . Author's interview with McGeorge Bundy.
211. *Soviet manoeuvre in East Berlin* . . . National Security files, JFK Library.
211. *Clay had formally volunteered* . . . National Security Files, JFK Library.
211. *Action,not words* . . . Schlesinger, op. cit.
212. *Johnson approached anybody else's decision* . . . Author's interview with McGeorge Bundy.
213. *Two years later* . . . Author's interview with Dean Rusk.
214. *Suppose the Russians had tried to stop* . . . General Bruce Clarke interview with Honoré Catudal.
217. *There had been* . . . Brandt, op. cit.

Chapter 12 – THE ROGUE SYMBOL

223. *either rhetorical or long-range* . . . Author's interview with Willy Brandt.
224. *Brandt did not seem to him* . . . Author's interview with Sir Edward Tomkins.
226. A paper prepared by the Historical Studies Division of the State Department, December 1963.
226. *went over like a lead balloon* . . . Taped comment by Allan Lightner.
227. *Clay will be a burden* . . . National Security Files, JFK Library.
229. *to cool the hotheads* . . . Slusser, op. cit.
232. *was not quite aware* . . . Author's interview with Martin Hillenbrand.
234. *He was a loose cannon* . . . Author's interview with Arthur Day.
235. *little doubt that Clay* . . . Geoffrey McDermott, *Berlin – Success of a Mission.*
235. *Afterwards I called Norstad* . . . General Clarke interview with Honoré Catudal.
239. *Had it not been* . . . Trivers, op. cit.
239. *We didn't send him* . . . Curtis Cate, *The Ides of August.*

241. *So Clay got the go-ahead* . . . Transcript, oral history interview with Clay, JFK Library.

243. *over an essentially minor issue* . . . Cate, op. cit.

Chapter 13 – ENDGAME

247. *Carl, The Soviet Union is the enemy* . . . Author's interview with John Ausland.

247 *to consider American proposals* . . . Slusser, op. cit.

248. *Berlin is not such a problem* . . . Paul-Henri Spaak, *The Continuing Battle.*

248. *Westerners usually like to rush* . . . Author's interview with Dean Rusk.

249. *thus weaken our ties* . . . Schlesinger, op. cit.

251. *The tone of Clay's telegrams* . . . Taped comment by Allan Lightner.

251. *just didn't fit in* . . . Author's interview with John Ausland.

253. *the director of British European Airways* . . . Author's interview with Sir Edward Tomkins.

254. *Lord Home told the Soviet foreign minister* . . . Author's interview with Dean Rusk.

258. *British philosopher Bertrand Russell* . . . *Manchester Guardian*, 25 October 1962.

258. *Let's all go out* . . . Author's interview with Francis Meehan.

259. *When I heard that Kennedy* . . . Author's interview with Joachim Bölke.

260. *Their stationing of nuclear-armed ballistic missiles* . . . William Kaufmann, *The McNamara Strategy.*

263. *We had to look for new ways* . . . Author's interview with Willy Brandt.

263. *We had to adjust to reality* . . . Author's interview with Egon Bahr.

264. *come back to haunt us* . . . Author's interview with David Klein.

Selected Bibliography

Willy Brandt, *People and Politics*.
Curtis Cate, *The Ides of August*.
Honoré Catudal, *Kennedy and the Berlin Wall Crisis*.
Lucius Clay, *Decision in Germany*.
W. Philip Davison, *The Berlin Blockade*.
James Gavin, *On to Berlin*.
Erich Honecker, *From My Life*.
Frank Howley, *Berlin Command*.
Nikita Khrushchev, *Khrushchev Remembers*.
Gregory Klimov, *The Terror Machine*.
Wolfgang Leonhard, *Child of the Revolution*.
Kenneth O'Donnell and David Powers with Joe McCarthy, *Johnny, We Hardly Knew Ye*.
Jack Schick, *The Berlin Crisis*.
Arthur Schlesinger Jr, *A Thousand Days*.
Hugh Sidey, *John F. Kennedy, President*.
Robert Slusser, *The Berlin Crisis of 1961*.
Jean Smith, *The Defense of Berlin*.
Theodore Sorenson, *Kennedy*.
Carola Stern, *Ulbricht: A Political Biography*.
Philip Windsor, *City On Leave*.

Index